APARECIDA:
QUO VADIS?

APARECIDA:
QUO VADIS?

Robert S. Pelton, C.S.C.
General Editor

University of Scranton Press
Scranton and London

Library of Congress Cataloging-in-Publication Data

Aparecida: quo vadis? / [edited by] Robert S. Pelton.
p. cm.
Includes bibliographical references and index.
ISBN 978-1-58966-143-1 (pbk. : alk. paper)
1. Aparecida 2007 (2007 : Aparecida de Goiânia, Brazil)
2. Catholic Church—Latin America—Congresses.
I. Pelton, Robert S., 1921-
BX1426.3.A63 2008
282'.8090511—dc22
2008035131

Distribution:

University of Scranton Press
Chicago Distribution Center
11030 S. Langley
Chicago, IL 60628

PRINTED IN THE UNITED STATES OF AMERICA

In Gratitude to:

The Council of Latin American Bishops—
CELAM—who have kept alive the Spirit of the
Second Vatican Council

The initiative of Pope John Paul II, whose call for
the 1997 Synod for America prepared the way for
the Fifth General Conference of Latin America
and the Caribbean

Rev. Edward L. Cleary, O.P., for his carefully
researched study of the Latin American Catholic
Church, especially since the Conference of
Puebla in 1979

The hosts of the Aparecida conference, who made
it possible for official participants and other
members of the faithful to come together in
supportive daily prayer throughout the
conference sessions

TABLE OF CONTENTS

ACKNOWLEDGMENTS

In a personal way, I wish to thank the staff of the Kellogg Institute for International Studies for their efficient assistance during the preparation of this publication.

I am also grateful to both the administration of the Kellogg Institute and the Department of Theology for providing me with the time and space to carry on this project.

The editors of *Notre Dame Magazine* obtained Vatican press credentials for me and the officials of the U.S. Secretariat for Latin America facilitated interviews that were important to fully appreciate the conference process.

Mr. Jeff Gainey—director of the University of Scranton Press—and Mr. Robert Ball—a very skillful editorial advisor—were most helpful.

Sister Patricia Ann Thompson, Ms. Betsy Station, and Ms. Susan Hamilton provided excellent translations, and Emmy Lou Papandria provided meticulous proofreading.

Monsignor Carlos Quintana took the fine photographs in this book.

Finally, Mr. Christopher Lund made the arrangements for my travel in Brazil.

May 2008
Robert S. Pelton, C.S.C.
Notre Dame, Indiana

PREFACE

This book has been prepared as a commentary on the official documents of the Fifth General Conference of the Bishops of Latin America and the Caribbean. Also included are the Inaugural Address of Pope Benedict XVI and the Message of the Fifth General Conference to the Peoples of Latin America and the Caribbean.

My essay, "Medellín and Puebla: Dead or Alive in the 21st Century Church?" provides overview and context for the Fifth General Conference. It concludes that Medellín and Puebla are in fact alive *because of* the achievements of Aparecida. While these achievements provide clear hope for the future, specific challenges remain as the Church works to fulfill her mission.

The next two essays focus on the contemporary Catholic Church in the Americas: "The Challenge of Aparecida for the Church in America" by Bishop Ricardo Ramirez, and "Aparecida and Hispanics of the U.S.A." by Father Virgilio Elizondo.

The themes of the next two chapters are essential to understanding the principal objectives of Aparecida: "The Preferential Option for the Poor at Aparecida" (Rev. Gustavo Gutiérrez, O.P.), and "Base Communities, A Return to Inductive Methodology" (Rev. Jose Marins).

Globalization assumes particular significance at this time in history. Rev. Ernest Bartell, C.S.C. provides context for this vital issue in "Aparecida and Global Markets." Professor Javier Maria Iguiñiz Echeverria even more specific in "Globalization and Economics at Aparecida." The third essay on globalization, "An Analysis of the Aparecida Document in Terms of Structural Sin" by Professor Margaret Pfeil, is one of the most challenging of the series. It describes clearly the seeds of social transformation that we must sow if we are to meet the recommendations of the Aparecida document.

Rev. Sergio Torres' "Amerindia: Return from Internal Exile" is a fascinating and positive expression of dialogue within the Church, one that could serve as a model for other fruitful exchanges between theologians and Church officials in the future.

The concluding essays, "Aparecida and Pentecostalism in Latin America" by Rev. Edward L. Cleary, O.P., and "The Future as Seen From Aparecida" by Daniel H. Levine, elucidate the challenges remaining for the Catholic Church. We need to consider these challenges carefully, along with reasons for hope, especially those implied in an ongoing and deeper commitment to a preferential option for the poor.

May 2008
Robert S. Pelton, C.S.C.
Notre Dame, Indiana

Inaugural Address of Benedict XVI

Pope Benedict XVI, Sunday, 13 May 2007

Dear Brother Bishops, beloved priests, religious brothers and sisters, and lay people. Dear observers of other religious confessions: It is a great joy for me to be here with you to open the Fifth General Conference of the Bishops of Latin America and the Caribbean, which is celebrated at the Shrine of Our Lady of Aparecida, Patroness of Brazil. I would like my first words to be of thanksgiving and praise to God for the great gift of the Christian faith of the peoples of this Continent.

The Christian Faith in Latin America

The faith in God has animated the life and culture of these peoples during more than five centuries. From the encounter of this faith with the original ethnicities, the rich Christian culture that emerged is expressed in the art, the music, and the literature. Above all, it has been expressed in the religious traditions and the idiosyncrasy of its peoples, united by a same history and creed, and forging a great harmony in the diversity of cultures and languages. Presently, it is this same faith that has to face serious challenges, since what is at stake is the harmonic development of society and the Catholic identity of its peoples. In this regard, the Fifth General Conference will reflect upon this situation to help the Christian faithful live their faith with joy and coherence, to acknowledge that they are disciples and missionaries of Christ, sent by Him to the world in order to announce and bear witness of our faith and love.

However, what has the acceptance of the Christian faith meant to the Latin American and Caribbean peoples? For them it has meant to know and welcome Christ, the God unknown by their ancestors, who without knowing were searching for Him in their rich religious traditions. Christ

1

was the Savior whom they were silently longing for. It has also meant to have received, through the waters of baptism, the divine life that made them children of God through adoption. It meant to have received also the Holy Spirit that has come to make their culture fruitful, purifying them and developing the numerous seeds that the incarnate Word had laid on them, guiding them through the paths of the Gospel.

Indeed, the announcing of Jesus and his Gospel did not presuppose in any moment an alienation of the pre-Columbian cultures, nor was it an imposition of a foreign culture.[1] The authentic cultures are not closed in themselves or petrified in a determined point in history; rather, they are open. Moreover, they seek the encounter with other cultures; they hope to reach universality in the encounter and dialogue with other lifestyles, as well as with the elements that can bring a new synthesis in which always is respected the diversity of expressions and the concrete cultural development.

Ultimately, only truth unifies, and its proof is love. That is why Christ, who is truly the incarnate Logos, "love to the end," is not foreign to any culture or any person; rather, the answer longed for in the heart of all cultures is what gives them their definite identity, uniting humanity and at the same time respecting the richness of diversities, opening to all the possibility of growth in a true humanization, in an authentic progress. The Word of God, taking flesh in Jesus Christ, became also history and culture.

The utopia of giving life again to the pre-Columbian religions, separating them from Christ and the universal Church, would not be a progress but a drawback. It would truly be an involution towards a historic moment anchored in the past.

The wisdom of the first peoples fortunately led them to form a synthesis between their cultures and the Christian faith offered by the missionaries. From there, the rich and profound popular religiosity was born, in which the soul of the Latin American peoples appeared:

> Love to the suffering Christ, the God of compassion, forgiveness,
> and reconciliation; the God who has loved us to the point of giving himself
> to us

---

[1] There was some tension in the way these words were interpreted. The Holy Father clarified his intended meaning at his General Audience on 23 May 2007, available from http://www.vatican.valholy_fathct-Benedictxvi/audiences/2007/documents/hfben-xviaud20070523en.html.

Love to the Lord present in the Eucharist, the God incarnate, dead and risen to be the Bread of Life

The God who is near the poor and the suffering

Profound devotion to the Most Holy Virgin of Guadalupe, of Aparecida, or of the various national and local devotions

When the Virgin of Guadalupe appeared to the Indian St. Juan Diego, she said these meaningful words: "Am I not here, I who am your mother? Are you not under my shadow and watch? Am I not the source of your joy? Are you not in the fold of my mantle, in the crossing of my arms?" (Nican Mopohua, nn. 118–119)

This religiosity is also expressed in the devotion to the saints, manifested in the celebration of their feasts, in the love to the Pope and to the Shepherds, in the love to the Universal Church as the great family of God who cannot and should not ever leave her own children in misery. All this shapes the great mosaic of the popular religiosity which is the precious treasure of the Catholic Church in Latin America, and which she must protect, promote, and, whenever necessary, purify.

CONTINUITY WITH THE OTHER CONFERENCES

This Fifth General Conference is celebrated in continuity with the other four that preceded it in Rio de Janeiro, Medellín, Puebla, and Santo Domingo. With the same spirit that animated them, the Shepherds want to give now a new impulse to the evangelization, so that these peoples will continue to grow and mature in their faith, so that they may be light for the world and witnesses of Jesus Christ with their own lives.

After the Fourth General Conference in Santo Domingo, many things have changed in society. The Church, who participates in the happiness and hope, the sorrows and joys of her children, wants to walk alongside them in this time of so many challenges, to always instill in them hope and consolation. (cf. *Gaudium et Spes*, 1)

In today's world, we see the phenomenon of globalization as a complicated weaving of relations at a planetary level. Even though in certain aspects it is an achievement of the great human family and a sign of its deep aspiration to reach unity, it also, nonetheless, brings about the risk of great monopolies and of converting profit into a supreme value. As in every field of human activity, globalization must be also guided by ethics, putting everything at the service of the human person, created in the image and likeness of God.

In Latin America and the Caribbean, as in other regions, there has been an evolution towards democracy, even though there are reasons of concern in the face of governments that are either authoritarian or subject to certain ideologies that were believed to have been overcome and which do not correspond to the Christian vision of men and society, as taught by the social Doctrine of the Church. On the other hand, the liberal economy of some Latin American countries must consider equity, because those social sectors which are ever more put to the test by enormous poverty or even stripped of their own natural goods continue to grow.

In the ecclesial communities of Latin America, it is noteworthy to see the maturity of the faith in many lay men and women, active and committed to the Lord, along with the presence of many generous catechists, of so many young people, of new ecclesial movements and recent Institutes of consecrated life. We can see how vital are many of the Catholic educational, assistencial, and hospitalarian works. We perceive, however, a certain weakening of the Christian life in the whole of society and of the sense of belonging to the Catholic Church due to secularism, hedonism, indifferentism, and proselytism of several sects, animist religions, and new pseudo-religious expressions.

All this configures a new situation that will be analyzed here in Aparecida. In the face of this new challenge, the faithful expect from this Fifth Conference a renewal and revitalization of their faith in Christ, our only Master and Savior, who has revealed to us the unique experience of the infinite Love of God the Father to humankind. From this source, new paths and creative pastoral projects will be able to unfold, and they will infuse a firm hope to live the faith in a responsible and joyful way, as well as to irradiate it in their own environments.

DISCIPLES AND MISSIONARIES

This General Conference has as its theme: "Disciples and missionaries of Jesus Christ, so that our peoples may have life in Him, 'I am the Way, the Truth, and the Life.'" (Jn. 14:6)

The Church has the great task of watching over and nourishing the faith of the people of God, and of reminding the faithful of this continent that, through their baptism, they are called to be disciples and missionaries of Jesus Christ. This implies following Him, living in intimacy with Him, imitating His example, and giving witness. Every baptized person receives from Christ, like the Apostles, the commandment of the mission: "Go out to the whole world and proclaim the Good News to all creation. He who believes and is baptized will be saved," (Mk. 16:15) because to be disciples and missionaries of Jesus Christ and to seek life "in Him" implies to be deeply rooted in Him.

What is it that Christ really gives us? Why do we want to be disciples of Christ? Because we hope to find life in the communion with Him, the true life worthy of this name, and for this reason we want to make Him known to others, to communicate to them the gift we have found in Him. But is it truly this way? Are we really convinced that Christ is the way, the truth, and the life?

In the face of the priority of faith in Christ and of life "in Him," expressed in the title of this Fifth Conference, another question could arise: couldn't this priority be an escape towards intimism, towards a religious individualism, an abandonment of the urgent reality of the great economical, social, and political problems of Latin America and of the world, and an escape from reality towards a spiritual world?

Firstly, we can answer this question with another one: What is this reality? What is real? Is "reality" only the material goods, the social, economical, and political problems? Precisely here is the great mistake of the dominant tendencies of the last century, a destructive error as has been evidenced through the results of the Marxist system and even that of the capitalist ones. They falsify the concept of reality with the amputation of the founding reality; since it is founding, it is also decisive: God. Whoever excludes God from his horizon falsifies the concept of "reality" and, in consequence, can only end up in wrong paths and with destructive ideas.

The first fundamental affirmation is the following: only he who knows God, knows reality and can respond to it in an adequate and truly human way. The truth of this thesis is evident before the failure of all the systems that put God in parentheses.

But then, immediately, another question is raised: Who knows God? How can we know Him? We cannot enter here into a complex debate about this crucial question. For the Christian, the core of the answer is simple: Only God knows God, only his Son who is God of God, the True God, knows Him. He "who is in the bosom of the Father, has told us." (Jn. 1:18)

Here we find the unique and irreplaceable importance of Christ for us, for humanity. If we do not know God in Christ and with Christ, all reality will be transformed in an indecipherable mystery; there is no way, and thus, there is neither life nor truth.

God is the founding reality, not only a God who is thought of or hypothetical, but a God with a human face; He is God-with-us, the God of love to the point of the cross. When the disciple reaches the comprehension of this love of Christ "to the end" he cannot not respond to this love but with a similar love: "I will follow you wherever you go." (Lk. 9:57)

We can still ask ourselves another question: What does faith in this God give us? The first answer is that it gives us a family, the universal family of God in the Catholic Church. Faith frees us from the isolation of the "I," because it leads us to communion. The encounter with God is, in itself and as such, encounter with our brothers and sisters, an act of convocation, unification, and responsibility towards others. In this sense, the preferential option for the poor is implicit in the christological faith in that God who became poor for us, so that he would enrich us with his poverty. (cf. 2 Cor. 8:9)

However, before facing what is brought by the realism of the faith in God made man, we must continue to deepen on the question: How can I truly know Christ so that I can follow Him and live with Him, so that I will find life in Him and communicate this life to others, to society, and to the world? Above all, Christ made himself known to us in his person, in his life, and in his doctrine through the Word of God. As we begin this new time that the missionary Church of Latin America and the Caribbean is willing to undertake, after this Fifth General Conference in Aparecida, it is an absolutely necessary condition to have a profound knowledge of the Word of God.

For this reason, we must teach the people in reading and meditating on the Word of God: may it become its nourishment, so that, through their own experience, they may see that the words of Jesus are spirit and life. (cf. Jn. 6:63) Otherwise, how are they going to announce a message of content and spirit they don't know deeply? We must base our missionary commitment and all our life on the rock of the Word of God. For this reason, I encourage Shepherds to do their best to make it known.

A great means to introduce the people of God to the mystery of Christ is catechesis. In it, the message of Christ is transmitted in a simple and substantial way. It is convenient, thus, to intensify catechesis in the formation in the faith of children, youth, and adults. A mature reflection about the faith is light for the path of life and strength to be witnesses of Christ. For this, we have very valuable instruments such as the Catechism of the Catholic Church and its shortened version, the Compendium of the Catechism of the Catholic Church.

In this area, we must not be limited only to homilies, conferences, Bible or theology courses, but we must seek also the media: the press, radio and television, websites, forums, and so many other systems to effectively communicate the message of Christ to a great number of people.

In this effort for knowing the message of Christ and making it the guide for our own lives, we must recall that evangelization has been always united to human promotion and to an authentic Christian liberation. "Love to God and love to the neighbor become one: in the most humble we meet Christ himself and in Jesus we meet God." (*Deus caritas est,* 15) For the same reason, also necessary are a social catechesis and an adequate formation in the social doctrine of the Church. The "Compendium of the Social Doctrine of the Church" will be very useful for this. The Christian life is not only expressed in personal virtues, but also in the social and political virtues.

The disciple, rooted in the rock of the Word of God, feels himself encouraged to share the Good News of salvation with his brothers and sisters. Discipleship and mission are like the two faces of the same medal: when the disciple is in love with Christ, he cannot help but to announce to the world that only He saves us. (cf. Acts 4:12) In fact, the disciple knows that without Christ there is no light, there is no hope, there is no love, and there is no future.

"So that We May Have Life in Him"

The Latin American and Caribbean peoples have the right to have a full life, fitting of the children of God, with more humane conditions: free of threats of hunger and all sorts of violence. For these peoples, their Shepherds are to promote a culture of life that allows, as my predecessor Paul VI said: "The rise from poverty to the acquisition of life's necessities . . . acquiring refinement and culture . . . an active interest in the common good. . . . Then man can acknowledge the highest values and God Himself, their author and end." (*Populorum progressio,* 21)

In this context, I am pleased to recall the encyclical *Populorum progressio,* whose 40th anniversary we commemorate this year. This pontifical document evidences that an authentic development has to be comprehensive: this is, oriented toward the promotion of every man and of all mankind (cf. n. 14) and invites all to abolish the grave social inequalities and the enormous differences in the access to goods. These peoples yearn, above all, for the fullness of life that Christ has brought: "I came that they may have life, and have it abundantly." (Jn. 10:10) With this divine life, the human existence is also developed in fullness, in its personal, family, social, and cultural dimensions.

In order to form the disciple and sustain the missionary in their great task, the Church offers, besides the Bread of the Word, the Bread of the Eucharist. In this regard, we are inspired and enlightened by the page of the Gospel about the disciples of Emmaus. When they sit at the table and receive from Jesus Christ the bread blessed and broken, their eyes are opened, they discover the face of the Risen One, and they feel in their hearts that all that He has said and done is true, and that the beginning of the redemption of the world has already begun. Every Sunday and every Eucharist is a personal encounter with Christ. On hearing the divine Word, the heart burns because it is Him who explains and proclaims it. When in the Eucharist the bread is broken, it is Him who is personally received. The Eucharist is the absolutely necessary nourishment for the life of the disciple and missionary of Christ.

THE SUNDAY MASS, CENTER OF THE CHRISTIAN LIFE

Hence, the need to give priority in the pastoral programs of giving importance to the value of Sunday Mass. We have to motivate the Christians to participate actively in Mass, and if possible, even better with their family. The attendance of the parents with their children to the Sunday Eucharistic celebration is an efficient way to teach and to communicate the faith, and is also the close bond that keeps unity among them. Sundays, throughout the life of the Church, have meant the privileged moments of encounter of communities with the Risen Lord.

It is necessary that Christians experience that they are not following a character of the past, but the living Christ, present in the today and now of their lives. He is the Living One that walks by our side, revealing the meaning of the happenings, of pain and of death, of joy, and of celebration, entering into our homes and remaining in them, nourishing us with the bread that gives life. Therefore, the Sunday celebration of the Eucharist has to be the center of the Christian life.

The encounter with Christ in the Eucharist brings about the commitment to evangelization and the thrust to solidarity; it awakens in the Christian the strong desire to announce the Gospel and witness it in society so that it may become more just and human. From the Eucharist has sprung throughout the centuries an enormous flow of charity, of participation in the difficulties of others, of love and justice. Only from the Eucharist will spring the civilization of love, which will transform Latin America and the Caribbean, so that besides being the Continent of Hope, it may also be the Continent of Love!

THE SOCIAL AND POLITICAL PROBLEMS

On arriving to this point, we can ask ourselves how the Church can contribute towards the solution to the urgent social and political problems, and answer to the great challenge of poverty and misery. The problems of Latin America and the Caribbean, as those of the world today, are manifold and complex and cannot be faced through general programs. However, the fundamental question of the way in which the Church, enlightened by the faith in Christ, should react to these challenges is of concern to all of us. In this context, it is inevitable to talk about the problem of structures, above all those that create injustice. In fact, the righteous structures are a condition without which it is not possible to have a just order in society. But how do these begin? How do they work?

Both capitalism and Marxism promised to find a way for the creation of righteous structures and affirmed that once these had been established, they would work by themselves. They affirmed that not only was it unnecessary to have a precedent of individual morality, but that these in fact would foster a common morality. And this ideological promise has been proved false. The facts make this clear. The Marxist system, wherever it has governed, has not only left a sad inheritance of economic and ecological destructions, but also a painful oppression of the soul. And we see the same thing in the Western Hemisphere, where there is a continuously growing separation between the poor and the rich, and there is a troubling degradation of the personal dignity through drugs, alcohol, and the subtle mirage of happiness.

The righteous structures are, as I said, an absolutely necessary condition for a more just society, but they do not begin and work without a moral consensus of society about the fundamental values and the need of living these with the necessary renounces, including those that are against personal interests.

Wherever God is absent—the God of the human face of Jesus Christ—these values are not shown with all its strength, nor is a consensus upon them produced. I do not want to say that the nonbelievers are unable to live an elevated and exemplary morality; I am simply saying that a society in which God is absent does not find the necessary consensus on the moral values and the strength to live according to the norm of these values, even against its own interests.

On the other hand, the righteous structures have to be sought and elaborated in light of the fundamental values, with all the pledge of the political, economic, and social reasoning. It is a question of the *recta ratio* and does not come from ideologies or its promises. There certainly exists a treasure of political experiences and knowledge on social and economic problems that make evident the fundamental elements of a just state and the paths that should be avoided. However, in diverse cultural and political situations, and in the progressive change of the technologies and the world historic reality, there has to be a rational search for adequate answers, and the consensus about the structures that should be established—with the crucial commitments—must be created.

This political work is not an immediate responsibility of the Church. The respect of a healthy laity—including the plurality of political positions—is essential in the authentic Christian tradition. If the Church began to transform itself into a direct political subject, it would not do more for the poor and for justice; rather it would do less, because it would lose its independence and moral authority, identifying itself with only one political option and with debatable partial positions. The Church is the advocate of justice and of the poor, precisely by not identifying herself with the politicians or the interests of a party. Only by being independent can it teach the great criterions and the irrevocable values, orient the consciences, and offer an option of life that goes beyond the political sphere.

To form consciences, to be advocate of justice and truth, and to educate in the individual and political virtues is the fundamental vocation of the Church in this sector. And the Catholic laity has to be aware of their responsibility in the public life; they have to be present in the formation of the necessary consensus and in the opposition against injustices.

The righteous structures will never be complete in a definite way; due to the constant evolution of history, they need to be continuously renewed and updated; they have to be always animated by a political and human "ethos," which presence and efficiency one is always to seek. In other words, the presence of God, the friendship with the incarnate Son of God, the light of His Word, are always essential conditions for the presence and efficiency of justice and love in our societies.

Given that it is a continent of baptized people, it is convenient to fill the critical absence in the realms of politics, media, and the universities with voices and initiatives of Catholic leaders of strong personality and a tireless vocation that are coherent with their ethical and religious convictions. The ecclesial movements have here a vast field to remind laity of their responsibility and mission of bringing the light of the Gospel to the public, cultural, economic, and political life.

To bring about the renewal of the Church entrusted to you in these lands, I would like to draw to your attention some areas that I consider a priority in this new phase.

THE FAMILY

The family, "heritage of humanity," constitutes one of the most important treasures of the Latin-American peoples. It has been, and is, a school of faith, platform of human and civic values, and a home in which human life is born and where it is generously and responsibly welcomed. However, presently it suffers adverse situations caused by secularism and ethic relativism, through the diverse external and internal migrations, due to poverty and social instability and due to civil legislations against marriage that, by favoring contraceptives and abortion, threaten the future of the peoples.

Regrettably, in some families in Latin America, a "macho" mentality still persists, ignoring the novelty of Christianity that recognizes and proclaims the equal dignity and responsibility of women in regards to men.

The family has no substitute for personal serenity and for the education of the children. Mothers who wish to fully dedicate themselves to the education of their children and to the service of the family should have the necessary conditions to be able to do so, and thus have the right to rely on the support of the State. Indeed, the role of the mother is paramount for the future of society.

The father has the duty to be truly a father, who exercises his absolutely necessary responsibility and collaboration in the education of his children. The children, for their comprehensive growth, have the right of having a father and a mother who will care for and accompany them towards the fullness of life. It is necessary, therefore, to promote an intense and vigorous family ministry. It is also absolutely necessary to promote authentic family policies that respond to the rights of the family as an essential social subject. The family is part of the heritage of the peoples and the entire humanity.

THE PRIESTS

The first promoters of discipleship and mission are those who were called "to be with Jesus and were sent to preach," (cf. Mc. 3:14) that is, the priests. They are to especially receive attention and paternal care of their Bishops, since they are the primary agents of an authentic renewal of Christian life in the people of God. To them I want to address some words of paternal affection, wishing "that the Lord be part of their portion and cup." If the priest puts God as the foundation and the center of his life, only then will he experience the joy and fruitfulness of his vocation. The priest has to be firstly a "man of God," (1 Tim. 6:11) a man who knows God "first hand," who cultivates a deep personal friendship with Jesus, who shares the "sentiments of Jesus." (cf. Fil. 2:5) Only in this way, the priest will be capable of bringing God—the God incarnate in Jesus Christ—to mankind, and of being the representative of His love. To fulfill this lofty mission he needs to have a solid spiritual structure and to live all his existence driven by faith, hope, and charity. He has to be like Jesus: a man that seeks, through prayer, the face and the will of God, equally cultivating his cultural and intellectual preparation.

Beloved priests of this continent and all those who as missionaries have come here to work: the Pope follows your pastoral activity and wishes that you are filled with consolations and hope, and prays for you.

RELIGIOUS AND CONSECRATED MEN AND WOMEN

I would like to address also the religious and consecrated lay men and women. The Latin-American and Caribbean society needs your witness: in a world that so many times searches, above all, for well-being, richness, and pleasure as the ultimate aim of life, and that highlights freedom disregarding the truth of man created by God, you are witnesses that there exists another way of living meaningfully. Remind your brothers and sisters that the Kingdom of God is at hand, that justice and truth are possible if we open ourselves to the loving presence of God our Father, of Christ our brother and Lord, of the Holy Spirit our Consoler. With generosity and up to the point of heroism, continue working so that love, justice, goodness, service, and solidarity may reign in society, according to the charism of your founders. Embrace your consecration with deep joy, because it is the instrument of sanctification for you and of redemption for your brothers and sisters.

The Church of Latin America is grateful for the work you have been carrying on throughout the centuries for the Gospel of Christ, in favor of your brothers and sisters, especially those who are poor and marginalized. I invite all of you to collaborate always with the Bishops, responsible for the pastoral work, working united with them. I also exhort you to a sincere obedience to the authority of the Church. Do not have an ideal other than holiness, according to the teachings of your founders.

THE LAITY

In this time that the Church of this continent gives itself fully to its missionary vocation, I remind the laity that you are also the Church, an assembly called by Christ to bear witness to the whole world. All baptized men and women must be aware that they were configured to Christ Priest, Prophet, and Shepherd, through the common priesthood of the people of God. You must be stewards in the building of society according to the criterion of the Gospel, with enthusiasm and boldness, in communion with your Shepherds.

There are many faithful who belong to ecclesial movements, in which we can see the signs of the manifold presence and sanctifying action of the Holy Spirit in the Church and in today's society. They are called to take to the world the witness of Jesus Christ, and to be leaven of the love of God in society.

THE YOUTH AND VOCATIONAL MINISTRY

In Latin America, most of the population is young. In this regard, we have to remind them that their vocation is that of being friends of Christ, disciples, and sentinels of tomorrow, as my predecessor John Paul II used to say. The youth are not afraid of sacrifice, but surely of a meaningless life. They are sensitive to the calling of Christ, who invites them to follow Him. They can answer to this calling as priests, as consecrated men or women, or also as fathers and mothers, fully dedicated to serving their brothers and sisters with all their time, their ability of giving of self, and with their whole lives.

The youth face existence as a continuous discovery, not limiting themselves to fashions and common trends, going beyond, driven by a radical curiosity about the meaning of life, of God the Father Creator and God the Son Redeemer in the heart of the human family. They should commit to a constant renewal of the world in light of God. Moreover, they are called to the task of opposing themselves to the easy illusions of immediate happiness and of the deceitful paradise of drugs, pleasure, and alcohol, along with all forms of violence.

"Stay with Us"

The work of this Fifth General Conference encourages us to ask with the disciples at Emmaus: "Stay with us, for it is nearly evening and the day is almost over." (Lk. 24:29) Stay with us Lord; accompany us although we have not always known how to recognize you. Stay with us, because around us the shadows become ever more dense, and you are the Light; hopelessness is subtly suggested in our hearts, and you make them burn with the certainty of Easter. We are tired of the way, but you comfort us with the fraction of the bread to announce to our brothers that you are truly raised and that you have given us the mission of being witnesses of your resurrection. Stay with us Lord, when our Catholic faith is surrounded by clouds of doubt, of weariness, or difficulty. You, who are the Truth itself as the revealer of the Father, shed light on our minds with your Word; help us to feel the beauty of believing in you.

Stay in our families, shed light on their doubts, sustain them in their difficulties, console them in their sufferings and in the fatigue of every day, when they find themselves surrounded by shadows that threaten against their unity and nature. You, who are the Life, stay in our homes, so that they may continue to be the nests where human life is born in abundance and generosity. A place where life is welcomed, loved, and respected from its conception to its natural death.

Stay, Lord, with those who in our societies are most vulnerable, stay with the poor and humble, with the indigenous and Afro-American, who have not always found spaces and support to express the richness of their culture and the wisdom of their identity. Stay, Lord, with our children and our youth, who are the hope and wealth of our continent; protect them from so many attacks that threaten their innocence and threaten their legitimate hopes. Oh, Good Shepherd, stay with our elderly and our ill. Strengthen all in their faith so that they may be your disciples and missionaries!

CONCLUSION

On concluding my stay amongst you, I wish to invoke the protection of the Mother of God and Mother of the Church upon you and all Latin America and the Caribbean. I implore to Our Lady, under the name of Guadalupe, Patroness of America and of Aparecida, Patroness of Brazil—that she accompanies you in this beautiful, demanding pastoral work. To her I entrust the people of God during this stage of the third Christian millennium. I ask her to guide the work and reflections of this General Conference and to bless with abundant gifts the beloved peoples of this continent.

MESSAGE OF THE FIFTH GENERAL CONFERENCE TO THE PEOPLES OF LATIN AMERICA AND THE CARIBBEAN

The Bishops of Latin America and the Caribbean

Gathered in the National Shrine of Our Lady of the Conception Aparecida, in Brazil, we greet in the love of the Lord all the people of God and all men and women of good will.

From 13 to 31 May 2007, we were gathered in the Fifth General Conference of the Bishops of Latin America and the Caribbean, inaugurated with the presence and the words of the Holy Father Benedict XVI. In our works, developed in an environment of fervent prayer, fraternity, and affective communion, we have sought to give continuity to the path of renewal that the Catholic Church undertook since the Second Vatican Council and in the four prior General Conferences of the Bishops of Latin America and the Caribbean. At the conclusion of this Fifth Conference, we announce that we have embraced the challenge of working to give a new impulse and vigor to our mission in and from Latin America and the Caribbean.

JESUS THE WAY, THE TRUTH, AND THE LIFE—"I AM THE WAY AND THE TRUTH AND THE LIFE." (JN. 14:6)

In the face of the challenges presented by this new time in which we are immersed, we renew our faith, proclaiming with joy to all men and women of our continent: we are loved and redeemed in Jesus, Son of God, the Risen One who is alive in our midst. Through Him, we can be free of sin, of all slavery, and live in justice and fraternity. Jesus is the way that allows us to discover the truth and to achieve the total fulfillment of our life!

CALLED TO THE FOLLOWING OF JESUS—"SO THEY WENT AND SAW WHERE HE WAS STAYING, AND THEY STAYED WITH HIM" (JN. 1:39)

The first invitation that Jesus makes to every person who has lived an encounter with Him is to be His disciple, so as to follow in His footsteps and to be part of His community. Our greatest joy is that of being His disciples! He calls each one by name, knowing our history in depth, (cf. Jn. 10:3) so that we may share our lives with Him and be sent forth to continue His mission. (cf. Mk. 3:14–15)

Let us follow Jesus! The disciple is the one who after having responded to this calling, follows Him step-by-step through the paths of the Gospel. As we follow Him, we hear and see the happening of the Kingdom of God, the conversion of each person, starting point for the transformation of society, at the same time that the paths to eternal life are opened to us. In the school of Jesus, we learn a "new life," moved by the dynamism brought by the Holy Spirit and reflected upon the values of the Kingdom.

Identified with the Master, our life is moved by the impulse of love and in the service to others. This love implies a continuous option and discernment to follow the path of the Beatitudes. (cf. Mt. 5:3–12; Lk. 6:20–26) Let us not be afraid of the cross, intrinsic in the faithful following of Jesus, because it is illuminated by the light of the Resurrection. In this way, as disciples, we open paths of life and hope to our peoples who suffer from sin and all kinds of injustice.

The calling to be disciples-missionaries demands from us a clear option for Jesus and His Gospel, coherence between faith and life, embodiment of the values of the Kingdom, insertion in the community, and to be a sign of contradiction and novelty in a world that promotes consumerism and disfigures the values that dignify the human being. In a world that is closed to the God of love, we are a community of love, not of the world, but in the world and for the world! (cf. Jn. 15:19; 17:14–16)

MISSIONARY DISCIPLESHIP IN THE CHURCH'S MINISTRY—"GO, THEREFORE, AND MAKE DISCIPLES OF ALL NATIONS" (MT. 28:19)

We see how the path of missionary discipleship is a source of renewal of our ministry in the continent and a new starting point for the new evangelization of our peoples.

A Church that Becomes a Disciple Herself

In the parable of the Good Shepherd, we learn to be disciples who are nourished from the Word: "the sheep follow him, because they recognize his voice." (Jn. 10:4) May the Word of Life (cf. Jn. 6:63) tasted in prayerful reading and in the celebration and living of the gift of the Eucharist transform and reveal to us the living presence of the Risen One who walks with us and acts in history. (cf. Lk. 24:13–35)

With firmness and decision, we will continue to exercise our prophetic task, discerning where the way for the truth and the life is, raising our voices in the social spheres of our peoples and cities, and especially in favor of those who are excluded in society. We want to stimulate the formation of Christian politicians and legislators, so that they may contribute in the building of a society more just and fraternal, according to the principles of the Social Doctrine of the Church.

A Church Which Forms Disciples

Everyone in the Church is called to be disciples and missionaries. It is a duty to form ourselves and to form all of God's people in order to fulfill this task with responsibility and boldness.

The joy of being disciples and missionaries can be seen in a special way in the places where we create fraternal communities. We are called to be a Church with open arms, who knows how to welcome and value each one of her members. Therefore, we encourage the efforts made in the parishes to become "home and school of communion," animating and forming small communities and basic church communities, as well as in the lay associations, ecclesial movements, and new communities.

We commit to strengthen our presence and proximity. Thus, in our pastoral service we invite to dedicate more time to each person, to listen to them, to be with them in the important events of their lives, and with them, to help seeking the solutions for their needs. Let us bring about that everyone, in feeling valued, may also experience the Church as their own home.

As we reaffirm the commitment with the formation of disciples and missionaries, this Conference decided to pay closer attention to the stages of the first announcement, of Christian Initiation, and of growth in the faith. With the reinforcement of Christian identity, let us help each brother and sister to discover the service that the Lord asks of them in the Church and in society.

In a world thirsty for spirituality and aware of the centrality of the relationship with the Lord in our life as disciples, we want to be a Church who learns to pray and teaches how to pray: a prayer that springs from our life and heart, and which is the starting point for lively and participative celebrations, which animate and nourish the faith.

MISSIONARY DISCIPLESHIP TO THE SERVICE OF LIFE— "I CAME SO THAT THEY MIGHT HAVE LIFE AND HAVE IT MORE ABUNDANTLY." (JN. 10:10)

From the cenacle of Aparecida, we commit to begin a new stage in our pastoral journey, declaring ourselves in permanent mission. With the fire of the Spirit, we will inflame our continent with love: "You will receive power when the Holy Spirit comes upon you, and you will be my witnesses . . . to the ends of the earth." (Acts 1:8)

IN FAITHFULNESS TO THE MISSIONARY COMMANDMENT

Jesus invites all to participate of His mission. May no one stay with crossed arms! To be a missionary is to announce the Kingdom with creativity and boldness in every place where the Gospel has not been sufficiently announced or welcomed, especially in the difficult or forgotten environments and beyond our borders.

AS LEAVEN IN THE DOUGH

Let us be missionaries of the Gospel not only in word, but also with our own lives, giving it in service, even to the point of martyrdom.

Jesus began His mission by forming a community of missionary disciples, the Church, which is the beginning of the Kingdom. His community was also part of His announcement. Inserted in society, we must make visible our love and fraternal solidarity (cf. Jn. 13:35), and let us promote the dialogue with the different social and religious agents. In an ever more pluralistic society, let us integrate forces in the building of a world with more justice, reconciliation, and solidarity.

SERVERS OF A SHARED TABLE

The acute differences between rich and poor invite us to work with greater effort in being disciples who know how to share the table of life—the table of all the sons and daughters of the Father—an open table, inclusive, in which no one is left behind. Therefore, we reinforce our preferential and evangelical option for the poor.

We commit to defend those who are weak, especially the children, the ill, the disabled, the at-risk youth, the elderly, the imprisoned, the migrants. We watch over and respect the right that the peoples have, "defending and promoting the underlying values in all social levels, especially in the indigenous peoples." (Benedict XVI, Speech in Guarulhos, n. 4) We want to contribute so that dignified living conditions, in which the needs such as food, education, housing, and work are guaranteed for all.

Faithfulness to Jesus demands from us to fight against the evils that harm or destroy life, such as abortion, wars, kidnapping, armed violence, terrorism, sexual exploitation, and drug dealing.

We invite all the leaders of our nations to defend the truth and to watch over the inviolable and sacred right to life and dignity of the human person, from conception until natural death.

We make available to our countries the pastoral efforts of the Church to contribute in the promotion of a culture of honesty that will heal the root of all forms of violence, illegal enrichment, and generalized corruption.

Coherent with the project of the Father who is the Creator, we call upon all living forces of society to take care of our common house, the Earth threatened of destruction. We want to favor a human and sustainable development based upon a just distribution of wealth and the communion of goods among all peoples.

TOWARDS A CONTINENT OF LIFE, LOVE, AND PEACE— "THIS IS HOW ALL WILL KNOW THAT YOU ARE MY DISCIPLES." (JN. 13:35)

We, participants of the Fifth General Conference in Aparecida, and with the entire Church "community of love," want to embrace all the continent to transmit to it the love of God and our own. We hope that this embrace will also reach out to the whole world.

At the closing of this Conference of Aparecida, in the vigor of the Holy Spirit, we summon all our brothers and sisters so that united with enthusiasm we may carry out the Great Continental Mission. It will be a new Pentecost that impels us to go, in a special way, in search of the fallen-away Catholics, and of those who know little or nothing about Jesus Christ, so that we may joyfully form the community of love of God our Father. It is a mission that must reach everyone, must be permanent and profound.

With the fire of the Holy Spirit, let us move forward, building with hope our history of salvation in the path of evangelization, surrounded by so great a cloud of witnesses, (cf. Hb. 12:1) the martyrs, saints, and blesseds of our continent. With their witness, they have shown us that faithfulness is worthwhile and possible up to the end.

United to all prayerful peoples, we entrust to Mary, Mother of God and Our Mother, first disciple and missionary at the service of life, love, and peace, called upon under the titles of Our Lady of Aparecida and Our Lady of Guadalupe, the new impulse that springs from this day onwards, in all Latin America and the Caribbean, under the breath of a new Pentecost for our Church, from this Fifth Conference which we have celebrated here.

In Medellín and Puebla, we concluded by saying, "WE BELIEVE." In Aparecida, as we did in Santo Domingo, we proclaim with all our strength: "WE BELIEVE AND WE HOPE."

We hope . . . to be a lively Church, faithful and credible, which is nourished from the Word of God and the Eucharist . . . to live our being Christians with joy and conviction as disciples-missionaries of Jesus Christ . . . to form lively communities that nourish the faith and encourage missionary action . . . to value the diverse ecclesial organizations in a spirit of communion . . . to promote a mature laity, steward in the mission of announcing and making visible the Kingdom of God . . . to impel the active participation of women in society and in the Church . . . to maintain our preferential and evangelical option for the poor with a renewed effort . . . to accompany the youth in their formation and search for identity, vocation, and mission, renewing our option for them . . . to work with all the people of good will in the building of the Kingdom . . . to strengthen with audacity Family and Respect Life Ministries . . . to value and respect our indigenous and Afro-American peoples . . . to advance in the ecumenical dialogue "so that all may be one," as well as in the interreligious dialogue . . . to make of this continent a model of reconciliation, justice, and peace . . . to be stewards of creation, home of all, in fidelity to the project of God . . . to collaborate in the integration of the peoples of Latin America and the Caribbean.

May this continent of hope also become the continent of love, life, and peace!

—Aparecida, Brazil, 29 May 2007

MEDELLÍN AND PUEBLA: DEAD OR ALIVE IN THE 21ST CENTURY CATHOLIC CHURCH?

Robert S. Pelton, C.S.C.

Having participated in the Second Vatican Council and, in various roles, in all of the CELAM conferences since Vatican II, I was delighted to be selected as an observer at CELAM V, the Fifth General Conference of the Bishops of Latin America and the Caribbean, held in Aparecida, Brazil, during 13–31 May 2007.

Although it would have been unrealistic to expect CELAM V to equal the extraordinary successes of the Medellín Conference in 1968, my hope was that CELAM V would strongly reaffirm the distinctive identity of the Latin American Catholic Church, offer strong encouragement and support for the basic Christian communities (CEBs), and find new and creative ways to apply the spirit and the thrust of the Second Vatican Council to the dynamics of twenty-first century Latin America. Despite excellent work by the 260 delegates and despite numerous positive outcomes, those hopes were not fully realized. I can only conclude that Medellín (1968) and Puebla (1979) are alive in the twenty-first century Catholic Church, but that they continue to be challenged.

Like the watershed conference in Medellín, Colombia, and the two intervening Conferencias Episcopal de America Latina, CELAM V conceptualized its conclusions relevant to the signs of the times by viewing the rapidly changing religious, social, economic, political, and cultural dynamics of the continent in the light of the Gospel. What emerged from Aparecida is a clear affirmation that the Catholic Church in Latin America and the Caribbean remains committed to full and creative expression of the Second Vatican Council, that it faces very different but no less daunting challenges in the twenty-first century than it did in the final decades of the twentieth century, that it has retained its own distinctive identity, and that it has much to share with the world.

Significantly, the bishops readopted the inductive "See-Judge-Act" method of discernment that proved so fruitful at Medellín and Puebla, whereas the 1992 Santo Domingo Conference employed a deductive and more theoretical methodology. CELAM V unequivocally endorsed and expanded three key concepts of the Latin American Catholic Church: the preferential option for the poor, ecclesial base communities (CEBs), and opposition to structural sin within the modern context of globalization and neoliberal economic models. It did so in an enlightened and collegial manner that may diminish the controversy that has sometimes arisen from popular misunderstanding of these principles.

Small ecclesial communities received an endorsement that underscores an inclusiveness that always existed in reality, but was not universally perceived in terms of their relationship with the institutional Church. The "preferential option for the poor" was expanded at Aparecida to become the "preferential and evangelizing option for the poor," making it clearer that the option is not solely a matter of socioeconomics. In a concrete demonstration of the necessity for and potential of that preferential and evangelizing option for the poor, the bishops issued a statement to the leaders of the G-8 nations, calling for the elimination of extreme poverty from all the world's nations before 2015, and making that goal "one of the most urgent tasks of our time," one that is "inseparably linked with world peace and security." The bishops also criticized "environmental aggression" against the Amazon rainforest, warning that Amazonia—which replenishes much of the world's atmospheric oxygen supply, contains twenty percent of the world's fresh unfrozen water, and nourishes thirty-four percent of the world's forests—will cease to exist within thirty years if present patterns of corporate, profit-driven destruction continue.

Many bishops displayed acute concern about the challenges posed by globalization, rapid urbanization, the changing roles of families and youth, and the demand for real dialogue with the indigenous and Afro-American communities, despite the lack of concrete action in these areas. They recognized also the need for greater decision-making roles for women in the Church and for greater clarity on the roles of ministry and the laity.

That the bishops are now focusing more attention on these issues than at any other time in CELAM's history suggests their deepening understanding of the full scope of Medellín and Puebla, and their growing commitment to adaptation of the mandate of promoting social justice to address the demands of present realities. Optimism about the full realization of

Vatican II was strong in the 1970s, but it gradually receded throughout much of Latin America as Pope John Paul II's episcopal appointments rarely challenged the status quo maintained by the national security states of that era.

COHERENT IMAGE OF THE CATHOLIC CHURCH IN THE 20 LATIN AMERICAN COUNTRIES?

The Catholic Church throughout Latin America is almost as diverse as Latin America itself, with little coherence other than that created by Scripture, CELAM and its declarations, and, to a lesser degree, communications networks formed by CEBs and other lay groups. The array of parish plans, liturgical forms, and concepts of Church that can vary greatly from parish to parish as well as from nation to nation arise from a unique blend of theology, history, necessity, and conscious choice. Following more than four centuries as an appendage of the Spanish Church, the Catholic Church in Latin America finally acquired an identity of its own from the Second Vatican Council's efforts to transform the Catholic Church into a "World Church" that integrates its values within the cultures of the various nations. The Latin American Bishops enthusiastically embraced the Council's teaching and followed the methodology of the Council's *Pastoral Constitution on the Church in the Modern World* by studying the facts, reflecting upon them, and then taking the appropriate actions.

It is widely understood that the culture of Latin America, the prevailing realities that the bishops studied, and the appropriate actions for which they called had combined to produce a theology and a concept of church that was, in some respects, quite different from that of Europe or North America. Less obvious, however, is the enormous range of cultures and diverse and rapidly changing realities that exist side by side within Latin America, demanding a multiplicity of responses from the Church at the most local levels. The bishops realized that the challenge for pastors and bishops alike is to find effective ways to meet both the spiritual and temporal needs of parishioners within each individual parish and to simultaneously maintain close bonds with the universal Church, while remaining mindful that a very different pastoral plan may be needed in adjacent parishes.

DOES THE VATICAN MAINTAIN A CENTRALIZING
MENTALITY OR DOES IT PRACTICE SUBSIDIARITY?

The current Vatican position is closer to centralization than to the principle of subsidiarity. It is centralized to a significantly greater degree than was envisioned by the Second Vatican Council and more than is favored by many of the Bishops of Latin America and the Caribbean. However, there has been no indication of Vatican intent to restore the degree of centralization that existed during the early 1950s, the era that ended the European worker-priest movement and silenced progressive theologians including Yves Congar, Henri de Lubac, and Marie-Dominique Chenu.

The pontificate of Pius XII (1939–1958) marked the completion of the near-absolute papal supremacy, initiated by Pius IX (1846–1878). Over the intervening century, the Pope and the Roman Curia, for the first time in history, had come effectively to hold the power of appointment of all the bishops in the Church. A neoscholastic orthodoxy was imposed on the Church in Leo XIII's 1879 encyclical, *Aeterni Patris*, and was consolidated by Pius X's intervention and simultaneous condemnation of "Modernism" in *Pascendi Gregis* (1907). Although surprising to some, John XXIII (1958–1963), who attempted to reassert the importance of the study of Latin (*Veterum Sapientiae*, 1962) also convoked the Second Vatican Council (1962–1965), which ended the excessive centralization of the preceding century. In the Council's central document on the Church, *Lumen Gentium*, the bishops returned to the early Church's emphasis on the significance of the local church and explicitly recognized that the local bishop's office is acquired through his consecration, not through papal delegation. In an obvious attempt to finesse the ancient battle between conciliarism and an autocratic papacy, the Council fathers proclaimed the ultimate authority of the college of bishops, though never without the presidency of the Bishop of Rome.

Joseph Ratzinger, during his tenure as theologian and *peritus* at Vatican II, expressed concern about *Gaudium et Spes* (*The Pastoral Constitution of the Church in the Modern World*), the conciliar decree so important for its definition of the role of the Catholic Church in the contemporary world. Both before he became cardinal-archbishop of Munich in 1977, and later, while serving as prefect of the Congregation for the Doctrine of the Faith during succeeding decades, he expressed displeasure with the manner in which some postconciliar reforms were implemented.

To date, however, there have been no papal reinterpretations of *Gaudium et Spes* or other conciliar documents. The first years of Benedict's papacy have been moderate and conciliatory for the most part and have respected both orthopraxis and Catholic social teaching. While attending the World Congress of Families in Valencia, Spain in July 2006, the pope explained why he refrained from criticizing Spanish social policies that are strenuously opposed by the Spanish Church and chose instead to offer the Catholic vision of family as a positive alternative.

> Christianity, Catholicism isn't a collection of prohibitions; it's a positive option. It's very important that we look at it again because this idea has almost completely disappeared today. We've heard so much about what is not allowed that now it's time to say: we have a positive idea to offer . . . The human person must always be respected. But all this is clearer if you say it first in a positive way.[2]

As John L. Allen, Vatican correspondent for *The Tablet*, (U.K.) has written, "This effort to phrase the Christian fundamentals in a positive key has become something of a leitmotif. Having been responsible for expressing the 'nos' of the Catholic Church for 20 years, Ratzinger as pope appears determined to articulate what he sees at its much deeper 'yes'. . . . To date [April 2007], expectations of a 'Catholic fundamentalist' papacy have been confounded."[3]

Promotion of Christian fundamentals without becoming rigidly fundamentalist lies at the core of Pope John XXIII's (1958–1963) insistence that the Catholic Church—a diverse and broadly inclusive Church, both by choice and necessity—must continuously learn from, and adapt to, the rapidly changing modern world. Since his papacy, progressive churchmen and women have reiterated this concept of church: that it must encourage the free exchange of ideas, not silence free exchange; that it must value orthopraxis over orthodoxy; and that it must never forget that the mission is far more important than the mechanisms. This is the *ecclesia semper reformanda*—a pilgrim Church, self-criticizing rather than self-congratulatory, desiring to learn and to grow, constantly striving for better

---

[2] John L. Allen, "The Real Ratzinger Revealed," *The Tablet*, 14 April 2007.
[3] John L. Allen, "The Real Ratzinger Revealed," *The Tablet*, 14 April 2007.

understanding of the great Mystery—that Karl Rahner, S.J. (1904–1984) and other theologians have been continuously articulating since Vatican II (1962–1965).

THE PREFERENTIAL OPTION FOR THE POOR AMONG PARISH PRIESTS AND RELIGIOUS ORDERS TODAY

Among the vast majority of experienced Latin-American priests, the preferential option for the poor, which was broadened at Aparecida into the "preferential and evangelizing option for the poor," is regarded not only as a guiding principle but also as one of the most crucial elements of their pastorates. Younger priests—who increasingly come from wealthier families and who grew up under conditions quite different from those experienced by most of their parishioners—often leave the seminaries with more conservative viewpoints, but pastoral realities frequently teach them that the preferential option is essential to the physical, social, and spiritual well-being, and not infrequently to the very survival of many millions of destitute persons. This reality is clearly reflected in the Synthesis of Contributions Received for the Fifth General Conference (May 2006):

> In many Latin-American countries, most of [the] Catholic
> population is made up of poor people who live excluded from the material,
> cultural, and social riches present in our countries. The preferential option
> for the poor distinguished the Church of the region and was influential in
> other churches. Today, this option faces new challenges that demand its
> renewal, so that it may manifest the fullness of its evangelical roots, its
> urgency, and its gospel riches.[4]

The Bishops of Latin America and the Caribbean repeatedly reaffirmed the option for the poor during the Fifth General Council, citing it as one of "the pastoral aspects that had the greatest resonance in the life of the Church," (N. 21) calling for a new integrating synthesis between the option for the poor and care for the middle class, (N. 82) affirming the option

---

[4] *Synthesis of Contributions Received for the Fifth General Conference,* 2006, N. 346.

as a major christological criteria for the missionary path of the Church, (N. 165) recognizing the evangelization of the poor as the great messianic sign that Christians are called to live as Church, cf. Lk. 7–22, (N. 165) and citing weaknesses in the option as a sin within the individual Christian that must be repented and corrected. (N. 79) Significantly, the bishops called for further renewal, consolidation, and permanence of the option for the poor.

> In our time, we tend to defend excessively spaces of privacy and enjoyment, and we let ourselves be infected by individualistic consumerism. Hence, our option for the poor runs the risk of remaining on a theoretical or merely emotional level, without really affecting our behaviors and our decisions. This generic option must be turned into a permanent attitude that is reflected in concrete options and gestures (cf. DCE 28.31). That means first devoting time to the poor, giving them friendly attention, listening to them with interest, accompanying them in the most difficult moments, choosing them for sharing hours, weeks, and years of our lives, and seeking them for the transformation of their situation. Jesus proposed it with how he acted and with his words: "When you hold a banquet, invite the poor, the crippled, the lame, the blind." (Luke 14:13)[5]

In 1968, at the conference at Medellín, the Bishops of Latin America sought "the presence of the Church in the current transformation of Latin America in the light of Vatican Council II." The preferential option for the poor was one of many creative applications of conciliar renewal to a continent gripped by poverty, acute social injustice, and institutionalized sin, but it soon became a keystone of the Latin-American Church's new dedication to a Christianity that unites faith with justice, with promotion of people and societies, and with service to the Kingdom in accord with the teachings of Jesus Christ.

Nearly four decades later, the option continues to serve as a lifeline to countless millions of marginalized persons and as a key element of the Church's social mission. Once controversial, it has since been almost universally accepted and has been incorporated into canon law, which states: "[The Christian faithful] are also obliged to promote social justice and, mindful of the precept of the Lord, to assist the poor from their

---

[5] *Synthesis of Contributions Received for the Fifth General Conference,* 2006, N. 224.

own resources."[6] The option has been reaffirmed by the Latin-American Bishops at four consecutive CELAM conferences and by four successive pontiffs, most recently by Pope Benedict, who said in Aparecida on 11 May 2007, "The poor are the privileged audience for the Gospel." Clearly, the preferential and evangelical option for the poor is in place as intended on the continent of its birth and within the Church.

ARE THE CEBS STILL ALIVE?

Contrary to periodic reports of their impending demise, the *Comunidades Eclesiales de Base* are alive, thriving, and continuing to fulfill a multiplicity of vital roles across Latin America and on the other continents as well. Some Latin-American CEBs now exist in forms that would be almost unrecognizable to the pioneering CEB members of the late 1960s and 1970s, and many of these may well transform themselves into still other forms. Conversely, other CEBs have changed little since they were formed in the immediate aftermath of the Medellín Conference. Both models, and the countless others along the continuum, are fulfilling their intended roles as perennial works-in-progress that exist to meet the needs of particular groups of individuals in a specific time and place, and to adapt themselves to new missions as soon as they have fulfilled their original purpose. Thinking "on their feet" and adapting rapidly to the changing needs of their communities is a clear indication of their success, not of failure or disarray.

An excellent summary of contemporary CEBs is contained in *Do Vaticano II: a um novo Concilio* (2004) by Dom Luiz Alberto Gómez de Souza: "The CEBs continue to play an active role in society, from assistential activities to mobilizations and involvement in associations, syndicates, and parties as well as in national campaigns."[7]

This study further reports that CEBs in Brazil appear as a consolidated experience. The most successful CEBs make special efforts to attract young people, both to better serve the youth and to revitalize

---

[6] 1983 CIC, canon 222 § 2.

[7] Luiz Alberto Gómez, S.J., *Do Vaticano II: a um novo Concilio.* São Paulo: Loyola, 2004.

the communities. Women are in the majority (comprising approximately 62 percent of the membership), which contributes to a certain empowerment of women in the Church and in local civic society. Most of their members come from the middle and lower-middle socioeconomic classes. Most CEBs emphasize the role of the Mass, which also provides a space for communion.[8] Active support from the Church hierarchy has waxed and waned over the years, but reports of condemnations of CEBs are unfounded. There have been instructions to the CEBs from the Vatican and from the Latin-American bishops, but these have been intended as constructive criticism and guidance, not as efforts to constrain. *The Instrumentum Laboris* (1997) for the Synod of America, in Rome in 1997, calls base ecclesial communities "the primary cells of the Church structure" and views them as being "responsible for the richness of faith and its expansion, as well as for the promotion of the person and development." In his post-synodal Exhortation, *Ecclesia in America* (1999), Pope John Paul II recognized the CEBs' ability to renew parishes by enabling each to become a community of communities, (N. 41) and their ability to promote interpersonal bonds within the Catholic Church. (N. 73) In *Redemptorio Missio* (1990), John Paul II emphasized the evangelizing roles of CEBs (N. 51) after personally observing some of the results produced by Chilean CEBs, which have remained a pastoral priority of the Chilean Episcopal Conference since 1969.

In May 2006 in Quito, Ecuador, CELAM sponsored a continental meeting, "Small Christian Communities: Schools for the Followers and Missioners of Jesus Christ." Approximately fifty bishops, priests, male and female members of religious orders, and lay members of CEBs from eighteen nations gathered to share detailed information about the successes, failures, and challenges of CEBs across the continent, and to form realistic assessments of the communities' future. Many of the delegates reported difficulties in recruiting committed members in large cities and among increasingly transient segments of society—a difficulty shared by many urban churches as well—but they concluded that CEBs are doing well overall.

---

[8] Luiz Alberto Gómez, S.J., *Do Vaticano II: a um novo Concilio.* São Paulo: Loyola, 2004.

After three days of intensive discussion, the delegates were able to offer specific recommendations to help CEBs overcome challenges and avoid pitfalls:

1. reduction of the CEBs' dependence upon individual bishops who might or might not consider CEBs a priority within their dioceses
2. recognition that CEBs are, and must remain, works-in-progress and that they must be provided with "missionary space" to take on new forms and to move in new directions, true to their roots
3. heightened respect for the works of the Spirit in the grass roots of the Church, and for the prophetic role of the CEBs
4. greater awareness that CEBs are not merely mass movements, but are the nucleus of the present and future Church, as well as its ancestor
5. renewed support for CEBs, both as concepts and as fully functional entities that flow from the teachings of the Second Vatican Council and from the Medellín and Puebla Conferences

The participants at the Quito meeting took these recommendations back to their homelands and to the planning sessions of CELAM V. Although the Conference of Latin-American Bishops gave strong support for the CEBs in their text issued before the Fifth General Conference in May 2007, the Vatican's view was that the General Conference did not do so in its vote on May 30. Cardinal Giovani Batista Rey, the chair of the Pontifical Commission for Latin America, stated that although the text as a whole received a clear majority of the votes cast, the sections concerning CEBs received only 72 votes out of a possible 261 voters. According to the official procedures of the conference, passage requires that two-thirds of delegates vote in favor.

Thus, the Vatican-approved document presents a more minimalistic vision of the CEBs. There is no mention of their prophetic role and no recognition of the need for support from their parishes and their dioceses. Instead, the document implies fear of the CEBs and of leadership from "below." The final document respects the Medellín emphasis of CEBs as basic cells of the Church, but it mixes them with an array of other essentially unrelated ecclesial movements, increasing the risk that the CEBs may lose their identity. I am confident that the CEBs will continue to function as a model of the Church at the service of the poor, struggling against structural sin, but there is little question that the alterations made to the final document have made the fulfillment of the CEBs' mission more difficult.

THE CHURCH AND SOCIAL ISSUES: REPRODUCTIVE RIGHTS, HOMOSEXUALS, ROLES OF WOMEN

Dom Luiz Alberto Gómez de Souza, former Executive Director of the Centro de Estatística Religiosa e Investigacöes Sociais research center in Rio de Janeiro, and a former Visiting Fellow at the University of Notre Dame's Helen Kellogg Institute for International Studies, has presented a succinct and accurate overview of these and other issues which, though currently unresolved, cannot be allowed to remain so indefinitely.

Today, there are many restricted areas of sexuality and reproductive behavior, celibacy of the clergy, and access of women to the various ecclesiastic ministries. In spite of some overtures, such as that of John Paul II at Assisi, the ecumenical and interreligious exchanges are frustrated by many manifestations like the Eucharistic document of the same pope. Some voices have been heard suggesting a new Council, but at the moment it seems premature in view of the prevailing ecclesiastic conditions. However, a conciliar process must be prepared. The most important thing is the continuance of an ecclesial and pastoral practice that is experimental and renewing, silent, subversive, and patient, steadily staying ahead of today's institutional politics, and perhaps preparing underground surprises for tomorrow.

In the Church today, there is, therefore, a growing demand to reopen a debate on themes noted above that had remained frozen, from sexuality, participation of women in the religious ministries, imposed celibacy of the clergy, interreligious dialogue, and, especially, shared participation, which is nothing other than democratic ecclesial practice.

Who knows, this may form part of a long conciliar process in a future pontificate, while probably not in that of Benedict XVI. If the Church of the second millennium was a Church with power concentrated in the clergy, a Church may arise with the active and decisory presence of all the faithful.[9]

---

[9] Luiz Alberto Gómez, S.J., Kellogg Institute Working Paper 334, *Latin America and the Catholic Church: Points of Convergence and Divergence 1960–2005.* Notre Dame: Helen Kellogg Institute for International Studies, 2007.

Somewhat less controversial than many other issues, the role of women within the Church and within secular society is by far the largest issue in terms of the number of persons it directly affects. Section 2 of the Synthesis of CELAM V, entitled "Faces that Question Us," presents a troubling portrait of the realities encountered by all too many Latin-American women:

> Countless women of every condition have suffered a double exclusion by reason of their socioeconomic situation and their sex. They are not valued in their dignity, they are left alone and abandoned, they are not sufficiently recognized for their selfless sacrifice and every heroic generosity in the care and education of their children or in the transmission of the faith in the family, nor their indispensable and special participation in building a more humane social life and building up the Church in the merging of its Petrine and Marian dimensions sufficiently appreciated or promoted.[10]

Several years ago, Sister Aline Steur, C.S.C., a veteran missioner in Latin America, made similar observations: "Women continue to offer the main support of the Church and to comprise the overwhelming majority of its active members, but the inclusion of women and women's issues does not reflect their numbers, their contributions, or their needs."[11]

CELAM V, which included 25 women among the 267 participants (religious, laity, *periti*, and observers gave the role of women more attention than at any previous General Conference of CELAM. The Vatican-approved final document praises motherhood as "an excellent mission of women" but also states that motherhood "does not exclude the need for their active participation in the construction of society." A later paragraph calls for women to have decision-making roles in the Church, and decries "discrimination against women and their frequent absence in organisms of ecclesial decision."

Pope Benedict has made few statements on the role of women, but he has expressed strong opposition to divorce, same-sex marriages, and "the risk of deviations in the area of sexuality," and he has pledged that the Church will not compromise on these issues. Many Catholics oppose these practices as threats to traditional family structure, but those who cite violations of

---

[10] *Synthesis of Contributions Received for the Fifth General Conference.* 2006, N. 51.
[11] Interview of Sr. Aline Steur, C.S.C., 1 Nov 2005.

"natural law" and "universal binding norms" stand on weak foundations. Catholic scholars have responded that "natural law," "absolute truth," and "universal binding norms" are elements of ancient Greek metaphysics— not of Scripture.

It is hardly surprising that complex issues with powerful religious, emotional, and social components are causing divisions within the Catholic Church, between the Catholic Church and churches of other denominations, with civil authorities, and with secular society—none of which think with one mind or speak with one voice. It is understandable that millions of Catholics, clergy and lay alike, especially those who see merits and shortcomings on both sides of pressing social issues, may prefer to avoid struggling with such challenging issues, or may retreat to familiar, comfortable, but ultimately non-fruitful habits and thought patterns. As the Latin-American Bishops warn, however, failure to apply the Church's social teachings to questions that impact human lives is an abdication both of Christian vocation and of civic responsibilities. Relying on authority figures to make difficult choices is "one more way of being childishly and massively dependent rather than being involved with creativity and constancy."[12]

How, then, are Catholics to seek conditions in which a healthy politics and consequently solutions to social problems can mature? One possible answer may lie in the CELAM bishops' attempt to translate belief in the possibility of a "more just world" into a concrete reality, making the defense of life "pro-life" in the much broader sense of promoting better lives for every segment of society.

THE ROLE OF DEACONS AND LAY MINISTERS

"I am the only Bible that most people will ever read," a laywoman said recently, while leading scriptural study at a *casa culto*, a "house church" in Havana, Cuba. Her statement may sound overblown and self-aggrandizing to those of us who hear it with a North American or European mentality but it accurately reflects the prevailing reality faced by the many millions of Latin Americans who must find ways to cope with shortages of ordained

---

[12] *Synthesis of Contributions Received for the Fifth General Conference.* 2006, N. 280.

clergy, limited seating capacities of churches, lack of transportation, ethnic or socioeconomic differences that make the poor fear they will be unwelcome in the churches of their "betters," and countless other obstacles.

For these and many other members of the Latin-American faithful, lay catechists and deacons are often the primary source of pastoral care and teaching. Recently, for example, Father José Oscar Beozzo, a leading expert on Brazil's religious vocations and training, pointed out that 80 percent of all the Sunday celebrations in Brazil are led by laity, either because there are not enough priests to celebrate Mass or because the faithful are unable to attend traditional churches.

Working within a multiplicity of initiatives at the grass roots of the Church with different degrees of success, lay ministers have long been essential both to the faithful and to the Church, and their role continues to grow. They preach the Word to those who would otherwise rarely hear it or might not understand it in more formal modes of expression. They preside at the celebrations, comfort the ill and the bereaved, and find countless other ways both to animate the journey and to contribute decisively to the role of the laity as protagonists within the Church. For this reason Edward Cleary, O.P., Director of Latin American Studies at Providence College, cites the 1.1 million lay catechists currently active in Latin America as a basic strength of the Catholic Church there.[13]

The Bishops of Latin America and the Caribbean are keenly aware both of the lay ministers' contributions and of the need to promote a still more active laity, as the *Synthesis* of CELAM V makes clear:

> The whole Church is missionary. What is needed for this truth to become reality is that lay people be trained, the Christian and secular character of their vocation be promoted actively without fear, room be made for them in the Church, they be respected in their opinions and initiatives, and that room be opened for them to participate in the decisions of the community; in short, that they be treated as adults in a line of communion and participation (cf. p. 11), as is proper to their baptismal vocation which they subsequently confirmed sacramentally.[14]

---

[13] "Featured Q&A With Our Board of Advisors," *Inter-American Dialogue*, 27 March 2007.

[14] *Synthesis of Contributions Received for the Fifth General Conference.* 2006, N. 349.

Although there is nothing new in the bishops' position, there seems to have been a significant rise in Vatican support for lay involvement in the Church's ministries. Rome has long endorsed lay ministries, but it has often done so cautiously. In Aparecida, however, Pope Benedict urged the laity to join with priests and religious in an ambitious program of evangelization and missionary and pastoral outreach, especially at the urban peripheries, and he strongly endorsed the growth of lay ministries while stressing the need for their ministries to remain in alignment with their pastors and in conformity with the orientation of the diocese.

IS THERE A CRISIS OF VOCATIONS?

Fr. José Oscar Beozzo has repeatedly warned that Brazil has just over 18,000 priests to serve a Catholic population of 140 million—a clergy-to-lay ratio of approximately 1 to 8,600.[15] Both the numbers and the ratios vary from diocese to diocese and from country to country, but all twenty Latin American nations are experiencing shortages of priests and nuns so pronounced that they leave gaping holes in the Church's pastoral nets.

Conversely, Edward Cleary, O.P., recently reported that the number of seminarians throughout Latin America has increased approximately 400 percent since 1972, and that there has been a 70 percent increase in the number of Latin-American clergy replacing missionaries from other continents—a reversal of the 1960s, when the Vatican was asking that ten percent of North American clergy go to Latin America to alleviate the critical shortage of priests.[16] Additionally, there are increasing numbers of lay catechists, as well as tens of millions of lay men and women fulfilling Christian vocations within thousands of CEBs and within faith-in-daily-life endeavors in both urban and rural communities throughout every nation of Central and South America.

Despite the apparent contradiction, both of these observations are accurate. Every continent is experiencing a crisis of vocations, but Latin

[15] John L. Allen, "Benedict's Priorities: Feeding Humanity's Spiritual and Material Hunger," *NCRcafe*, 11 May 2007.

[16] "Featured Q&A With Our Board of Advisors," *Inter-American Dialogue*, 27 March 2007.

America is responding to this challenge imaginatively and with great success. Certainly, the shortage of priests, sisters, and brothers throughout Latin America is nothing new, nor is it as pronounced as it was throughout most of the past 500 years. At Medellín in 1968, there was a "crisis of vocations" that was even more profound than it is today. The Latin-American Church partially overcame that crisis as it has overcome many daunting obstacles in its long history.

THE RELEVANCE OF CHARISMATIC MOVEMENTS

Both the Vatican and the Latin-American bishops have expressed concerns about the number of Latin Americans being drawn away from the Catholic Church by the various Pentecostal movements and by Evangelical Protestant churches, but those concerns are frequently misunderstood. Declines in Church rolls do not threaten the existence of the Catholic Church in Latin America, nor were they the raison d'être for CELAM V, as some media reports have suggested. The Catholic Charismatic movement, sometimes blamed for drawing members away from the mainstream Church, is actually having the opposite effect.

Nevertheless, the decrease in the per capita percentage of Catholics in Latin America is very real. In Brazil, for example, the national census reveals that 74 percent of Brazilians identified themselves as Catholics in the year 2000, compared to 89 percent in 1980. Those who self-identified as Pentecostal, Evangelical, or fundamentalist Protestants grew from seven percent to 15 percent during the same period.[17] Similar trends have been documented in three Mexican states and in four Central American and South American nations in addition to Brazil, and a 2007 study conducted by the Pew Hispanic Center/Pew Forum on Religion and Public Life found very similar trends among Hispanic-Americans in the United States.[18] Despite such declines, South America is home to more Catholics than all other continents combined, and Brazil remains the nation with both the highest

---

[17] "Pope Calls Latin America 'Continent of Hope'," Associated Press, 13 May 2007.

[18] Patricia Zapor, "Study Finds U.S. Hispanics Drawn to Charismatic Churches," Catholic News Service, 4-26-2007.

per capita percentage and the greatest number of Catholics, approximately 140 million.[19]

Pope Benedict undoubtedly had both facts in mind when he made his call at Aparecida for the members of the Latin-American religious community to remain "courageous and effective missionaries" in order to maintain Catholicism as the dominant religious force on the continent. The bishops had already conducted a comprehensive study of what they termed "the expansion of the sects," a terminology that itself presents issues. They concluded that much of the attraction of the Evangelical and Pentecostal churches resulted from proselytizing efforts that are, in some cases, more a matter of marketing than of evangelization. Significantly, however, the bishops identified four specific weaknesses within Catholic parishes: shortage of pastoral agents, inadequate evangelization in the past, deficient pastoral care for the poor and the alienated, and lack of pastoral outreach to those who were baptized but no longer participate. The bishops called for concerted pastoral actions to minister more fully to the underserved and disaffected, as well as campaigns to reassure inactive Catholics that the Church will welcome those who wish to return.[20]

Although most of those who join Evangelical or Pentecostal churches come out of the Catholic Church, most researchers agree that the majority come from the nonpracticing sector of Catholicism.[21] Their dropout rate from their new churches is high, probably in the 40 percent range. Some continue to "church hop" for years, while others give up religious practice altogether.[22]

Except for a shared need for a more evangelical style of faith and a more animated liturgy than many Catholics are accustomed to, Charismatic Catholics seem to share few of the characteristics of those who choose fundamentalist Protestant churches. This is but one of the conclusions reached in the detailed 2007 survey conducted by the Pew Forum on

---

[19] John L. Allen, "Benedict's Priorities: Feeding Humanity's Spiritual and Material Hunger," *NCRcafe*, 11 May 2007.

[20] *Synthesis of Contributions Received for the Fifth General Conference*, 2006, N. 348.

[21] "Featured Q&A With Our Board of Advisors," *Inter-American Dialogue*, 27 March 2007.

[22] *Synthesis of Contributions Received for the Fifth General Conference*, 2006, N. 347.

Religion and Public Life. As its title implies, "Changing Faiths: Latinos and the Transformation of American Religion" surveyed only U.S. Hispanic Catholics, but the Pew Hispanic Center's analysts are convinced that many of the findings are equally true among Charismatic Catholics across the American continents.

The Pew study of 4,016 Hispanic-American adults, conducted between August and October 2006, made many significant discoveries:

1. a decline in the percentage of U.S. Hispanics who self-identify as Catholic, primarily due to those who joined evangelical or Pentecostal churches
2. approximately one-third of all U.S. Catholics are of Latin American origin or ancestry, a percentage that is growing due to immigration and birthrate
3. Hispanics differ little from the general U.S. population in most respects, but "renewal Christianity" has attained much more resonance among Hispanic Catholics than among non-Hispanic Catholics, only 12 percent of whom consider themselves charismatics
4. Conversely, the analysts identified 54 percent of Hispanic Catholics as charismatics, based upon "displays of excitement and enthusiasm such as raising hands, shouting, or jumping" during Masses, or participating in prayer groups where participants pray for miraculous healing or deliverance, or speak in tongues
5. Hispanic Protestants were even more likely to join "renewal" churches, with 57 percent in that category: 31 percent Pentecostal and 26 percent charismatic Protestants; in contrast, less than 20 percent of non-Hispanic Protestants are renewalists
6. Conversion from Catholicism to other faiths was much more common among second or third generation Hispanic-Americans than among recent immigrants
7. The large majority of those who left Catholicism joined evangelical churches
8. 61 percent of former Catholics who became evangelical Protestants said they found the Mass "unexciting," and 36 percent said that was a factor in leaving the Church; 46 percent disapprove of Catholic restrictions on divorce but only 5 percent claimed this as their reason for leaving.

Among Catholic Charismatics, "there's absolutely no evidence that [charismatic religious practices] diminish or undercut their Catholic orthodoxy or their connection to parish life," says Luis Lugo, Director of the Pew Forum. To the contrary, involvement in the charismatic style of religious practice strengthens religious identity. "Whether Catholic, Anglican, or mainline Protestant, Latinos who adopt a more charismatic style of practicing their faith remain within their original churches and become stronger in their religious commitment," Lugo reports.

Far from hastening loss of Church membership, the rapidly growing Catholic Charismatic movement is helping the Church to share in the religious renewal that is sweeping across many areas of Latin America. The charismatics also help retain those active Catholics who seek a "high energy" Mass and the practice of charisms, and who might otherwise leave the Church to join one of the fundamentalist Protestant denominations. In Brazil and many other nations of Latin America—as in portions of Africa, Europe, and the United States as well—the rapid growth of the Catholic Charismatic movement has made charismatics a major constituent in many parishes.

Pope John Paul II regarded the Catholic Charismatic movement as integral to the renewal of the Catholic Church. Pope Benedict XVI has cautioned charismatics to remain fully grounded in the universal Church, but has otherwise acknowledged the many positive elements of the movement.

Concerning those persons who turn away from both traditional and charismatic Catholicism, and possibly from a succession of other churches as well, the Latin American Bishops have stated, "The example of Christ also asks from us a respectful relationship with our brothers and sisters in other Christian communities and with those who follow other religions." (21)

Unfortunately, this degree of ecumenism was not always evident in Aparecida. Although CELAM V welcomed seven observers representing the Anglican, Baptist, Judaic, Lutheran, Methodist, and Presbyterian denominations, many observers—both Catholic and non-Catholic—have expressed agreement with *The Tablet,* a prominent independent Catholic newspaper published in the United Kingdom, which headlined a recent story "Conference Weak on Ecumenism." Bishop Ricardo Ramirez of Los Cruces, New Mexico, said, "If [CELAM] has any weaknesses from a North American perspective, it is its very limited acknowledgement of ecumenism, which is totally subsumed under the challenge of the 'sects'—the term used in Latin America for proselytizing Christian groups."[23]

Although there had been agreement at the Synod for America in 1997 to cease using the word "sects," the disparaging term was used repeatedly during the General Conference. Despite several clarifications and expressions of respect from prominent members of CELAM, the perception of a general ecumenical weakness—extending beyond semantics—persists in some quarters. "The Rev. Néstor Míguez, an Argentine Methodist observer at Aparecida, agreed with Bishop Ramirez about the lack of ecumenism," *The Tablet* reports. "This was 'not envisaged in the prior agenda and the Pope said not a single word about it. Curial cardinals came from several dicasteries, but no one from the Council for Promoting Christian Unity . . . There should always be an ecumenical approach to reading the Bible in Christian communities.'"[24]

RELIGIOUS PLURALISM AND THE CATHOLIC CHURCH

Although religious pluralism is often perceived as a synonym for ecumenism or religious tolerance, the late Cardinal Giacomo Lecaro was much more accurate when he defined religious pluralism as "a struggle toward a Church that is truly Catholic yet truly catholic." His point, of course, was that mutual respect and understanding, harmonious coexistence, righteousness without self-righteousness, willingness both to teach and to learn, and ability to disagree without animosity must be fostered within the Church as well as between the Church and other religious denominations. His use of "yet" instead of "and" reflects the fact that positive goals are all too frequently at odds with each other.

Nearly half a century later, the difficult but vitally important struggle toward catholic Catholicism continues, a fact reflected in Section 4.1 of the Synthesis of Contributions Received for the Fifth General Conference:

> The cultural and religious pluralism of contemporary society
> impacts strongly on the Church. There are other sources of meaning
> competing with it, relativizing and weakening its social impact and its

---

[23] "Conference Weak on Ecumenism," *The Tablet*, 2 June 2007.
[24] "Conference Weak on Ecumenism," *The Tablet*, 2 June 2007.

pastoral action. Not all Catholics were prepared to resist this multiplicity of discourses and practices present in society. Indeed, this fact has been manifested in a certain silent distancing from the Church by many who join other religious beliefs or institutions with little thought. This situation is aggravated by the ethical and religious relativism of contemporary culture. However, pluralism opens spaces for personal freedom and conscious religious option. All this shows the urgent need for greater Christian formation of the laity, so as to allow it to develop a posture of convinced identification with its Christian vocation and evangelical discernment in the face of this pluralism.

Moreover, the emergence in our time of subjectivity, accompanied by a growing participation of our contemporaries in cultural conquests, also represents a challenge to the Church. A statement is no longer accepted merely because it comes from an authority. An adequate foundation must be offered for doctrinal or ethical discourse, because everyone wants his or her personal autonomy and freedom to be respected; thus as Pope Benedict XVI says, the Church should intervene on the various issues in the life of society "through rational argumentation."[25] The Christian message undoubtedly offers solid frameworks for personal integration and shared social life. It must be announced to our contemporaries with an open and dialogue-oriented posture.

The Catholic Church of Latin America did indeed come into its own with the Second Vatican Council and the CELAM convocations. It is continuing that mission today, concretely confronting the challenges of Latin American reality, displaying deep commitment and perseverance in its quest to become *ecclesia simper reformanda.*

BENEDICT XVI'S EPISCOPAL APPOINTMENTS

Many of the Episcopal appointments that Pope Benedict made early in his pontificate had been initiated by Pope John Paul II. Thus, these appointments may or may not accurately reflect the type of churchmen that Pope Benedict sees as models for the Church in the twenty-first century. The majority of the more recent appointments in the Holy See and in dioceses

---

[25] Pope Benedict XVI's encyclical, *Deus caritas est,* 2005.

throughout Latin America have been ideological moderates who have a strong pastoral orientation. If continued, such appointments bode well for Latin America, but it will take time to see what direction these bishops will go and to what extent Aparecida will influence them.

A relatively small number of appointments, many of which were "in the pipeline" during John Paul II's pontificate, do not permit sweeping generalizations about the impact that Pope Benedict's Episcopal appointments will have in coming years. The new cardinals are not of a single mind, and any suggestion that they are likely to move in only one direction is incorrect. Much will depend upon subsequent appointments, and upon how the prelates respond to the realities of life in Latin America and to the pastoral directives of Aparecida.

National Catholic Reporter believes that the pope's visit to Aparecida may offer some clues about his future appointments and about the relationship between the Latin American Church and the Vatican:

> Brazil has offered an intriguing mix of what many regard as 'the real Ratzinger,' with tough talk on abortion, marriage, priestly celibacy, and ecclesiastical discipline, along with the more pastoral Benedict—praising the late Archbishop Oscar Romero of El Salvador; urging work on behalf of the poor, the Amazon rain forest, and in general for 'a more just and fraternal society' and, by virtue of his very choice to be here, offering an olive branch to a Brazilian church long seen as estranged from Rome.[26]

On 9 May 2007, while flying to Brazil to inaugurate CELAM V, reporters reminded the pontiff that Pope John Paul II designated Archbishop Romero as one of the "new martyrs" of the last millennium.[27] Pope Benedict responded: "I have no doubt he [Romero] will be beatified. I know that the cause is proceeding well at the Congregation for the Cause of the Saints . . . He was certainly a great witness for the faith, a man of great Christian virtue who was committed to peace and against dictatorship."[28]

---

[26] John L. Allen, "Benedict's Priorities: Feeding Humanity's Spiritual and Material Hunger," *NCRcafe*, 11 May 2007.

[27] *Commemorazione ecumenical dei testimony della fede del XX secolo, cetta del Vaticano 2000*, p. 104.

[28] Reported by the Italian news agencies ANSA and APCOM on 9 May 2007.

Although definitive conclusions cannot be drawn from a few remarks or from a single papal visit, the pope's esteem for Archbishop Romero—who was, above all, the ultimate pastoral leader—may shed some light on Pope Benedict's vision of his own pastorate of the universal Church and of the bishops that should lead the Latin American Church in this new millennium.

Nor can there be doubt that many Latin American churchmen and millions of Latin American laypersons who revere "Saint Romero" would agree that the Church needs bishops who strive to model themselves after Óscar Arnulfo Romero y Galdámez, fourth Archbishop of San Salvador. Speaking at Notre Dame in 2002, Cardinal Óscar Andrés Rodríguez Maradiaga, S.D.B. said, "In pastors like Monsignor Romero, we have the figure of the 'Bishop who is a servant of the Gospel of Christ for the hope of the world.' With bishops like him, the Church can truly be the hope for the world."[29]

In closing, I would like to quote a passage from the Conclusion of the Aparecida document that encapsulates much of CELAM's vision of the future of the Latin American Church, a vision of integrating synthesis that offers "prophetic wisdom" for the world.

> In the twentieth century, the life of the Latin American Church was marked by various tendencies, sometimes at odds with one another. We believe that the time has come to create, through a great love for the truth and a fraternal openness and a respectful dialogue, new integrating syntheses. For example: between evangelization and "sacramental-ization" between witness and proclamation, between proclamation and denunciation, between ministry among the popular masses and formation of the lay people, between preferential option for the poor and care for the middle class and leadership groups, between ministry and spirituality and social commitment, between traditional values and contemporary searching, between social liberation and developing the faith, between theology and praxis, between worship and life witness, between local and national causes and openness to Latin America and

---

[29] *Monsignor Romero: A Bishop for the Third Millennium.* Notre Dame, IN: University of Notre Dame Press, 2004.

the world, between Catholic identity and openness to dialogue with those who are different. The aim is not to weaken or relativize any of these demands, but rather that the Person of Jesus Christ enlighten all these realities and allow them to be properly interconnected.[30]

---

[30] *Synthesis of Contributions Received for the Fifth General Conference,* 2006, N. 82.

THE CHALLENGE OF APARECIDA FOR THE CHURCH IN AMERICA: DISCIPLESHIP AND MISSION

Bishop Ricardo Ramirez, C.S.B.

The Fifth General Conference of the Bishops of Latin America, held in Aparecida, Brazil in May 2007, offers powerful challenges to the Church in the United States. Yet, while these challenges most directly apply to Latin America and the Caribbean, much of what is in the final document says a great deal to the Church in the entire hemisphere, including the U.S. Church.

Clearly, the Synod for the Church in America, with the resulting post-synodal exhortation by John Paul II, *Ecclesia in America*, was in great measure the inspiration for Aparecida. It was the vision of John Paul II to group together the entire Church of the Western Hemisphere at the Synod, as a witness of communion and as a practical instrument for addressing the common concerns of all the Catholics of all America. *Ecclesia in America* was present in the Aparecida Conference, from its preparatory stages and throughout the discussions during the Conference, and its influence is apparent in the final document.

Aparecida—as the Fifth General Conference is now called—should not be seen as just one more Latin American Church document. Indeed, this chapter is written to show how its message is an urgent one, especially for us in the United States, as it challenges *all* Catholics of America to be authentic disciples and missionaries of Jesus Christ.

THE CONSULTATION PROCESS OF APARECIDA

The Aparecida experience was in many ways a model of the ecclesiology of Vatican II. The methodology used by organizers, *Consejo Episcopal Latinoamericano* (CELAM), is noteworthy first of all in the preparatory stages. This Conference was different from the previous four held in Rio de Janeiro (1955), Medellín (1968), Puebla (1979), and Santo Domingo (1992). There was more consultation in preparation for this conference compared to the former conferences, and preparation for the Aparecida Conference was a good example of consultation at its best.

The period of consultation took place over two years and actively solicited the thoughts of lay movements, women and men religious, groups of women, priests, indigenous peoples, economists, theologians (including liberation theologians), Mariologists, and missionologists. The preparatory commission, called the *Comisión Permanente*, included representatives from various countries, who joined the executive governing body of the Latin American Council of the Bishops of Latin America (CELAM). Invited also to be a part of this commission was this writer, appointed representative of the United States Conference of Catholic Bishops by its president, Bishop William Skylstad.

This Commission prepared the *Documento de Preparación,* the paper used to spark discussion and input from the grass roots communities. A series of study pamphlets based on the *Documento* were distributed throughout Latin America and the Caribbean. Results of the discussions were compiled at parish, diocesan, and national conference levels and these were sent to the CELAM headquarters for further compilation. Ultimately, this process created the *Sintesis de Consulta*, which became a major reference during the actual Conference, along with John Paul II's *Ecclesia in America* and the Inaugural Address by Benedict XVI.

The *Documento de Preparación* was studied and discussed in the United States by Hispanic communities, with these discussions eliciting input from about forty U.S. dioceses. The U.S.C.C.B. Secretariats for the Church in Latin America and Hispanic Affairs prepared the compilation from the U.S. and sent the results to CELAM.

NON-LATIN AMERICAN PARTICIPANTS

For the first time, there were participants (who went not just observers) from the Episcopal conferences of Spain, Portugal, Canada, and the United States. The presidents of these conferences had both voice and vote, while other bishops from these countries had voice only. Besides Bishop Skylstad, three others from the United States participated: Bishop Plácido Rodríguez,

Bishop Jaime Soto, and this writer. The inclusion of Canada and the United States was clearly in keeping with the spirit of *Ecclesia in America*. There were also representatives from the Symposium of the Episcopal Conferences of Africa and Madagascar, the Council of the Episcopal Conferences of Europe, and the Federation of the Episcopal Conferences of Asia. Representatives of the Orthodox, Anglican, Lutheran, Presbyterian, and Evangelical communities were invited as observers and there was also a representative of the Jewish faith. These representatives were invited to speak at the general assemblies.

THE MAJOR THEME OF DISCIPLESHIP

The theme of the Conference, "Disciples and Missionaries of Jesus Christ, that Our People May Have Life in Him –'I am the Way, and the Truth and the Life' (Jn. 14:6)" is indicative of the major challenge to Catholics in America, that the call to be disciples of Jesus Christ carries with it a missionary dimension. We cannot only be disciples, i.e. *followers* of Our Lord, but we must also be emissaries of his message. The bishops saw that a disciple is, at the same time, a missionary, and throughout the final document, the two words appear as one hyphenated expression: *disciple-missionary*.

The bishops at Aparecida made a very important decision when they chose to follow the "see, judge, and act" methodology used at the Medellín and Puebla Conferences. They recognized that this method was a practical way to discuss the theme of the Conference and the best way to arrive at a conclusive document.

The first part of the final document describes the reality lived by the disciple-missionary in Latin America and the Caribbean. That reality is the one in which Catholics have to live out their discipleship and in which they will exercise their mission:

> "As disciples of Jesus Christ, we are compelled to discern the 'signs of the times.' in the light of the Holy Spirit, to place ourselves at the service of the Kingdom, announced by Jesus, who came that all might have life and that they have it to the full." (Jn. 10:10)[31]

---

[31] *Aparecida Document* N. 33.

Just as Jesus in his incarnation reveals the love of God to a particular time and place, so the Church must always respond to the situations in the here and now. Disciples of Christ must see the task of responding to the signs of the times as having a permanent character, a task that needs constant renewal. Recently, profound changes have been happening at an accelerated pace in economics, politics, and culture, as well as in religion—including Christianity. To these the Church must interpret in the light of the Gospel and the Kingdom announced by Jesus Christ.[32]

PREFERENTIAL OPTION FOR THE POOR

Aparecida reaffirmed the "preferential option for the poor," a phrase that has also been adopted by the U.S.C.C.B.—it appears in the 2007 version of "Faithful Citizenship." The bishops at Aparecida state: "We reassume with new vigor the option for the poor."[33] Moreover, in a remarkably strong expression of commitment for the poor, the bishops at Aparecida assert: "We pledge to work so that our Church in Latin America and in the Caribbean will continue with greater zeal to accompany the poorest of our brothers and sisters, even to the point of martyrdom."[34]

Pope Benedict XVI inspired the reappearance of the phrase. In his inaugural address, he said, "Faith frees us from the isolation of the ego, because it leads to communion: the encounter with God is in itself and as such, is an encounter with our brothers, an act of convocation, of unification, of responsibility toward others. . . . The preferential option for the poor is implicit in Christological faith in that God who made himself poor for us, in order to enrich us with his poverty (cf. 2 Cor. 8:9." (Inaugural Address 3)

The bishops repeated from *Ecclesia in America*: "Our faith proclaims that Jesus Christ is the human face of God and the divine faith of man. (EA N. 67)"[35] Thus, the preferential option for the poor is eminently deduced from Christological faith. "This option is born from our faith in Jesus Christ, God made man, who has become our brother." (Heb. 2:11–12)[36]

---

[32] Aparecida Document N. 33, 44.
[33] Aparecida Document N. 399.
[34] Aparecida Document N. 396.
[35] Aparecida Document N. 392.
[36] Aparecida Document N. 392.

While it is true that the preferential option for the poor had already been part of the teachings of three previous CELAM conferences, Aparecida, with its precise and vigorous language, has made this theme the indelible characteristic of the Church in Latin America. It is the "axis of life" of the entire document and an indispensable source of reflection for every follower of Jesus.[37]

In continuity with previous conferences, Aparecida refers to the poverty of indigenous peoples and African descendants. It takes note of the "faces of the newly excluded"—immigrants, victims of violence, displaced persons, and refugees, as well as victims of human trafficking, kidnapping and those who have disappeared. It also lists the victims of HIV, the chemically dependent, and victims of prostitution and pornography. It makes special mention of the continued plight of women, who suffer from domestic violence as well as from sexual and economic exploitation. Among the newly excluded are those who are technically illiterate.[38]

THE MAJOR THEME OF MISSION

Aparecida recognizes the origin of the disciples' mission as nothing less than that of the Blessed Trinity. Jesus, it says, revealed the mystery of the Trinitarian communion of God as the origin of mission. This Trinitarian communion is synonymous with love.[39] Jesus is the revelation and witness of this intra-trinitarian love.[40] It is out of divine love that God's mission in Jesus Christ takes place.

God sends the Son in the Holy Spirit in the mission to inaugurate the new covenant, announcing a new commandment as the Good News for the re-creation of the world and of humankind.[41] Furthermore, all Christians since their baptism share in this "mission of God"[42] and see themselves entirely at the service of others.[43]

---

[37] Gutirez, *Aparecida: Renacer de una esperanza.* Amerindia, 2007, p. 131.

[38] Aparecida Document N. 402.

[39] Aparecida Document N. 109, 157.

[40] Aparecida Document N. 348.

[41] Aparecida Document N. 241.

[42] Aparecida Document N. 153.

[43] Aparecida Document N. 240.

Mission and communion are closely associated in the Aparecida document. All the baptized, because of the common priesthood of the People of God, are called to live out and transmit communion with the Trinity.[44] The Church is missionary and its names relate its mission to the Trinity: "People of God," "Body of Christ," and "Temple of the Holy Spirit." Because it is the Temple of the Holy Spirit and it is also "the house of the poor,"[45] she convokes and gathers everyone into the mystery of communion and does not discriminate nor exclude anyone for reasons of gender, race, social condition, or nationality.[46]

The mission of the Church is both *ad intra* and *ad extra*. The Church is sent at the same time to the core and center and to the periphery of the world. Aparecida calls all the baptized "to be who they are"—missionaries of Jesus Christ who live out their Christian vocation, not so much in terms of a variety of tasks to be done, but to recognize themselves always being in the "state of mission"[47] to announce the Gospel of the Kingdom. Its mission is at the service of the Kingdom and, as such, at the service of the poor taken in the widest sense.[48]

The signs of the Kingdom are the personal and communitarian living out of the beatitudes, the evangelization of the poor, the knowledge and fulfillment of the will of the Father, martyrdom, access to the goods of creation by everyone, and mutual forgiveness.[49]

The Kingdom is in our midst but always in process, transforming the reality of our societies and of the Church. Indeed, the challenge of transformation appears numerous times in the document.[50]

Aparecida challenges parishes to be "communities of communities" and to cease being "preservers," rather becoming "centers of missionary radiance."[51] They are also called to be places where permanent missionary formation takes place.[52]

------

[44] Aparecida Document N. 157.
[45] Aparecida Document N. 524.
[46] Aparecida Document N. 524.
[47] Aparecida Document N. 213.
[48] Aparecida Document N. 516.
[49] Aparecida Document N. 383.
[50] Aparecida Document N. 44, 90, 151, 219, 283, 336, et al.
[51] Aparecida Document N. 306.
[52] Aparecida Document N. 306.

In the concept of mission in Aparecida, all are messengers and at the same time subjects of the Good News: everyone is called to give as to receive.[53] "The mission must take place in an ambience of joy inasmuch as the encounter with Jesus Christ whom we recognize as the Incarnate and Redeeming Son of God is victorious over sin and death. We are called to make him known with our words and actions, and this is our joy."[54]

The follow up to the conference of Aparecida is a "continental mission." Its purpose is the re-evangelization of "cultural Christians" and of non-practitioners. "We have a high percentage of Catholics who lack the missionary conscience to be salt and leaven in the world and whose Christian identity is weak and vulnerable."[55] The continental mission promises "a new Pentecost which will free us from the fatigue, the disillusion, the accommodation to the status quo; the new coming of the Spirit will give new birth to our joy and hope."[56]

While at this writing, it is yet unclear how the continental mission will occur, CELAM has appointed a commission of bishops to plan this important endeavor, and national conferences in Latin America and the Caribbean have begun to plan their versions of the mission. It will probably not be a single event, but a process that will be ongoing in keeping with the principle that the Church is *always* in a state of mission.

CONCLUSION

The Final Document of Aparecida is an exciting and refreshing articulation of the contemporary mind and heart of the Church of Latin America and the Caribbean. What appears in this chapter is mostly the content of the document, yet the story of Aparecida has to include the events leading up to the Conference, including the positive way the Vatican, through the Commission for Latin America (CAL), oversaw the planning and preliminary documents. The involvement of the Amerindia theologians at the consultation stage and later as unofficial theological consultants during

---

[53] Aparecida Document N. 536.
[54] Aparecida Document N. 29.
[55] Aparecida Document N. 286.
[56] Aparecida Document N. 362.

the Conference proved to be most helpful. The great Brazilian National Basilica of Aparecida was an ideal venue, since it placed the bishops in daily contact with pilgrims, most of whom were from the working classes. It was estimated that almost 100,000 pilgrims were at Aparecida for the Solemnity of Pentecost.

The daily liturgies, the Eucharist, and the Liturgy of the Hours were beautifully executed, as were the solemn Rosary led by Benedict XVI and the Inaugural Mass. For those of us privileged to be there it was a stunning ecclesial event.

What remains, however, is the application of this remarkable document in the years to come. We can fervently hope that the message of Aparecida will be heard by the Church in the United States, for we too are challenged by the call to be disciples and missionaries in our own reality.

Aparecida and Hispanics of the U.S.A.

Virgilio Elizondo

It is important to note that for the first time at a CELAM conference, the Bishops of the U.S.A. and Canada had both a voice and a vote. This was an important recognition that a large portion of Latin America now exists within the United States and Canada. Hence, the deliberations and conclusions are not just for Latin America, but equally for us in the U.S.A. and Canada—especially for dioceses where the number of Latin American Catholics is growing rapidly, even to the extent where the majority of the parishioners are Latinos/as.

The Aparecida gathering was a carefully prepared Episcopal assembly critically searching for pastoral responses to the urgent needs of today's church and society. Pope Benedict XVI opened the gathering with a clear theological perspective that, along with the working document, served as the basis for the intensive discussions that took place during the following weeks of prayer, study, and discussion.

In the following reflections, I will not comment on many of the topics elaborated in the final document of Aparecida, to which all citations refer, but only on those that have a direct and immediate bearing on the ecclesial life of Latinos/as living in the U.S.A. In summary, I can say that the conclusions of Aparecida confirm, deepen, and expand the main pastoral lines we have been insisting upon in Hispanic ministry in the U.S.A.

Mestizo Culture

"The most widely extended culture of Latin America is the Mestizo Culture. In the midst of the many contradictions throughout history, it has sought to synthesize various cultural sources, thus facilitating a dialogue between

57

their respective cosmovisions, and opening the way for their convergence in a shared history." (56) The document goes on to refer to the three roots of the Mestizaje of Latin America: the indigenous, the African, and the European. This biological and spiritual mixture produced the Mestizaje of Latin America, which is the social and cultural base of the people. (88)

Mestizaje is the most profound difference between the cultures of Latin American and the mainline culture of the U.S.A. Mestizaje was the natural and encouraged way of the colonization and evangelization of Latin America while it was all-too-often prohibited and outlawed in the U.S.A. This is the reason why there is no decent translation of the word "Mestizo" into the English language. In the first encounters between settlers from the U.S.A. and Mexicans in former Mexican territories, which had been conquered by the U.S.A., the Mexican people were abhorred as mongrels whose presumptive imbecility and treacherous character was caused by the amalgamation of races.

The white, Anglo Saxon peoples construed their whiteness and racial purity as superiority and they often had difficulty mixing even with other white European groups. Furthermore, much of white Protestant U.S.A. regarded the Catholics of Mexico as superstitious, and as more pagan than Christian. Historically, because the culture of U.S. society was a strictly divided one between white and black with an exclusion of the darker skinned natives, it has traditionally had great difficulties and fears in accepting and incorporating the Mestizos of Latin America. U.S. society abhorred and feared that ethnic mixing would produce a weakening of the white/supreme race. Latin American Mestizos are the mixture of Europeans, Africans, and Native Americans. They do not fit into the black-white divide and are a profound challenge to the "either-or" divide of the U.S.A. I am sure this is one of the deep yet unspoken reasons for the strong anti-immigrant fever of the United States.

Yet, as my good friend, Jacques Audinet has stated, "Mestizaje is the human face of globalization." I am convinced that one of the greatest things we can offer the emerging globalizing humanity is the fact that we have been struggling and dealing with Mestizaje for the last 500 years. It has not been easy, and will never be, as long as one of the ethnic lines of the Mestizo is despised and looked down upon. It is only when all of the ethnic lines that converge in the Mestizo are looked upon with gratitude and grateful pride that the Mestizo will emerge as the new creature of the globalized society.

Because the U.S. Hispanics have been struggling to find ways of truly blending into a new synthesis of the great cultures of Latin American and the U.S.A., cultures that are part of our innermost being, we have something of value to offer to the new Mestizos that are being born out of the various ethnic and racial unions that are becoming more and more common. No one is promoting this, but it is happening and it will be the face and body of the new humanity of globalization. Mestizos are changing the Western notion of "race" from one of radical exclusion of "other" to one of a joyful inclusion of everyone.

GLOBALIZATION (60–73)

Since we in the U.S.A. are key players in the process of globalization, this section has serious implications for us today. There is no doubt that globalization has positive possibilities, but probably even greater are its dangers since most of globalization is guided by the desire for profit as the supreme goal. As it is happening, it creates gross inequalities and multiple structures of injustice. One of the great challenges of the Church is the creation of new forms of globalization that will be characterized not by the exploitation of the masses and the environment but rather by a solidarity based on justice, love, and respect for human rights. This is definitely a great ideal, but how will we help to bring this about? Certainly, we can do it only by helping everyone, without exception, to look upon the disfigured faces and broken bodies of today's victims of globalization.

The Final Document of Aparecida lists many of those that are the excluded from the benefits of today's globalizing society, referring to them as the exploited and disposable, who are used and thrown away like used paper cups. Reading through the long list of excluded I could not help but come to the shameful realization that the more humanity develops, the more groups of persons that it finds ways of excluding. The misery of these excluded groups has to be exposed and their cries must be heard. The world must know that massive profits are being gained through the human sacrifices of the exploited. Unfortunately, globalization has increased the various forms of human sacrifice offered to the god of profit.

This final expression, "disposable" speaks loudly to the situation of millions of undocumented Latin American immigrant workers in the U.S.A. Often they work for less then minimum wages with no protection of the law and no social benefits, and when through sickness or disability, often incurred precisely because of the work that they are no longer able to perform, they are simply dismissed. After all, others can easily take their place.

The millions of undocumented immigrants working in the U.S.A. are doing the work no U.S. citizen wants to do, or wants their children to do. Rather than thank the immigrants for their service, many are trying to criminalize them. Government raids have taken men and women from their place of work, leaving their young children in day-care centers, waiting for parents who will never come back. The leadership of the Church has made some attempts to protest this but, unfortunately, Catholics in general have remained silent or have even opposed the humanitarian treatment of these unappreciated servants.

POPULAR RELIGION

One of the deepest, most beautiful, most powerful and theologically most challenging sections of the document is contained in paragraphs 258 to 265, dealing with the encounter with Christ through popular piety. I say this because popular piety has so often been dismissed as simplistic folklore and even ridiculed by the more enlightened sectors of the Church. Many have tried to do away with popular piety by replacing it with what they consider "proper liturgy." Others have tried to discredit it because they claim it was simply the opium of the masses. It has often been attacked by Catholics, Protestants, and Evangelicals in any number of ways—that it is superstitious, pagan, idolatrous, primitive, syncretistic, and so on.

Speaking as a Mexican-American who grew up experiencing not only the deep spirituality and beauty of these expressions, and later reflecting on their life-giving source, I have always disagreed with these negative judgments of popular piety. I met a very personal, intimate, and loving Jesus, Mary, and saints through these communal celebrations; equally they were the language of resistance. In these celebrations, we were free to be who we were in the context of the alien culture of the U.S.A. These were the sacred spaces and moments where we experienced the various elements of the Christian message and entered into deep communion with the living God. Hence, I was overjoyed at the document's treatment of popular piety.

In 258, the document begins by quoting Benedict XVI, who refers to popular piety as "the soul and precious treasure of the peoples of Latin

America." He went on to invite the participants to promote and protect the popular expressions of the faith of the people since these are an authentic expression of our Catholic faith. It is the expression of a profoundly inculturated faith that is the most valuable dimension of Latin American culture. This has been the mission of the Mexican American Cultural Center in San Antonio since its very beginning, and the subject of much of my research and writings. Orlando Espin and Timothy Matovina, two of our leading U.S. Latino theologians, have written masterfully on this subject. Much of the pastoral work among the Hispanics in the U.S.A. has centered on the promotion of the popular expressions of our faith. Yet today the challenge is greater than ever, and it is important to take Benedict's admonishment seriously: to protect and promote.

Number 259 describes some of the main expression of this spirituality. My first comment is that it refers to it as a spiritually. It is a style of spirituality no less than the Franciscan, Jesuit, Theresian, Dominican, Opus Dei, etc. Like every form of spirituality, it has its particular characteristics. Popular Catholic spirituality is characterized by feasts, novenas, rosaries, *via cruces,* processions, love of the saints, personal intimacy with Jesus and Mary, and home altars. This spirituality is also characterized by the songs and dances that accompany popular feasts. In the context of these feasts, the faithful experience an intimate communion with all the others who, through the celebration, are walking together towards the God who is waiting for them. In their processions and feasts, they experience Jesus truly present among them, sharing their life and joining in their sorrows and joys, frustrations, and hopes. This was certainly my experience as we celebrated many of these feasts at San Fernando Cathedral, most especially during our annual feasts of Our Lady of Guadalupe, the Christmas *posada*, and the *Semana Santa Viernes Santo* processions. There was a profound sense of mystical communion with Christ-redeemer and with each other.

Often non-Hispanic tourists just walking by were pulled into the crowd by a sort of spiritual magnetism and their comments afterwards were fascinating. "Never before had I experienced such a profound and transforming religious experience" was the expression of many. For our own people, no explanation was necessary for they knew in their hearts that they were in real communion with Christ, his Mother, and all the saints.

Popular spirituality as a distinctive Christian spirituality is further developed in Number 263. It summarizes the theological aspects of this spirituality, such as its deep sense of transcendence, its spontaneous ability to depend totally on God, and its true experience of theological love. It is also an expression of supernatural wisdom because the wisdom of love does not depend directly on the illumination of the mind but upon the internal action of divine grace. It is truly a Christian spirituality because, through the encounter with the living Lord, it integrates the corporal, the sensual, the symbolic, and the deepest needs of the person and the community. "It is a spirituality incarnated in the culture of the simple people but it is no less spiritual than other forms of spirituality, it is simply a different form of spirituality." (263)

I had never really thought of popular piety as a school of spirituality or as another well-developed form of spirituality; yet the more I reflect upon this, the more I appreciate the depth and wisdom of the Aparecida document. Indeed, I would probably go a step further. In a beautiful prayer of praise by Jesus, he states, "I give praise to you, Father, Lord of heaven and earth, for although you have hidden these things from the wise and the learned you have revealed them to the childlike. Yes Father, such has been your gracious will." (Matthew 11:25)

Maybe it would be better to recognize popular piety not just as another form of spirituality, but as a privileged one since it is the spirituality of the poor, neglected, and excluded of society who are loved by God and closer to God since they have no one to depend upon, converse with, or celebrate with other than God. Hence, because they live in intimate communion with God, they can easily know God much better than the experts on religion who might know God well in their minds but might be a bit more distant in their hearts. We really can go even further; if God truly has a privileged option for the poor, then the God-expressions of the poor are privileged manifestations of God and privileged places of our personal encounters with the living God.

In working with poor people, praying with them, and doing Bible study with them, I have often been amazed and inspired by their insights into the mysteries of God's love. I remember the great spiritual wisdom of my grandmother, father, and mother who didn't know the catechism or the Bible; nevertheless, it was evident they knew God well and were on intimate terms with God. It becomes more evident to me how God dwells within the hearts of the believing poor in a very special and intimate way. They truly have the knowledge of a knowing and loving heart.

The simple expressions of popular piety (261) such as a rosary, holy card, crucifix, holy water, votive candle, medals, and other such objects are tangible gifts of God's love. They are like the little gifts that we give to a loved one so that we might live in their presence. In and by themselves they are nothing, yet their symbolic meaning and the emotions they evoke when we see or touch them are fantastic. They make the loved one present to us! These simple objects, which are easily accessible to anyone without exception, are great gifts of God's love, of God wanting to be ever present among His people, especially among the poor and neglected. Through these simple faith-objects we truly touch God and equally feel God's loving touch.

It is certainly true (262) that the faith expressed through popular piety can be deepened and purified, but this will only happen if, first of all, we recognize it positively as a fruit of the Holy Spirit. Purification does not mean elimination nor does it mean that popular piety is a false expression of the faith. This simply means that every expression of faith has to continually be purified through a direct contact with the Scriptures, participation in the sacraments, participation in the Sunday Eucharist, and service to those in need. The document is very insistent that we cannot consider popular piety as a secondary or inferior type of spirituality since it has come about through the action of the Holy Spirit, a gratuitous initiative of God's love.

Popular piety is a very legitimate way of living the faith (264) and feeling a part of the church. It is likewise a way of being a missionary because, through these expressions, the Christian life of Latin America is promulgated. These celebrations have a way of attracting others into them. They are a type of proclamation for many, as powerful as, or even more powerful than the reading of Holy Scripture, not because they are above the scriptures but precisely because they bring the content of the scriptures to life in very vivid and participatory ways.

This was the intent of the early missioners who devised popular theatrical religious celebrations to bring all the senses into the redemptive mystery of Christ. The various moments of the redemptive life of Christ are thus brought to life, and the local time and space is transformed into biblical time and space. The mysteries of our faith are not just remembered but truly brought to life, thus inviting anyone to enter easily into them and became a part of them. "They are a powerful confession of the living God that acts in history." (264) They are marvelous ways of affirming our faith and transmitting our faith to others.

Again I can testify to the evangelizing power of these celebrations. I have known many people who, having participated in one or more of these popular celebrations, then wanted to learn more about our faith. Some joined RCIA, others became active in Bible study groups, and still others became dynamic catechism teachers. There is nothing like experiencing the various core elements of the life of Jesus to quicken our desire to know a lot more about him, his mission, and his church. It is through these various expressions, from the simple home altar to the massive holy week processions, that the people often insulted and humiliated by society experience the tender *cariño* of our loving God and their true dignity as children of God. (265)

OPTION FOR THE POOR

I was very impressed in the strong and clear re-affirmation of the privileged option for the poor expressed by the Aparecida document. (391–405) The clear theological language of Benedict XVI that "the privileged option for the poor is implicit in the Christological faith in that God that makes Himself poor for us so as to enrich us with his poverty" brought out clearly that the option for the poor is not ideological but solidly theological. Again, it is not about abstract theology, but rather about living out the full extent of our Christian faith.

The privileged option for the poor begins by befriending the poor, seeing them not as objects of pity but as brothers and sisters. From there, precisely because they are brothers and sisters, the Church must be advocates for justice and defenders of the poor, especially of those that society does not tolerate or want. This is probably the biggest challenge facing the Catholic Church, and all Christian churches, of the U.S.A. today: are we willing to be the advocates for the human rights of our immigrant workers—most of them from the poorest of Latin America—in the face of mounting popular opposition?

The undocumented immigrant workers are the voiceless victims of a small but vociferous group of anti-immigrant groups in the U.S.A. I suspect, as many others do also, that the basis of this horrible anti-immigrant campaign is ultimately racist. Some of the white supremacy groups are afraid that the United States is being "invaded" by too many Latin American "mongrels" who are going to weaken our "American way of life." The Church cannot remain silent on this, yet Catholics cannot abdicate their responsibility by leaving it up to the bishops to issue statements. Individual

Catholics have to make their voice known and the Church can help by preaching about the Church as the "servant of charity" in its sermons and catechesis. We need to form a Catholic consciousness that can truly be concerned for the most vulnerable amongst us. At this particular moment, I feel that the undocumented immigrant is the most urgent issue because it includes not only the individual immigrant but also their wives and families. Most of these are Catholic but even if they were not, they are human beings; they are our brothers and sisters.

PASTORAL CARE OF MIGRANTS

The document begins (73) its treatment of migrants by pointing out that many people were forced to migrate either within their own country or into another country due to a variety of painful circumstances. Some migrate to escape violence and persecution while many others migrate because of dire economic necessity. Many of the immigrants from Latin America into the U.S.A. come in order to survive and to provide for their families. Some have stated that they have the choice between starvation or immigration. Prolonged misery without any hope of betterment induces many to take the treacherous risk of immigration into a foreign country. This is the story of the majority of immigrants from Latin America that come to the U.S.A.

Another aspect of the document that is especially relevant to us in the U.S.A. is the pastoral care of migrants. The church is a community of love without borders. For the Church, there are never any "illegals," but simply people in need. It reaches out to all her faithful wherever they might be and, as such, it considers it "her indispensable task to develop a mentality and spirituality of service to peoples on the move." (412) The migrants must never be looked upon as a problem to be solved or as a dreaded burden but rather as a great resource in the development of humanity. As Bishop McCarthy of Phoenix used to say, "They are not a problem to be solved but a people to be loved." This is especially important for us in the U.S.A. as the anti-immigrant mentality spreads throughout our country and even many Catholics turn their backs on the suffering of our immigrant brothers and sisters. Rather than being grateful for their contributions to our society, people seek to criminalize them and make them appear as lawless and violent.

The Church has a moral obligation to raise its voice against these forces of evil by bringing up the truth of the immigrant poor who come to do the backbreaking work that Americans refuse to do. (414) One of the most valuable things the Church can do at this moment of time in the U.S.A., where the anti-immigrant forces have become so emotional and so strong, is to work to give a different perspective of the immigrant—not as one who breaks the law but as one who has come to serve, who is a benefit to the welfare of our country, and who is seeking nothing other than what all previous immigrants have sought: a better way of life. They are not criminals, as they are often portrayed, but rather human beings struggling to survive.

At this point, Christians might sometimes need to go beyond the civil law in order to help our brothers and sisters in need. It is not that we disregard civil law but that when in conflict, we are bound to follow the higher law of Christ, the law of universal love. The deportation raids are creating great panic in our communities, breaking up families, leaving children abandoned and unprotected, and even deporting U.S. citizens who merely look "foreign" because of their dark skin and physical features. This is one of the most scandalous and inhumane things going on in our country at this time.

In ministering to the migrants, ministers must base their work on the religious and cultural expressions of the people. Since most of the migrants come from the lower classes of society, the popular expressions of the faith will be most meaningful to them and will be a good way of making them feel welcome and at home while away from home. The churches from which people migrate also have the obligation of sending clergy and religious to accompany them as they journey to new lands. The great difficulty here is that, whereas the European Church has an abundance of clergy and religious to accompany its immigrants to the U.S.A., Latin America has suffered from a lack of clergy and religious to accompany their immigrants.

Given the large numbers of Latin American immigrants in the U.S.A. and the fact that the greater number among them are among the poorest of the poor, this is probably one of the greatest pastoral challenges facing the Church today, especially in regard to the millions of undocumented Latin Americans who are working and living among us. Yet, since Christ comes to us in the person of the poor, the disfigured, the desolate, and the excluded, to the degree that we work to welcome these people into our society and our church, we will truly be welcoming Christ to come into our midst. It is in the defense of the rights of the excluded one finds the fidelity of the Church to Christ. (257)

IMPORTANCE OF CULTURE (476–480)

This section of the document deepened and reaffirmed one of the most important issues of our pastoral, liturgical, and theological work among the Hispanics of the U.S.A. The Catholic Latino/a leadership in this country has continued to insist that pastoral work must celebrate rather than destroy our Latin American Catholic religious tradition. This is not because of cultural nostalgic reasons, but the very basis of an evangelization that will proceed by way of the Incarnation, as all evangelization should.

The gospel comes not to destroy cultures, but to purify and enrich them while the missioners themselves become purified and enriched by the very peoples to whom they take the gospel. "The Church is enriched through the inculturation of the faith which produces new expressions and values that continue to manifest in even better ways the richness of the mystery of Christ." (479) Many of our U.S. Bishops and pastoral workers who have gotten to know and appreciate the popular spirituality of Latin Americans have recognized that it is a great gift to the Church of the U.S.A. I personally think this is the greatest thing we have to offer the United States: the many beautiful, festive, and participatory expressions of our Christian faith.

One of the main reasons why the Catholic Church of the U.S.A. has had such a difficult time appreciating Latin American Catholics and ministering to us in a meaningful way has been the vast cultural difference between the United States and Latin America. In many ways, mainline U.S. culture was born and shaped out of Calvinism, without interchange with the indigenous cultures of America. European Catholic immigrants came into this environment with a counter-reformation mentality and they established ethnic parishes without any contact with the indigenous populations. The underlying religious-culture basis of the U.S.A. is the WASP—white, Anglo-Saxon, Protestant. Culturally speaking, U.S. Catholics have adapted to this cultural-religious ethos in many ways while remaining in communion with Catholic tradition.

It was totally different in Latin America. From the very first contacts, there was cultural and biological exchange between the colonizers and the native peoples. A radically renewed and idealistic Iberian Catholicism found many ways of interacting with the native religions and cultures. Out of this encounter with its many pains and joys, lights, and storm clouds, Latin American Catholicism was born, in continuity with the Church of

Europe yet in many ways quite distinct. It could equally be said that the deep religious ethos of the pre-encounter religions continued, yet their innermost meaning was now quite different. One scholar has stated, "The native religions were recycled and came out Catholic." If Latin American is a Mestizo continent, so Latin American Catholicism is truly Mestizo Catholicism: "The Church in this continent has been throughout its history the creator and animator of culture . . . as expressed in the art, the music, the literature and most of all in the religious traditions and in the uniqueness of its peoples." (478) This has been one of our greatest treasures and source of unity, especially when living in a foreign country.

The Latin American Catholic tradition is characterized by the wealth of its popular expressions, which make religion easily accessible to everyone. From the very beginning, the gospel was presented not so much as the written word but as the visual word through paintings, shrines, and theatrical presentations. The doctrines of the Church were brought to life through intimate personal relations with the Trinity (we even name children "Trinidad") and with Jesus, Maria, and the saints. The real presence of Christ is called Jesus *sacramentado* (Jesus sacramentally present). The core moments of the Christian mystery are lived out through the annual celebrations of the feasts such as *Las Posadas* (Christmas novena), *La Presentacion del Niño* (Presentation of the child Jesus), *Semana Santa, Corpus Christi*, Patronal Saint, *Dia de los Muertos,* and many others.

Beyond these collective feasts, which gave our people a deep sense of communion, of being a united people sharing one divine soul, there were many personal practices that made the faith a very real and ever-present force in our lives. Candles, holy water and holy cards, medals, novenas, and rosaries served as small but powerful reminders of God's protective presence in our lives. The ubiquitous home altars—*altarcitos*—made every home a domestic sanctuary where the presence of God was made visible. These feasts and practices were the very basis of our culture because our culture had been a product of the evangelizing efforts of the missioners.

As beautiful and as powerful as these practices have been, there is no doubt that today they are being challenged in many ways by the many attractions of the consumer society we live in, and by the various religious groups that seek to discredit and destroy them. By promoting and celebrating these practices, the Church can play a key role in the preservation and transmission of these cultural treasures that are the basis of our Latin American identity and the crowning glory of the beautiful missionary process that gave birth to the faith throughout Latin America. Yet today, more is needed. Because these practices are loved, but frequently their meaning remains hidden, a good catechesis is desperately needed.

Those who do not understand us attack us for idolatry and paganism. Our people are often unprepared to respond and become confused. Hence, today we can no longer just celebrate them; we must also instruct the people in their meaning. In its preaching and catechesis, the Church must also engage, from the perspective of faith, the contemporary issues.

Because these religious-cultural celebrations and traditions have been the one place within the United States where the Mexicans, Mexican-Americans, and other Hispanics have been able to celebrate, affirm, and transmit our ethnic identity, the Church is in a privileged position to safeguard this cultural-religious heritage that Pope Benedict XVI has rightly identified as the "soul of Latin America." I am convinced that to the degree that they disappear, we will cease to exist as a distinct ethnic group. They have been the place and the language of ultimate resistance to an assimilation that would demand ethnic genocide. Uninformed U.S. Catholicism, Protestantism, and Evangelicalism have often demanded a radical break with our Latin American Catholic heritage in order to become what they consider true Christians.

ART (NUMBERS 499–500)

The production of distinctive styles of U.S. Latino art, especially the public art of murals, has been one of the striking characteristics of the Hispanic revival in the U.S.A. Hence, I think that these two paragraphs are especially significant for all those working in Hispanic ministry in the U.S.A. The first one deals with the use of art in catechetics. Our people have always communicated as much through the visual arts as through the verbal or written word. In fact, I have often stated that the western emphasis on the Word of God has limited itself to the alphabetic word and ignored the image word. Our earliest post-encounter manuscripts made wide use of both the written word and the image word. Our murals are a powerful example of the efficacy of the image word. This admonition has great possibilities for our catechetical programs.

Examples of this can already be found. Several years ago, I commissioned San Antonio artist Alex Rubio to paint a San Antonio version of

Our Lady of Guadalupe—it was beautiful. Father David Garcia, Rector of San Fernando Cathedral, commissioned a well-known local artist in San Antonio to paint the scene of the women at the tomb on Easter morning, using local women wearing traditional local dress. This follows the great tradition of European religious art that utilized local scenes and persons to portray the biblical themes. The Sisters of Charity of the Incarnate Word, also in San Antonio, just completed a beautiful and very Mexican crucified Christ—the people have been mesmerized by it. Juan Valdez produced a beautiful way of the cross through the life of a boxer.

These are good beginnings, but these efforts need to be helped and encouraged. In order to bring this about, the Church should begin to stimulate the creative imagination of children. Art contests would help. It could also invite local artists to paint their interpretation of sacred events.

Even more exciting is the instruction of Aparecida: "It is fundamental for liturgical celebrations to incorporate artistic elements that can transform and help the faithful for their encounter with Christ." This would include the artistic decoration of sacred spaces. Once again, Aparecida is building upon the earliest evangelization of Latin America that immediately started to prepare native artists to produce artistic works that could both adorn and edify the people and thus prepare them for an encounter with Christ. This has been one of the great characteristics of the first evangelization and I suspect one of the main reasons why evangelization was able to create what we know as Latin American culture today. I believe that to the degree that the New Evangelization, so dear to John Paul II, picks up on this tradition, it will produce deeper results than the mere preaching of the Word. It is not a matter of one or the other, but rather of each enriching and deepening the other.

THE PREFERENTIAL OPTION FOR THE POOR AT APARECIDA

Gustavo Gutièrrez, O.P.

As in the case of the preceding Latin-American Episcopal Conferences, that of Aparecida will mark out the life of the Church on the continent and will have far-reaching repercussions.

The conferences form a basis, and are the results of lengthy processes in which many important representatives of the People of God have participated. They follow, from Medellín on, in the focus begun by Vatican II Council, including the development of the conferences themselves, the participation of a number of important lay persons, priests, religious, and members of other Christian churches and of other religions, a contribution that was equally present in Conference V.[57]

The remote preparation of Aparecida during the preceding years was conducted in the commitment and fidelity of many to the Gospel and to the poor of this continent, in spite of all the difficulties including misunderstandings. It is, as Aparecida recognizes, in the "brave testimony of our men and women saints, and of those who, although they have not been canonized, have lived radically the gospel and have offered their lives for Christ, for the Church, and for their people. (A. 99)[58] Many of them are known and many others remain anonymous, but all are "witnesses to the faith" as the document says (a recognition and tribute which we had excluded in the

---

[57] In this article we shall cite the Conclusive Document, according to its last version. In the citation to it we shall identify it as A.

[58] "This has permitted the Church to be recognized socially on many occasions as an example of confidence and credibility. This endeavor in favor of the poorest and their fight for the dignity of each human being have occasioned, in many cases, persecution and even the death of their members, whom we consider witnesses for the faith. We want to record their testimony."

previous conferences). Therefore, for those—silent, but always alive—who have followed closely this position with commitment and surrender to the Latin-American Church, Aparecida is no surprise.

The immediate path which led to this conference was marked out by dialogs and consultations with persons in different positions, as well as in different meetings of CELAM in which the outline of this assembly was defined. This openness was also operative during the days of the conference and contributed to making it an important moment in the life of the Latin American and Caribbean Church. This environment will undoubtedly have future influence in the acceptance of the event of Aparecida, and its conclusions will play a decisive role.

The Marian sanctuary in which the assembly took place put it in close contact with the religiosity of a people who participated in the assembly with their interest and their prayers. It is said that Aparecida signifies a ratification of the theological-pastoral position taken for granted in the last decades in the preceding continental meetings.[59] This is true in several aspects. At the same time, or more correctly for that same reason, it creatively looks to the future, realizing the present challenges of living and announcing the gospel message. It is necessary to pay attention to the above-mentioned faithfulness and openness if we want to see the significance and great importance of an event like the document of Aparecida.

These pages do not attempt to comment on the whole document,[60] but simply treat one of the core ideas, central as it is, which definitely gives structure to the whole of the text and gives us a fundamental criterion for reading it: the preferential option for the poor. Precisely as it is

---

[59] The document says in numerous texts that it places itself in continuity with the preceding Conferences; an observable point already in the Inaugural Discourse of Benedict XVI: "This Fifth General Conference is celebrated in continuity with the other four which preceded it" (n. 2). In no less numerous opportunities, the document affirms again and again with renewed strength the perspective of seeing, judging, and acting as the preferential option for the poor. Throughout the document the prefix 're' is used frequently: revitalize, retake, renew, etc.

[60] It can be noted in the article of Agenor Brighenti, "Criteria for Reading the Document of Aparecida: The pretext, the context, and the text." (The original Portuguese will be published in the Conference of Religious of Brasil magazine, *Convêrgencia.*)

said in the final document, this perspective is "one of the characteristics which identify the features of the Latin American and Caribbean Church." (A. 391) This emphasis is the expression of the maturity of a Church which, since the second half of the past century, pledges itself to look squarely at the social and cultural reality of a continent which ought to give witness and announce the Good News in fidelity to the command of Jesus to seek the kingdom and justice of God. (Mt. 6:33)[61]

We shall see in the first place the insistence of knowing how to read the signs of the times, as John XXIII asked, by convoking the Council. We shall examine how, at Aparecida, the foundation and the implications of the option for the poor are presented. Finally, we shall emphasize one of the most important consequences: the relation between the proclamation of the Gospel and the transformation of history.

TO DISCERN THE SIGNS OF THE TIMES

The process used at Aparecida affirmed anew the necessity of the method of see, judge, and act. The believable story of the historical reality (because this is what it is about) is considered of major importance in order to outline the evangelizing presence of the Latin American Christian community. With the fact that the conference took place in the forward-looking perspective of the council days (through the encyclicals of John XXIII, in *Gaudium et Spes* and other texts) its presence is well known in Medellín, Puebla, and somewhat less in Santo Domingo.

From the beginning Aparecida presents itself as a credible story of reality and places it in relation to the central theme, "As disciples of Jesus Christ we feel strongly called to scrutinize 'the signs of the times,' in the light of the Holy Spirit, in order to put ourselves at the service of the Kingdom announced by Jesus, who came in order that all may have life and "may have it in its fullness. (Jn. 10:10)" (A. 33)

---

[61] An indication of that growth was the persistence of the bishops of the large majority of the countries—before the doubts of some—in asking that, as in previous situations, there be a document of the conference's conclusions.

In Continuity

Discernment presumes "an attitude of permanent pastoral conversion" as a personal disposition in order to "listen attentively" to what the Lord tells us. (A. 366) As is known, it was John XXIII who put the topic up for discussion in our era. Taking his inspiration from Matthew 16:3, he did this in the convoking text of the council, *Humanae Salutis* (1960). In relation with the prophetic books are found what we could call pedagogy of discernment of the signs of the times (see Jeremiah 1:11–19, for example). A pedagogy that translates into a demanding apprenticeship, along with a look to the historical development, must continually refine itself. The Pope also appealed to that focus in two great encyclicals: *Mater et Magistra* (1961) and *Pacem in Terris* (1963). It was a call "to look further ahead," as John XXIII enjoyed saying.

In the encyclical *Ecclesiam Suam,* a decisive influence in Vatican II, Paul VI turned openly to the matter. Finally, we have the council documents, beginning with *Gaudium et Spes*. Well-known texts establish the need of the relationship between the Church and the world, of scrutinizing the signs of the times and "interpreting them in the light of the Gospel so that, accommodating them to each generation, the Church can respond to the perennial questions of humanity on the meaning of the present and future life and the mutual relationship of both." (n. 4)[62]

This impressive and intense joint position (occurring besides at the high level of the Magisterium) during the five-year council period has made this point of view one of the most relevant strongholds and far-reaching consequences of Vatican II. The Episcopal Latin American Conferences, beginning with Medellín, make this perspective the methodological axis of their texts. The repercussion in the life of the Christian community has been and continues to be immense, opening courses of action for Christian commitment.

A Permanent Commitment

The acceptance extended to Pope John XXIII's proposal proves its agreement with the Christian message and the believing experience. It is obvious

---

[62] After the goings and comings during the conciliar works, no mention was made of the Mattean text noted by John XXIII.

that it is connected with the Incarnation of the Son of God, who reveals the love of God for the human race and continues to be present in the historical incertitude. That is its theological foundation. To discern what in human history corresponds to the demands and presence of the Kingdom or what, on the contrary, represents its absence, is the task of the entire Church.[63] In fact, from the start of this ongoing development of historic events that ought to be scrutinized, there are not only positive events but also those that are clearly not in line with gospel values. This attempt to understand history is key to the task of proclaiming the gospel; on this horizon are placed the documents of John XXIII and of the Council.

We have before us a permanent task. It must renew itself continually, as is understood at Aparecida. A series of events during the last years, many of them within the economic, political, and cultural order, as well as with the religious and Christian fields, are pointing out a rapid rhythm hitherto unknown, one which moves the foundation of many of our certainties and makes tremble not a few historic positions held until recently. It is undoubtedly a result of a long journey, but it is certain also that history intensified the tempo in recent times.

Undoubtedly, the means of entrance of the poor and oppressed into the historic scenario, which were assumed in the past, are not the same today. They are in crisis and have even regressed; nevertheless, it is necessary to be attentive to the new routes that they presently take. They express with greater clarity than in previous periods well-defined characteristics of the condition of insignificance and discrimination. One cannot identify what we have called the rising up of the poor to only one of these historic manifestations. In this way the outline of the complex reality of the poor continues through trial and error but finally it becomes more necessary and more compelling, a condition of which Aparecida takes note. In other words, we have before us a plan in process, which as yet has not been given full approval.

The question of method at Aparecida, the path that should guide one in identifying specifically the tasks of the present day Christian community in Latin America and the Caribbean, was a matter debated in preparation for Aparecida and included in the Conference itself.

---

[63] The Constitution *(Gaudium et Spes), The Church in the Modern World*, n. 4, the text which we have cited, speaks of a task of the church, and in Numbers 11 and 44 repeats it, but refers to it as the People of God.

SEE, JUDGE, AND ACT

As we have recalled, to start from the analysis and the interpretation of the social and historic reality constituted a decisive element in the documents of Medellín and Puebla. This did not happen in Santo Domingo due to fear that beginning in that manner would give approval, would affirm, a certain socialism that loses or at least makes it very difficult to adopt a Christian faith perspective. This view ignored the sense of that method, which supports precisely that seeing, in fact, is credible. Those who practice it, after the manner of promotion by the Young Catholic Workers and later by Cardinal Cardijn, know it well. Some commissions in Santo Domingo made an effort to maintain it, but the general disposition that dissuaded it impoverished the final document in spite of certain successes. From that, a clear conscience stood firm in Aparecida.

We have remembered this fact because it explains, in good part, the insistence of the great majority of bishops that another look be taken at that method, which leads to a reading of the signs of the times. The Document of Participation did not touch the theme, but it was addressed in the Synthesis Document, owing to the contributions of different Episcopal conferences of the continent, recognizing that that method had been used fruitfully in the previous Latin American Conferences. (See Numbers 34–36.) The first schemas of the final document—which remained only as drafts—do not mention it; nor do the first two redactions, other than references to it in part. In the face of a subsequent insistence, the Conference accepts it explicitly; the matter was then ratified and accepted through a large majority vote. The document summary[64] expresses it with all the desired clarity, as does the final Document itself (See A. Number 19, which remains with the third redaction).[65] In fact, after a chapter on missionary disciples the final text is arranged according to three stages.

---

[64] "The text has three main parts which follow the method of theological-pastoral reflection 'see, judge, and act.' Thus one sees reality with eyes illumined by faith and a heart full of love; proclaims with joy the Gospel of Jesus Christ in order to illuminate the goal and the way of human life, and search, by means of open community discernment of the inspiration of the Holy Spirit, common plans of truly missionary action, which give to all the People of God a permanent status of mission." (Summary N. 3)

[65] In the revised version, to this number were attached some lines which deal, as we know, with a reading from the point of view of faith.

THEOLOGICAL POSITIONS

The discernment of the signs of the times and the method of seeing, judging, and acting are dealt with in relation to the traditional manner of theological positions. It deals with a decisive contribution for the theological method, which comes from Melchor Cano, a theologian from the School of Salamanca. The new assessment of human history in the 16th century is not far from that theme.[66] Cano makes an effort to keep in mind that fact, and proposes a systematic way, perhaps at times with a certain rigidity, that he calls theological places; he sees them as fountains that provide material for theological reflection. Cano names ten places, but all are not at the same level. Scripture and Tradition are the fundamental ones and are the starting point; among the other eight points are the life of the Church and its magisterium, as well as theology, philosophical thought, and human history. Maintaining, it seems to us, the characteristic of a fountain, there is at present a tendency to consider that the theological position is actually an ecclesial and social position from which the treatise on faith is made.[67] That which gives a foundation to this function, including the nuances mentioned, is the biblical data concerning the presence of God in history.

THE "LAW OF THE INCARNATION"

M.D. Chenu[68] used the expression "law of the Incarnation" as an interpretive key—whose fountain is the Incarnation of the Word of the Father into history—in order to understand the Christian message and historical development of humankind. The discourse of Benedict XVI, with great influence on the conclusions of Aparecida, insists on God with a human

---

[66] A. Gardeil "Theological Places" in the *Dictionnaire de Théologique*. Paris: Librairie Letouszey at Ané, Première Partie, col. 712–747. 1926.

[67] See the article by Victor Fernandez about the notification received by J. Sobrino, "The Poor and Theology in the Notification on the Works of Jon Sobrino" researched on http://www.uca.edu.ar/esp/secfteologia/novedades.

[68] The presence of theme on the signs of the times in *Gaudium et Spes* owes much to its contributors; see his article "Signs of the Times: A Theological Reflection"; Y.M. –J. Congar and M. Peuchmaurd, *The Church in the Modern World*, Vol. II pp. 205–225.

face and for that reason on his presence in history. "God is the foundational reality, not a God only thought of or hypothetical, but a God with a human face; He is God with us, the God of love even to the cross." (N. 3) The Matthean theme of Emmanuel with its emphasis on ancestral lineage informs his words and offers strong support for speaking of commitments that Christians and the Church as a whole must assume in view of the Latin American and Caribbean situation.

In the beginning of his discourse, with a language that, in the past, some saw as lacking in confidence, the Pope gives affirmation: "the Word of God, making himself flesh in Jesus Christ, also incarnated Himself in history and culture." (DI. N. 1)[69] Upon becoming man, he enters into human history and places himself in a culture; there are necessary dimensions and weighty consequences for an appropriate understanding of the Christian message, a message that is given in history and which, at the same time, transcends it.

REAFFIRMATION OF THE PREFERENTIAL OPTION FOR THE POOR

The bond between God and the poor impregnates the entire Bible. Bartolomé de Las Casas says it in a beautiful, expressive thought, which he made a standard of conduct in his solidarity and defense of the original inhabitants of these lands. It is worth citing once more, in speaking of the continental ecclesial assembly: "from the smallest to the most forgotten, God has a most vivid and fresh memory." It is a memory that is present in Aparecida and on which is based the preferential option for the poor, a contemporary expression of the central point of the Christian message.

We assume "with new strength this option . . ." (A. 399) "our option is confirmed . . ." (Summary N. 6) "we reaffirm our option . . ." (Message N. 4) we maintain "with renewed effort our option . . ." (id. N. 4) . . . The texts of Aparecida multiply all of these declarations; with them is manifested clearly the intention to be identified in continuity, strengthened and creative, with the preferential option for the poor, a perspective adopted by

---

[69] The text, which was not withdrawn in Aparecida, is so very true that its content is present in various places in the final Document.

the Latin American and Caribbean Church in the last decades. That option outlines what a text already mentioned says, "the physiognomy of the church" (A. 391) on the continent. It is a conviction that Aparecida establishes as a point of no return in the Church that lives on this continent.[70]

FUNDAMENTAL CHRISTOLOGY

Undoubtedly, one of the most relevant assertions of the inaugural discourse of Benedict XVI, and of great influence on the final text, concerns the theological foundation of the option for the poor. Touching upon the theme and doing it in very clear terms, before the continental Episcopal Conference in which it arose, the formulation of that solidarity with the poor was especially significant.

The Pope summarizes the expressed option, recalling that Christian faith makes us depart from individualism and creates communion with God, and therefore, for the same reason, among ourselves: "Faith frees us from the isolation of the ego, because it brings us to communion; the encounter with God is in oneself and as such, a meeting with brothers and sisters, an act of calling together, of unification, of responsibility toward the other and toward all others." The option for the poor is a way toward communion, and we can find in it a very deep and demanding meaning. The text which we have just cited continues in immediate expression in the following way: "In that sense, the preferential option for the poor is implicit in Christological faith in which God has made Himself poor for us, in order to enrich us with his poverty. (2 Cor. 8:9)" It is faith in a God who has made himself one of us and who manifests himself in the witness of the primordial love of Jesus Christ for the poor.

On that matter of the Incarnation, the text of Aparecida is cited. "Our faith proclaims 'Jesus Christ is the human face of God and the divine face of man.'"[71] The quotation from the Pope's discourse follows: "For that reason the preferential option for the poor is implicit in Christological faith

---

[70] The expression preferential option for the poor is found 11 times in Aparecida, the shorter form option for the poor, 4 times. From these 15 citations eight are found in Chapter 8, which deals directly with the matter. Nevertheless, in addition to this must be added numerous texts which refer to the same issue with synonymous expressions.

[71] *The Church in America* N. 67.

in which God has made himself poor for us, in order to enrich us with his poverty." (DI. N. 3)

"For that reason," equivalent to "in that sense" from the papal discourse, as well as the mention of the face of Christ, human and divine, reaffirm equally the foundation of that option: faith in Christ. There is the root. In a very clear way, Aparecida supports it: "This option springs from our faith in Jesus Christ, the God made man, who has made himself our brother. (Heb. 2:11–12)"[72] The brotherhood between Christ and human beings, the communion of which the inaugural address spoke, is accentuated in Aparecida by means of the reference to the Hebrew text.

Two numbers further on take up again the idea of the option for the poor as implicit in Christological faith or as flowing from it: "from our faith in Christ comes forth also solidarity as a permanent attitude of encounter, brotherhood, and service." These diverse terms underline the relation between Christ and the option for the poor.

This bond is pointed out in the theological reflection, which accompanied these considerations and is found in the previous Latin American conferences. In them appears clearly the fundamental Christological option for the poor.[73] All are referred, furthermore, to the same text in 2 Cor. 8:9 to which Benedict XVI and Aparecida alluded: undoubtedly, the formulation which we find in their texts give precision, current importance, and a great vigor to a perspective which has put an indelible seal on the life of the continental Church and far beyond. In this way, the option for the poor is established on the essential axis of the Aparecida Document, and it is the reason precisely that it is regarded as the axis of life and of reflection for a follower of Jesus.[74]

---

[72] A. 394—The authorized Document attaches a sentence to this text: "It is not, nevertheless, exclusive nor excluding"; it emphasizes the meaning of the word preferential.

[73] Medellín, Poverty, NS. 4c and 7; Puebla, 1145 and 1147 and Santo Domingo, 178 and 164.

[74] It is interesting, in this regard that a first draft of the Message, presented in only one sentence "the preferential option for the poor and for youth." But before interventions which recorded the global nature, based on its evangelical root of the option for the poor and the pastoral aspect of the option for youth, it was decided to separate those two affirmations and the text remained as follows: To accompany youth in their formation and search for identity, vocation and mission, renewing our option for them." This accompaniment is a pastoral aspect, important without doubt, as the final document says in the context of the Pastoral on Youth (See A. 446a).

THE FACES OF THE POOR

The Document deduces an important consequence of what is said regarding the foundation of the option for the poor: "If this option is implicit in Christological faith, Christians as disciples and missionaries are called to contemplate in the suffering faces of our brothers, the face of Christ who calls us to serve Him in them." It has recourse to a text from Santo Domino (N. 178) in order to see the significance of its affirmation: "The suffering faces of the poor are the suffering faces of Christ." (A. 393) That recognition implies an "expression of faith." (A. 32)

The theme, with evident gospel inspiration, emerges, as is known, in Puebla, No. 31–39. Its acceptance in the Christian communities of the continent and in many liturgical celebrations was immense. Santo Domingo returned to it, extended the list of those faces, and asked that it be extended. This is what Aparecida has done, taking on as its own this relevant element of the Latin American ecclesial tradition of the last decades.

And what is more, we have in the Document two lists, which Santo Domingo had suggested extending, with the new faces of the poor in whom we must recognize the face of Christ.[75]

In this precise and strong way, the challenge that comes from these suffering faces goes to the depth of things: "They beg for help from the working core of the Church, from the pastoral level and from our Christian attitudes." (A. 393) The reason is clear and demanding, because "whatever one must see with Christ, one must see with the poor and all that is related to the poor. Jesus Christ reclaims: 'Whatever you did to the least of my brothers, you have done it to me' (Mt. 25:40)" (id.) It tightens the relationship between Christ and the poor. The essential point of the text of Matthew 25, a long-standing testimony in the history of evangelization and in solidarity with the poor of this continent, is the foundation of this perspective. For that reason it is the biblical passage most often drawn upon in liberation theology.[76]

The number of Aparecida, which we are citing, ends with a new Christological point: "John Paul II emphasized that this biblical text

---

[75] See N. 65, 402.

[76] G. Gutiérrez, "Where the Poor Are, There is Jesus Christ" in *Páginas*, Feb. 2006, pp. 6–22.

'illuminates the mystery of Christ.'"[77] Because in Christ the great is made the least, the strong is made weak, the rich is made poor." (A. 393) In effect, the text of Matthew does not limit itself to a question of Christian behavior, to an ethical matter of evangelical inspiration; it indicates to us the clue for understanding Immanuel, the God with us, the God present in human history. If we do not move to that point, we do not understand its depth and significance. The contrasts, which the quoted phrase presents, prove to be particularly significant and meaningful.

The final text of the first chapter of Aparecida summarizes very well what was said in this paragraph: "In the face of Jesus Christ, dead and risen, disfigured by our sins and glorified by the Father, in that suffering and glorified face[78] we can see, with a gaze of faith, the humiliated face of so many men and women of our peoples and at the same time their vocation to the freedom of the children of God, to the full realization of their personal dignity and to the brotherhood among all. The Church is at the service of all human beings, sons and daughters of God." (A. 32)

It treats of an option that embraces strong solidarity and commitment; it is an option that is not optional, as has been said many times. It is rather a preference for the poor, a preferred determination in behalf of the poor. Both words, option and preference, are deeply penetrated into the document of Aparecida.

A KAIRÓS MOMENT: THE EMERGENCE OF THE POOR

What has been called an eruption of the poor in the life of the continent has given place to a reflection, in the life of faith, to that sign of the times. That road led to a biblical study that results in the proposal of the option for the poor. The solidarity that it implies goes back, consequently, to the actual poor, those who live in a situation of injustice and of social insignificance, contrary to the intended life of the God of love. The document assumes this approach. In the first place, it sketches a perception of the *complexity* of poverty, which is not limited to its economic dimension, as important as that is. "The scourge of poverty . . . has diverse expressions: economic, physical,

---

[77] John Paul II, *Novo Milenio* 49.
[78] *Aparecida Documento Conclusivo* 1.32.

spiritual, moral, etc." (A. 176) Hence its sensitivity to the continental "cultural diversity" takes this "into account." (A. 56)[79] It values and considers it a "kairos" event, a propitious moment, the new presence of the natives and Afro descendents who can bring us actually to "a new Pentecost."[80]

Clearly, the conclusions say, "there are, above all, different 'others' who demand respect and recognition. Society tends to look down on them, not recognizing their difference." (A. 89)[81] In effect, the poor are the "other" in a society that does not recognize, except theoretically, their human dignity.

In the same vein, accentuating the complexity of the world of marginalization and social insignificance, Aparecida addresses the situation of the woman. At this time in Latin America and in the Caribbean, it urges becoming aware of the precarious situation that affects the dignity of many women (A. 48 and 451–458). Women suffer an ominous exclusion for various reasons: "they are excluded, by reason of their sex, race, or socio-economic situation." (A. 65)[82] For them, likewise valid is the question of the type of otherness mentioned in the lines above, of the certain manner in which the woman is 'other' in regard to present-day society, one in whom human dignity and rights are not fully recognized.

---

[79] The text continues: "There exist in our region diverse native cultures, African descendents, mestizas, country folks, city dwellers and suburban residents. . . . To this cultural complexity it would be necessary to add also that of the many European immigrants who established themselves in the countries of our region." (A. 56).

[80] Aparecida sees the emergence of those groups as an evangelizing opportunity: "The indigenous and the African descendents immerge now into society and into the Church. This is a 'kairos' moment, for making more profound the encounter of the Church with these human groups who reclaim full recognition of their individual and collective rights, to be taken into account in Catholicism with its global vision, its values and its particular identities in order to live a new ecclesial Pentecost" (A. N. 88–97 and 529–533).

[81] The text continues in these terms: "Their social situation is marked by exclusion and poverty. The Church accompanies the indigenous and Afro-Americans in their battle for their legitimate rights." (A. 89) With regard to the presence of indigenous people at Aparecida, see the interesting article by Eleazar López, "Aparecida and the Indigenous," *Analysis Bulletin* 10, pp. 1–6.

[82] Another text speaks of the necessity of "overcoming a *machista* mentality that ignores the new Christian message, where the 'equal dignity and responsibility of the woman relative to man is recognized'" (A. 453) Let us note the clarity of the language used.

The text places emphasis on the women who belong to populations that are particularly marginalized; at the same time it underscores the current importance and the pressure with which this state of things must be addressed. "At this time with Latin America and the Caribbean, it urges listening to the clamor, so many times silenced, of women who are submitted to many forms of exclusion and violence in all its forms and in all stages of life." Among them, poor women, the indigenous, and the Afro-descendents have suffered a double marginalization, about which the text "Preferential Option for the Poor" at Puebla had already called attention. (N. 1135)

There remains much more to say on the new faces of poverty and of the groups who suffer more cruelly exclusion and social and cultural insignificance. But in this case, as in many others, Aparecida does not offer close analysis or reflection on these realities.

The document points out equally the causes of the various types of poverty.[83] Let us limit ourselves to mentioning what it says in regard to globalization, a theme present at various times in the text of Aparecida. Let us begin by an overall affirmation: "Globalization makes emerge in our peoples new faces of the poor." (A. 402) The reason is that "in globalization, the dynamic of the market easily absolutizes efficiency and productivity as controlling values of all human relations. This special characteristic makes of globalization a process promoting multiple inequities and injustices." (A. 61) This is due to the tendency which globalization favors and that privileges profits and stimulates competition . . . increasing inequalities which sadly mark our continent and which keep in poverty a multitude of persons." (A. 62) Let us determine clearly that at all times the conclusions they leave so clearly are referred to "globalization such as it is presently configured," (A. 61) because it could take other courses of action.

Aparecida is attentive also to a central point of Latin-American practice and reflection about the option for the poor: the poor themselves must be *stewards of their own destiny*. It is not a matter of speaking for the poor; what is important is that they themselves have a voice in a society that does not listen to their plea for liberation and justice. That is their most profound aspiration; they feel "the necessity to build their own destiny." (A. 53) Appropriately with the process of the recovery of identities of marginalized peoples, it is said that those efforts make of black women and

---

[83] Numbers 43–82 treat the socio-cultural, economic and socio-politico situations.

men constructive individuals in their history and in a new history which is going to sketch itself into present-day Latin-American and Caribbean reality." (A. 97) This matters for other insignificant persons and in various fields: "Daily the poor make themselves individuals of evangelization and of the promotion of integral human development." (A. 398)

PREFERENCE

In the 1960s at Medellín, and building upon the conference at Puebla, the option for the poor became a priority and synonymous expression for the poor. In fact, the words of the phrase "preferential option for the poor" correspond one by one to the approvals of the term poverty from the distinction that Medellín accepted: actual poverty as an unjust and inhumane condition, a spiritual poverty, and solidarity with the poor and the rejected.[84]

The term "preference" does not intend to moderate—and still less to forget—the demand of solidarity with the poor and with social justice. It is not understood except in relation to the love of God for every person. Scripture presents it as universal and preferential at the same time. John XXIII referred to this when he spoke of "a church for all and particularly a church of the poor." The two aspects are not in contradiction, but rather in a productive tension. To limit it to one of them is to lose both. Because of that, Aparecida says—at the beginning of Chapter 8, which deals especially with the option for the poor—that the mission of announcing the Good News of Jesus Christ has a universal destination. Its mandate of charity embraces all dimensions of existence, all persons, all environments of life together, and all peoples. Nothing of the human can prove to be estranged. (A. 380) In this framework, it is necessary to understand the meaning of the priority of the insignificant and the excluded.

It is what the Document does when, speaking of the option for the poor: it affirms that "to be preferential implies that it must cross all our structures and pastoral priorities. The Latin-American Church is called to be a sacrament of love, solidarity, and justice among our peoples." (A. 396) Across all these ecclesial demands, not encased in set groups, is a way of

---

[84] See a brief description of that process in G. Gutiérrez, "Poverty and Theology" in *Páginas* Number 191, Feb. 2005, pp. 12–28.

being sacrament of love and justice. The preference aims at this, not to the diminishing of the radicalness of the option. On one side the universality situates the privilege of the poor on a wide horizon and demands continual improvement in reaching eventual limits; at the same time, the preference for the poor gives concrete expression and historic importance to universal happiness and warns of the danger of remaining at a dishonest and nebulous level.

EVANGELIZATION AND COMMITMENT FOR JUSTICE

Several questions are derived from the manner in which the preferential option for the poor is re-affirmed at Aparecida. We shall limit ourselves to emphasizing one of them. In continuity with what we have said, which at the same time is the result of decades of review in which there was no lack of ups and downs, the document expresses a wide and profound vision of evangelization. It says early in the text that missionary disciple[85] know that the light of Christ guarantees hope, love, and the future, and it adds, "This is the essential task of evangelization, which includes the preferential option for the poor, the promotion of human holistic development, and authentic Christian liberation." (A. 146) In effect, one of the pursuits of this option concerns the testimony of the Good News.

SHARING AN EXPERIENCE

The proclamation of the Gospel proceeds from an encounter with Jesus. We have encountered the Messiah, the Christ, says Andrew to his brother Peter, and he brings him to Jesus. (cf. John 1:41–42) It is a simple story that tells us what is essential in the communication of the Good News. Remembering it allows the document to enter into considerations, which are related,

---

[85] Various participants in the Conference postulated correctly, and it remained visible in some texts of the Aparecida Document, that the "and" is eliminated in the expression "disciples and missionaries," in order to emphasize that every disciple of Jesus is necessarily a missionary. The disciple witness is precisely an indispensable prolongation in community of the Trinitarian mission of the Son and Spirit (cf. *Ad Gentes* Numbers 3–5).

form part of many experiences, and are registered in the same sense as the option for the poor.

THE HAPPINESS OF THE DISCIPLE

That sharing gives birth to the joy of "the encounter with Jesus Christ, whom we recognize as the incarnate, redemptive Son of God . . . we desire that the joyousness of the Good News of Jesus Christ conqueror of sin and of death come to all . . . to make it known through our word and works is our pleasure." (A. 397) Without this experience, the transmission of the message changes itself into something cold and distant that does not reach people. The option for the poor, in fact, does not escape the risk "of remaining on a theoretical and merely emotionless plane, without a real incidence of it in our behavior and in our decisions." (A. 397) The joyous experience of an encounter with Jesus widens our vision and raises our spirits.

The option for the poor asks us to "dedicate time to the poor, to give them our loving attention, to listen with interest to them, to accompany them in the most difficult times, choosing to spend with them hours, weeks, or years of our life and searching with them the transformation of their situation." It is not a question of condescendence, but of solidarity and friendship, and the friendship signifies equality, recognition of human dignity. The document implies this understanding of it; it warns, therefore, that one must avoid "every paternalistic attitude."

HIDDEN POVERTIES

"Only the neighborhood that makes us friends," Aparecida says, "allows us to appreciate the deep values of the poor of today, their legitimate anxieties, and their manner of living the faith. The option for the poor must lead us to friendship with the poor." (A. 398)[86] In fact, without such friendship there is neither authentic solidarity nor true sharing; the option is for real persons, for daughters and sons of God. This position will help us perceive,

---

[86] The text, which follows, we have cited before, and it deals with the poor as stewards of their destiny.

Aparecida says with sensitivity and refinement, "the great sufferings in which the majority of our people live and the great frequency of the hidden poverties." (A. 176) There are among the poor, modest poverties, little noticed deeds of daily life, so hidden that they are not spoken of, sordid views of deeds causing irreparable damage, that a certain shamefulness covers them with a mantle of silence. It happens especially with the women of the poor sectors, marginalized, many times in the very midst of their families, but it does not happen only with them. All these small or great miseries appear only on the surface after a long time of friendship and until one asks forgiveness for speaking about them, there is no way out.

In no way do these considerations stand in the way of what the option for the poor signifies, nor of a commitment to justice that implies solidarity with efforts to eliminate it, as we shall see in the following paragraph. Simply, they make us project more clearly the central aspects that can escape one's vision when it does not penetrate sufficiently into the deep—and humble—dimensions of the life of the poor, as in its most delicate, personal aspects.

THE CHURCH, ADVOCATE OF JUSTICE AND THE POOR

The option for the poor is included in the evangelization task, said Benedict XVI in a phrase cited in the lines above. This places it in a position of battle for justice in proclaiming the Reign of God.

A PROPHETIC WORD

Action for justice and promotion of human development are not far from evangelization. All to the contrary. They do not end where the proclamation of the Christian message begins; they are not a pre-evangelization. They constitute a part of the proclamation of the Good News. This vision today is more clearly evident each time, and it is in Aparecida the result of a process which was making understood the meaning of the expression "Thy Kingdom come." It is speaking of the transformation of history in which it is making itself present already, although not yet fully. It is walking that accelerates the pace since the time of the Council, where the presence of the Church in the world was taken more seriously.

The Episcopal conferences, beginning with Medellín, which affirms that Jesus came to free us from sin, whose consequences result in slavery that is present in injustice (Justice 3), deal with this issue in one way or another in the sequential continental assembles. The Roman Synod on Justice in the World (1971) takes this position: the mission of the Church includes the defense and the promotion of dignity and of the fundamental rights of the human person. (N. 37) Furthermore, from *Evangelii Nuntiandi* (N. 29) John Paul II said at Puebla, with almost the same words mentioned in the Synod, that the evangelizing mission "has as an indispensable part the action for justice and the promotion of man." (DI. III, 2)

For his part, Benedict XVI affirmed in his inaugural address: "Evangelization has been united always to the promotion of human development and to authentic Christian liberation. Love of God and love of neighbor are fused to one another: in the most humble, we find Jesus himself and in Jesus we find God. (*Deus caitas est,* 15)" (DI. 3) A question from the beginning, which historical infidelities to that assumption do not modify . . . is a permanent need.[87]

In that sequence of ideas, it declares openly in that very influential text in Aparecida, "The Church is advocate of justice and of the poor," and it repeats the idea several lines below: "the advocate of justice and of truth." (DI. N. 4) These texts were cited various times at Aparecida, with agreement that deepens its meaning. "The Holy Father has recalled that the Church is gathered together to be an advocate of justice and defender of the poor before intolerable social and economic inequalities." (A. 395) The point remains clear. The proclamation of the Gospel is a prophetic word that announces the love of God for every person, but primordially for the poor and insignificant, and it denounces the situation of injustice that they suffer.

The proclamation of the Gospel implies a transformation of history, a transformation that revolves around justice, a respectful evaluation of the differences of kind, ethnic and cultural, and of the defense of the most elementary human rights which must be found in a society based

---

[87] Aparecida gathers up the idea with an allusion to the attitude of the Samaritan who leaves his path to attend to a wounded person: "Illuminated by Christ, suffering, injustice, and the cross beg us to live as a Samaritan Church. (Cf. Lc. 10:25–37). Citing the Pope: evangelization has been united always to human development and to authentic Christian liberation (DI. N. 3)" (A. 26).

on equality and brotherhood, a society of the "most humane" conditions, according to *Populorum Progressio* (N. 21), cited by Benedict XVI in his inaugural discourse.

THE TABLE OF LIFE

Denouncing injustice and establishing justice are necessary expressions of solidarity with actual persons.[88] We believe in one God of life, who rejects inhumane poverty as nothing less than an unjust and premature death. All are called to participate in the banquet of life. "The sharp difference," affirms the Conference, "between the rich and the poor invites us to work with greater effort in being disciples who know how to share at the table of life, the table of all the sons and daughters of the Father, the open inclusive table with no one left out. Therefore we re-affirm our preferential and evangelical option for the poor." (Message, 4) We seek an open table, from which no one is excluded, but whose first-invited guests are the least of this world.

The Pope, in his inaugural discourse, made an interesting allusion to the danger in the world today of an individualistic and indifferent attitude to the reality in which we live. Aparecida addresses this with the following words: "Holiness is not a flight toward the most intimate or religious individualism," a marked tendency in society and in the religious world today, "nor an abandonment of the urgent reality of the great economic, social, and political problems of Latin America and of the world, and much less a flight from the reality toward an exclusively spiritual world" (DI. N. 3), text cited in A. 146.

Truly, it is a great contemporary temptation in the Christian life, to which many give, and from which they strive to be included; it provides a clear conscience at the price of abandoning their witness to Jesus. It is as if one intimate, pretentious, recollected posture of moving oneself in an exclusively spiritual sphere might respond faithfully to the gospel demands. In that sense, the Pope and Aparecida make a great appeal regarding that

---

[88] Taking up with new force this option for the poor, we make clear that the whole evangelizing process implies human development and authentic liberation "without which a just order in society is impossible (DI. N. 3)" (A. 399).

"purism" which does not correspond to the authentic clarity and the integrity of the gospel.[89]

The ecclesial Base Communities, which display their gospel and missionary commitment among the simplest and most separated people, are a visible expression of the preferential option for the poor. (A. 179)[90] They accentuate justly the solidarity born of the love of God and of neighbor, and form part of a "unique commandment." (Deus Caritas 18) In the Eucharist, in configuring ourselves with the Lord, and in prayerful listening to the Word, we commemorate His life, testimony, teaching, death and resurrection and we celebrate joyfully our communion with God and among ourselves. (cf. A. 142)

CONCLUSION

The Document has a unique thrust of hope, but not of illusions. Toward the end of the final text it is noted, "There is no other region that counts so many unifying factors as Latin America and the Caribbean. But it deals with a distasteful unity because it is crossed through by domineering positions and contradictions." In addition, it is "still incapable of incorporating in itself 'all the bloods' and of overcoming the breech of strident inequalities and marginalizations." (A. 527) The expression 'all the bloods' comes from José María Arguedas, the title of one of his novels in which he tries to characterize the complex reality of Peru, but which is valid, in fact, for the entire continent. It expresses our diversity and likewise our richness and potentialities. To point out the difficulties, which we encounter in the present, is a question of realism and an indispensable condition for confronting properly the challenges, which come from our situation.

Aparecida has made it possible to see face-to-face this reality without subterfuges and escapes. It makes demands on the disciples of Jesus Christ in order to carry out faithfully their mission to the Gospel. It is a reality that

---

[89] In the same line is the insistence of Benedict XVI and of Aparecida in signaling out that "the Christian life is not expressed only in personal virtues, but also in the social and political virtues." (A. 505).

[90] Among the modifications of the final text of Aparecida, more numerous than at previous Conferences, the most extensive was—surprisingly—to the paragraphs which concern the base communities.

"the preferential option for the poor impels us, as disciples-missionaries of Jesus, to look for new and creative ways for responding to other results of poverty" (A. 409) as well as to their various causes and their multiple consequences, that would be necessary to add. That option understands a lifestyle that has inspired commitments on three levels, diverse but related: proclamation of the Good News in pastoral and social positions being perhaps the most visible; the theological; and as a foundation for all the aforementioned, spirituality, the following of Jesus. This provides one of the transverse axes of the document.[91]

At the beginning of these pages, we said that the event and the document of Aparecida will characterize the life of the Latin American and Caribbean Church in the time to come, but it is necessary to complete this affirmation. This will depend upon the acceptance that we give to Aparecida. It is something that is in our hands,[92] in the hands of the local churches, of the Christian communities, and of different, urgent, ecclesial demands. The exegesis, the interpretation of texts like this, is accomplished in actions, in practice. To that, the Good News of the kingdom of God calls us here and now.

---

[91] Regarding themes worked into liberation theology and the Document of Aparecida, see John Allen, "The Lasting Legacy of Liberation Theology" on the blog *All Things Catholic*, 24 May 2007. Available at: http://ncronline.org.

[92] As Carlos Galli says, Aparecida "was an event, which with the passage of time, the ecclesial acceptance, and its influence, will come to be 'historic.'" See "Aparecida, A new Pentecost in Latin America and the Caribbean?" in *Criterion*, July 2007, pp. 362–371

BASE COMMUNITIES, A RETURN TO INDUCTIVE METHODOLOGY

Jose Marins

The method of "See-Judge-Act" (frequently used both by the people from the base communities and by the bishops' assemblies at the national and continental levels) was eliminated from the Fourth General Latin American and Caribbean Bishops Assembly (Santo Domingo).[93] The question of whether or not to employ this methodology caused such intense discussions in the beginning moments of the Aparecida Assembly that, after heated debates, it was re-implemented, and was included in the text of the document. The reason that many of the delegates would not give up on this option is explained in the following: "Many voices coming from all over the continent offered contributions and suggestions, such that in a sense affirming that this method has been collaborative in living more intensely our vocation and mission in the Church, having enriched the theological and pastoral work, and in general has motivated us to assume our responsibilities with regard to specific realities of our continent."[94]

In short, it existed for good reason.

It does not try merely to be a technique for antiseptic or largely irrelevant group work. On the contrary, the method is in its content and the

---

[93] The ecclesiastical critics see in the method an implicit relativism, as if the truth were to be manufactured through consensus obtained through the process "See-Judge-Act." Many also see in the outline of the three steps that it superimposes a "horizontal" spirituality associated with Liberation Theology that can bring with it an acceptance of Marxist analysis and its many ideologies as operatives. In fact, the method was in use for about 40 years before the creation of Liberation Theology and it was fully accepted by Pope Pius XI and Pope Pius XII, two anti-communist popes who cannot be accused of horizontalism.

[94] Final Document of Aparecida, n. 19.

content is in the method. It gives direction to the community; it permits the people to be co-responsible individuals; and it empowers them to carry out a group action, intelligently planned and perseveringly executed. It is a way of being and influencing,[95] which unites faith and life.

The Bishops in Aparecida said, "This method permits us to implement, in a systematic way, the believer's perspective of seeing reality; the elevation to a higher level of dignity the criterion that comes from faith and reason by its discernment and valued critical sense; and, consequently, the projection for acting as missionary disciples of Christ."[96]

In the synthesis from the Bishops Conferences, presented at the beginning of the Aparecida Assembly, it was evident how this method has helped our people find ways of liberation. It does part of the pastoral work and is present in the life of various individual Churches and parishes, in a more steadfast way and in the CEBs.[97]

IN LATIN AMERICA AND THE CARIBBEAN

The methodology was linked to being Church and it developed pastoral team action because it is about: Seeing "as community," Judging "as community," and Acting "as community." Prior to Medellin, some countries already were using the method extensively in the Catholic Action groups, in the CEBs, and even in official Church documents.[98] The ecclesial community,

---

[95] A way very deeply rooted in the biblical faith. The nucleus of the faith from Israel has as at its start Ex. 3—the scream of a people who suffer and who demand justice. God watches the oppression, hears the clamor, knows the suffering, and acts by freeing the people. Cf. Carlos Ayala Ramires, "Latin America, See-Judge-Act a method of being in reality," *Adital*, May 19, 2007.

[96] Final Document of Aparecida, n. 19.

[97] By that method, even the simplest of our communities have gained human and ecclesial security. Little by little, the people from the base (at the bottom), in fact do theology, not in a systematic and academic way, but in the way it is lived, learned, and related to community.

[98] It is worth remembering that the Brazilian Bishops from Brazil have been utilizing this method since the 1950s. Mons. Helder Camara, who was then Secretary of the CNBB, worked with the then-Nuncio Apostolico, Mons. Lombardi to name Bishop Advisors from Catholic Action who were accustomed to the method of See-Judge-Act. The method was then used to systematize pastoral action and to structure the Episcopal documents on the local, regional, and national levels.

unworried about alarmist suspicions, was able to use the method to define their mission and put their faith into practice. That is to say, the method allows for seeing with the eyes of the Father, judging coherently by the teachings and testimonies of Jesus and His community, acting under the influence of the Spirit. Santo Domingo imposed a rupture that provoked discontinuity in the path since Medellín. Aparecida comes to heal that pastoral trauma, allowing the method to take back its ecclesial citizenship.

In Aparecida, the bishops' "*pastoralistas*" sensed that the question regarding the method was at stake not only as an operative framework, but also as the appropriate way in which the ecclesial community professes its faith (discipleship) and carries out its mission. Aparecida decided not to set out from Santo Domingo but rather from Vatican II, from the Latin-American tradition assumed at the Medellin Assembly, and from the great Tradition that came from the first Christian communities of the New Testament.

However, it must be recognized that, in the text from Aparecida, the method remained an intention, orientation, and effort that was not always successful. In fact, taking up the method again did not mean that everyone understood its breadth. See, for example, how the proclaimed truth in the final text of Aparecida did not pass through a structural analysis; neither did the missionary action link with and respond to the problems enumerated throughout the greatly amplified text of 554 paragraphs.

THREE STEPS OR FIVE?

The pastoral practice of the CEBs has advanced farther than the framework for Catholic Action inherited from Cardijn, adding two new steps to the three known ones: Evaluate and Celebrate.

Synthetically, to See is understood not merely as talking about a reality but rather as one sees it, understands it, and assumes it. To Judge from the criterion of faith and from human reasoning is to evaluate people, structures, and the cultures of today in the context of their history, in which one receives truth and well-being; it invites one to enrich oneself with each reality that is known, studied, and discerned. To Act welcomes and transforms; it recognizes, purifies, and satisfies. It recognizes the new theological places and the new step, to Celebrate. These steps in the method are not separate compartments but are like communicant vessels, mutually connected in the role of Evaluation. In Aparecida specifically, to See is a matter of affirming that the Latin American and Caribbean Church must realize the truth about the contemporary world, and about where the people and the Church find themselves as a community of missionary disciples.

To Judge is a matter of making an evaluation of whatever was seen, in the light of revelation and also from the criterion of Tradition, the Magisterium, and the *sensus fidelium* of the local church. Although use of the instruments and of the available advisors has been the path taken by Aparecida, the people's reflections do not have the same value as Revelation; neither do the people enjoy mathematical evidence. Therefore, at the same time that they should be welcomed and valued by the Church they remain open to subsequent supplements. Reality always changes. The way of each local church and its theological-biblical-pastoral reflection eventually contribute new elements. Aparecida, more than the previous Assemblies from our continent, made use of a greater number of biblical references. The quotations taken from the documents on the teachings of John Paul and Benedict XVI are abundant.

To Act, the operative proposals must be an answer to the urgencies and needs mentioned at length in the texts. Three basic questions guide the proper implementation of the Act. First, what are we doing and confirming? Second, what new aspects are there to take on? Third, what moves us to correct or to set aside; for what must we ask forgiveness? The actions that confirm what is already done are more numerous than those that point out answers to the new challenges. Many actions are not the result of the explicit analysis in the See, but rather are expressions of options that were already of concern and/or were decisions from a sector of participants from the Assembly. Nor did it feel proportionate or equitable as far as the quantity of practical references made for the different sectors, as expressed in the Final Message.

To Celebrate is to confirm how far the method has been taken on in different ways as shown at the assembly. In the final document, there is no reference to the "fiesta" so present in the lives of the people, the ways in which the people revive their communal feeling of hope and celebrate their humanity and cultural way of life. It is necessary to ask oneself if the method has been accepted only as a way of writing a document, or as a vital dynamism that animates all that one does and says: study commissions, plenary assemblies, transportation, and editing teams, synthesis, press conferences, symbols, ways of celebrating, etc.

To Evaluate, we must consider the directions taken in relation to the fundamental goals of the Church. How does the Church critically examine this model? If the Kingdom is really the first reference, from where does one see the effectiveness of the human being and the ecclesial task? The Kingdom was mentioned many times in Aparecida, but it does not remain as clear in the Final Document.

LIGHTS, SHADOWS, AND QUESTIONS

Lights generated at the Aparecida Conference included the following. The bishops succeeded in making Aparecida a General Bishops' Conference in Latin America instead of a Synod in Rome. This gave the bishops greater freedom to speak about their own circumstances.

Aparecida began by listening to reports from each Episcopal conference.

It was experienced in a popular Marian Shrine where each day the participants had the opportunity to be close to the common people, generally the poorest people in the country.

It re-adopted the See-Judge-Act methodology, and justified it explicitly in the document.

It took on issues of diverse kinds: the CEBs, option for the poor, oral reading of the Bible, as well as new topics, particularly the indigenous, migrants, Afro-descendents, the integration of the people, sustainable development, ecumenism and religious dialog, Christians in political danger, women's issues, and the laity.

It supported the formation of a continent of peace and justice.

It showed concern for the environment: ecology and protection of Amazonia.

Throughout the document, there is an insistence about the Church that is community (discipleship) and community mission.

There was no internal ecclesial condemnation.

Those who were officially "outside," like Amerindia and others were not denounced as "a parallel conference" or as "undesired and disturbing groups, creators of antagonisms" but were considered helpful. That point was declared publically at the Assembly by the same CELAM.

Shadows included:

Representatives from the *pastorales sociales* and the CEBs were not present.

There was a dominant presence of members from movements that express a more intra-ecclesial line.

Alterations were made in the final document, regarding spirit and content without clear reasons as to why they were made and who made them. This shadow generated discomfort and frustrations, and it weakened the credibility of the institutional authority.

The Aparecida conference also posed many questions:

Why are the areas of prophecy not identified in the Aparecida Document?

Why didn't the social themes appear as part of the mission?

Why did the base community, which is considered the mission, appear more as nostalgia than as Christianity, with a vision of a self-referring Church? As one bishop said, "We continue thinking that the Church is the beautiful little girl, but no one wants to dance with her."

Why, for many contemporaries, does a taste remain from the document that communicates an impression that we have a monopoly on God and on Salvation?

CONCLUSION

The way of our Latin American and Caribbean Church is vital for all those for whom we spend our lives in order to be faithful, and in order that the Church be faithful to the mission that the Lord entrusted to her. Therefore, we are constantly asking ourselves, "Where are you going, our Church?"

The General Bishops Assemblies have been references, not the only ones, but references of great importance for seeing, evaluating, and celebrating our walk as the People of God in today's realities which arise from our history, and thus for adjusting our pastoral performance. Looking at the five Conferences together, in terms of their process (content-method), one is able to synthesize the following.

Medellín went beyond the pastoral-ecclesial dominant model in Latin America and the Caribbean, at that moment; it has been a prophetic and creative assembly.

Puebla reached as far as the majority of the Church on the Continent desired to reach, and it expanded some content regarding the poor, the youth, the CEBs, and the structures of sin.

Santo Domingo stated less of who we were, particularly in regard to the subject of the CEBs; it gave pastoral citizenship to the theme of lack of education; it proclaimed the "prominence of the laity," but without specifying it.

Aparecida did not present attractive dreams and it did not make prophetic declarations, but it gently resumed the long walk of the Church of Latin America and the Caribbean, reaffirming the foundation laid by Medellin, and saving what Santo Domingo had sacrificed. The spirituality from the pastoral methodology was not expressed.

Aparecida spoke of almost every topic that touches pastoral concerns, being clear about which need to be high priorities. (One major exception is the dream of a continental mission that would be the great operative conclusion for all individual Churches, but this will be addressed in the next CELAM meeting.) There was no axis that gives unity to the whole document, other than the instructions to the Disciples and Missionaries of Jesus for giving life to the world. That allows for all the pastoral and theological trends to make use of the document as their tacit or explicit approval.

However, in its totality, methodology, and content, the Aparecida Document has features of hope and it confirms for us the originality of the Gospel, the communion with Peter, and the one holy, catholic, and apostolic community of Jesus. It invites us to a real missionary discipleship with the aim of being part of the Reign of the Father, manifested by Jesus, with the strength of the Spirit, in the communion of the Trinity.

APARECIDA AND GLOBAL MARKETS

Ernest Bartell, C.S.C.

The application of Catholic social thought to economic markets dates back at least to the thirteenth century when Thomas Aquinas responded to a request from the Duchess of Brabant to affirm the moral legitimacy of the trading that took place within the "farmers' market" in her duchy. In those days, markets were local and predominantly agricultural with buyers and sellers largely known to one another as they bought, sold, and bartered their own produce. Aquinas was basically supportive of the terms of trade in the local duchy, assuming honesty and goodwill on both sides of the exchange.

By the time the first major papal social encyclical, *Rerum Novarum,* was issued by Leo XIII in 1891, well after the industrial revolution, markets for goods, services, capital, and labor, as well as the distribution of income generated in each market, were distinct and less personal but still relatively small and local. At the same time, the influence of Marxist economic thought in some industrializing countries had resulted in constraints on private ownership of productive capital and the emergence of state-owned industries and firms. So, Catholic social teaching, while critical of both unbridled capitalist and socialist regimes, focused on justice in relations between labor and management at the level of production, principally at the level of the factory or firm, while at the same time defending the right of private ownership of productive capital.

By the time the encyclical *Quadragesimo Anno* was issued by Pius XI in 1931 when markets were increasingly regional and national, Catholic social teaching focused on relations between large firms, often operating as employers in several locations, and workers, often represented by national labor organizations whose members shared the same skills or worked in the same industries but were employed by various firms in multiple domestic locations.

However, by the time the papal encyclicals *Mater et Magistra* and *Populorum Progressio* were issued respectively by John XXIII in 1961 and Paul VI in 1967, large corporations in the most developed countries had expanded their markets internationally, exporting to foreign markets or establishing production facilities in foreign countries to serve emerging domestic foreign markets. Latin American markets had already for many years been internationalized by trade with their colonial founders and later with their North American trading partners. As they sought to industrialize, they were especially significant targets for capital investment and trade by the expanding multinational corporations based in more advanced econo-mies of North America and Western Europe. That experience helped drive the development of Catholic social thought that defined the documents issued by the Latin American Episcopal Conferences at Medellin in 1968 and at Puebla in 1979.

By the time the bishops of Latin America met at Aparecida, John Paul II had already addressed the possibilities and problems that have emerged with the expansion of global markets.[99] Not surprisingly, the documents issued by the Latin American bishops at Aparecida, though concerned with the impact of globalization on contemporary life in Latin America, are faithful to a tradition of universal Catholic social teaching already influenced by the earlier internationalization of economic development in Latin America and other emerging economies. The critiques of globalization in the Aparecida documents are as broad as the scope of the issue itself, and they address the impact of aspects of globalization on cultural, political, and social life. However, the social teaching in the Aparecida documents is directed most forcefully toward the impact of contemporary global expansion of economic markets on the distribution of both the costs and benefits of that expansion, thereby amplifying what John Paul II had already noted.

The Economic Context

The social teaching in the Aparecida documents directly addresses contem-porary issues raised by the globalization of economic markets for goods, services, capital, and labor that impact not only the emerging markets of the low and middle income countries of Latin America, but also the

---

[99] John Paul II, *Ecclesia in America* (1992).

domestic and international markets of the most advanced economies and the emerging markets of other continents, especially Asia and Africa. Latin American economies themselves remain diverse in their size, composition, and growth. Brazil is highly industrialized and one of the world's four largest emerging economies, while Bolivia and Nicaragua remain largely unindustrialized and among the poorest countries in the world. Consequently, the Aparecida documents are careful to limit their critiques to generalized principles, which, though perhaps not satisfying to those seeking specific solutions to vexing problems, are foundational for the ethical appraisal of policies, strategies, and tactics adopted by those in both public and private sectors, whose actions shape those markets and determine their outcomes.

The ethical principles embodied in the Aparecida critique of economic globalization proceed from the Church's faith in the Gospel message of Jesus, as the bishops point out. However, those principles, as the Aparecida document makes clear, are grounded also in the fundamental dignity of the human person and so have a universal relevance that extends beyond Catholic belief to other religious and secular social norms.

In expanding on that fundamental principle, the Aparecida documents focus on the "preferential option for the poor." It is the centrality of this perspective in the moral and ethical evaluation of economic markets and institutions that has identified and characterized Latin American contributions to global Catholic social thought since its promulgation by the Latin American Episcopal Conferences at Medellin and Puebla. That priority has also influenced the evolution of Catholic social thought in countries worldwide at every level of economic development.

Within that perspective, the moral and ethical critiques of globalization in the Aparecida documents address basic economic principles and issues of efficiency and equity in economic markets that are topical and significant throughout contemporary society. Just as the principles of social justice that underlie the contemporary preferential option for the poor have a long history in the evolution of economic markets from local to global, so do the economic principles in the analysis of the efficiency and equity of market behavior. In one sense, globalization itself as a phenomenon of economic life has roots that date back at least to Marco Polo and Prince Henry the Navigator.

The basic economic principles reflected in the trade of goods and services in global markets need not differ fundamentally from those in national or local markets. When Adam Smith and other founders of market analysis defended the importance of individual initiative in competitive free markets to ensure the maximum productivity of scarce resources, they envisioned morally responsible actors in local markets which none of them could individually control, responding to competitive pressures with productive entrepreneurship that would improve the quantity and quality of goods and services traded at the lowest feasible prices in those markets.

What has changed since the time of Adam Smith and other founders of market analysis are the scope and impact of markets now grown global in geography; the quality and degree of competition in those markets and the outcomes of global market behavior in the allocation of the world's resources; and the distribution of the incomes generated by those resources in global markets. Like Adam Smith, today's advocates of free trade in the global economy tend to point out that free trade can and does result in a greater and more cost-effective diversity of goods and services at lower prices for consumers, along with expanded opportunities for investment in the income and wealth-creating activities that drive economic growth. In so doing, efficient markets at global, as well as local, levels can contribute to greater productivity of all resources, including human effort, and thus to more efficient economic growth and the opportunity for steadily rising standards of living.

However, elementary market economics stipulates that the efficiency of markets depends upon many crucial assumptions or conditions that have seldom been fully realized. In markets that are competitively efficient, all buyers and sellers, whether of goods, services, or labor, have full knowledge of prices and availability, and no individual seller (or buyer) can influence the price set competitively, i.e., by many competing sellers (and buyers) in the same market. In efficient global markets the same conditions should hold true for buyers and sellers, whether they are individuals, small business firms, multinational corporations, or government entities, such as the relatively recent sovereign wealth funds of national governments that invest in productive enterprises throughout the world.

Economic history has made it abundantly clear to all, including the bishops of Aparecida and students of elementary economics, that competition is imperfect in many markets where one or a few dominant sellers or buyers can manipulate prices and quantities, e.g., of goods and services being sold or of labor being hired, to their own advantage. In the history of international trade, it has not been unusual for emerging economies to have little control over the prices they receive for their exports, especially of tropical agricultural commodities, while being forced to pay administered non-competitive prices set by dominant suppliers for the imported goods, especially manufactures, and for capital expenditures necessary for the growth and modernization of their own economies.

As markets have expanded globally, however, competition has increased in the markets for many goods and services. For many Latin American countries, this has meant an improvement in their gains from international trade. Although the United States is still a principal trading partner for Latin American exports and imports, it can no longer dominate as many Latin American markets, including those for imports and exports, as it did, for example, when the bishops at Medellín issued their documents on social justice. Brazil, which now lends more to other countries than it borrows abroad, as do China, Russia, and India, accounts for forty percent of the total exports of all emerging economies. As a result, exports to the United States in 2007 accounted for only four percent of Brazil's total exports. On the other hand, Mexico, the second largest economy in Latin America, still depends on the United States for over one-quarter of its exports.[100]

Moreover, prices, though still volatile in recent years, have risen in global markets for many traditional export commodities, such as corn, soybeans, oil, copper and other minerals that have long been identified with traditional export strength in primary products of many Latin American economies. Much of that improvement is due to the exceptionally rapid increase in trade among emerging economies themselves, making them less economically dependent upon the developed markets of their traditional American and European trading partners. The rapid industrial growth of China, for example, has raised global prices of many Latin American commodities, such as Venezuelan oil and Chilean copper.

At the same time, the rapid development of industrial technology in emerging industrial economies, especially in Asia, has severely challenged the competitive capabilities of Latin American industries in global markets. This is especially true in global markets for high-technology products, where the share of Latin American exports in the world market continues to fall, while that of other emerging economies, especially China, grows.[101]

---

[100] *The Economist*, March 8, 2008, p. 80.

[101] Kevin P. Gallagher and Roberto Porzecanski, *Climbing up the Economic Ladder? High Technology Exports in China and Latin America*, Working Paper No. 20, Center for Latin American Studies, University of California, Berkeley, January 2008.

Virtually all Latin American countries have entered into bilateral or multilateral free-trade agreements with each other and/or with major trading partners outside of Latin America. Within Latin America itself, for example, there have been many attempts at regional economic integration, including current trade agreements among the Southern Cone countries (Mercosur) and among the Caribbean countries (CAFTA). These agreements aspire to varying levels of economic integration, including the elimination or reduction of various barriers to trade such as tariffs and quotas among the member countries. In principle, such agreements can benefit both consumers through lower prices, and producers through new and enlarged export markets, and may reflect a common movement toward greater integration into the global economy. However, such outcomes depend on the extent of barriers to trade with non-members, held in common or permitted by the terms of the agreement. Agreement on the terms of these treaties in law and in practice have proven difficult, and agreements in Latin America have languished as individual member countries have opted for bilateral agreements with major trading partners elsewhere in the world economy.

In any case, as cheaper imports, even from treaty partners, replace the products of domestic producers in domestic markets, some domestic production is adversely affected. Because of the North American Free Trade Agreement (NAFTA) signed by Mexico, Canada, and the United States, relatively inefficient small farms producing corn in Mexico suffered from the competition of cheaper imported corn grown by large, relatively efficient, mechanized agricultural firms in the United States, whose production enjoys the additional benefit of subsidies from the U.S. government. Therefore, it is not surprising that the Aparecida documents include a general reference to the distributional inequities among Latin American countries and within the populations of individual Latin American nations that can result from trade agreements.

It is also worth noting, however, that within Mexico some sectors have also benefited to some extent from NAFTA as American industrial firms have shifted production from locations with high labor costs in the United States to Mexico in order to take advantage of lower cost Mexican labor. Therefore, the human burdens of free-trade agreements are not limited to the emerging economies among the treaty partners. Indeed, domestic pushback against the displacements in the United States attributed to NAFTA has weakened American support for NAFTA and led to pressure within the United States for enforcement in subsequent trade agreements of more stringent government regulation of working conditions in Mexico to create a more level playing field for American labor.

The effects of the expansion of global markets on the distribution of the incomes generated by those markets have, for many emerging economies as well as most highly developed nations, resulted in greater inequalities in the distribution of the incomes generated by those markets. The benefits of global growth probably accrue most rapidly to those with the greatest access to all the ingredients in global growth, such as technology, education, and access to capital markets.

However, advocates of global free trade point out that even so, in most emerging economies, especially in Asia, the absolute income of the poorest fifth of income earners who have benefited to some extent from improvements in the economic infrastructure of their countries has at least risen somewhat in recent years. Not even that limited result, however, has been true for Latin America, where the absolute income of the lowest quintile of income earners has actually decreased slightly since the mid 1990s.[102]

Thus, in their emphasis on the option for the poor, the Aparecida documents understandably address the plight of economically active Latin Americans who are adversely affected by the dislocations and shifting outcomes created by competitive globalized markets. However, the Latin American poor also include those who are left out of market participation, for whatever reason, e.g., lack of marketable skills or access to existing employment opportunities, or who are simply too numerous to find employment at a subsistence wage, despite their actual or potential skills. As a result, those who control relatively scarce productive resources, such as financial and physical capital, are left to capture most of the gains from trade in local, domestic, or global markets.

That helps to explain why markets alone cannot be relied upon to distribute equitably the income generated by market activity for the well-being of both those who participate as well as those who cannot participate in the market economy, even in those markets that come close to meeting the conditions for competitive efficiency. It is typically argued that consumers worldwide benefit from the diversity and low prices of goods and services produced in efficient global markets. However, markets in themselves treat labor as a commodity and workers as objects rather

---

[102] *The Economist*, January 26, 2008, pp. 28–29.

than subjects, as Catholic social teaching has consistently noted and as is graphically illustrated in the Aparecida documents' reference to human trafficking.

Consequently, history repeatedly demonstrates that there is no guarantee that incomes generated, even in relatively efficient markets, will be distributed by the markets in ways that ensure even minimal access to basic goods and services, not only by those left out of the market economy, but even by many actively participating in the market economy.

The Aparecida documents criticize the priority typically given to efficiency over equity in economic activity. Even under strong and often unrealistic assumptions behind perfectly efficient competitive markets, such as full employment and the inability of individual employers to control wages, the wages set by impersonal market forces alone, i.e., by supply and demand, cannot be expected to reflect the full contributions to product value made by individual workers, especially the least skilled, who are typically in excess supply, i.e., unemployed or under-employed. In addition, just as market demand for goods and services is heavily weighted by the cultural values and specific tastes of consumers with the ability and desire to spend the most on consumer goods, so too the demand for, and wages of, those employed in their production may reflect those wishes in ways that discriminate against allocation of resources for basic human needs and which also discriminate on the basis of race, ethnicity, and gender.

Moreover, even markets that begin as relatively competitive can become less competitive and more monopolistic as individuals, corporations, and even nations strive to dominate the markets in which they compete as sellers or buyers in order to control prices and capture as "unearned rents" non-competitive shares of the total income generated. There is simply no necessary correlation in market analysis between market behavior and distributional equity.

Although underplayed in the Aparecida documents, traditional Catholic social teaching as well as analytic market analysis have made it clear that the assumptions and conditions of both supply and demand for efficiency in markets for goods and services, as well as in markets for the necessary labor, capital, and other resources required for production and trade, are seldom realized in actual practice. In addition, both economic history and analysis make it clear that, when left to the markets themselves, the distribution of income and wealth generated by market activity easily becomes skewed in favor of the few at the expense of the many.

The evidence is apparent from the days of the *hacendados* to the days of "golden parachutes" for failed CEO's.

The history of Latin American economies since colonial times is replete with market failures and imperfections that have thwarted development of market efficiency and have done so in ways that have exacerbated inequities in the distribution of incomes. From the initial *encomiendas* of colonial times to the contemporary concentration of financial capital, the skewed distribution of productive wealth, along with flawed business practices, trade rules, and discriminatory local laws, has left great numbers of people trapped in poverty and marginalized in economic life by the lack of access to productive resources, including adequate education and health care.

Economic history has also demonstrated, however, that grand schemes by national governments of emerging economies to create non-market command economies, substituting socialist economic policies and state ownership of productive enterprises for flawed market mechanisms, have failed to produce either consistently efficient economic growth or a sustainable equitable distribution of income and wealth.

Consequently, especially following Vatican II, the remedies for inadequate attention to the mal-distribution of incomes and wealth sought by proponents of Catholic social thought, including scholars and hierarchy, have stressed the centrality of human development within an economic system, rather than wholesale systemic change in the assessment of economic life and growth. They have done so with an emphasis on those segments of the population marginalized by or excluded from the uneven expansion of economic well-being in advanced and emerging economies.

One segment of the economically active population that is significant, within Latin America itself and in its relations with its neighbors to the north, is that of economic migrants, who also warrant specific mention in the Aparecida documents. Latin America has a long history of economic migration, dating back to colonial times when foreign mercantilist colonial administrators controlled domestic production and destiny of primary products, including precious metals and other minerals, to enrich the treasuries of the colonizing powers.

In the decades leading up to the Episcopal conference of Medellín, when newly industrializing Latin American economies were protected from international competition, rapid internal and domestic migration from the countryside to industrializing urban areas created the squalid *barrios, callampas* and *favelas* that helped define the original "preferential option for the poor" in Latin American social thought. Since then, Latin American migration has become international as, for example, Haitian migration to the Dominican Republic and, along with Mexicans and Central Americans, to the United States. In economic analysis, both domestic and international migration can be viewed as specific instances of the free movement of goods, services, and capital.

Migrants contribute to efficient global production and growth by seeking the most productive and presumably best-paid positions relative to their skills, wherever those positions exist. Highly skilled Indian technicians who migrated to California in recent years helped develop the high-tech industry of Silicon Valley in California. Even more recently, this brain drain has been partially reversed as many of those migrants returned to their home country, enriched with additional skills and experience, as more attractive job opportunities accompanied the recent rapid economic growth in India.

Meanwhile, the controversial migration to the United States of unskilled Mexican workers (whose remittances to families still in Mexico have become a major source of Mexican foreign income) to fill low-paying jobs in the United States has, in some ways, served as a substitute for moving productive capital from the United States to Mexico and hiring laborers there, or for importing the equivalent final products produced in Mexico by local firms there using local capital and labor. The market choices of all the participants are influenced by the economic costs and benefits of the various alternatives.

Increased access to transportation and communication facilities has also given rise to a phenomenon sometimes identified as transmigration, whereby migrants, unlike their predecessors a century ago, travel back and forth and maintain regular contacts and relationships with friends and relatives in their places of origin.[103] In addition to dependence on available resources, the ability to maintain such an array of options obviously depends also upon political measures in both countries to encourage or discourage their execution.

---

[103] Cf. Nina Glick Schiller, Cristina Szanton Blanc, "From Immigrant to Transmigrant: Theorizing Transnational Migration," *Anthropological Quarterly*, Vol. 68, No. 1, Jan., 1995. pp. 48–63.

The overall effects of migration on domestic and global economies as well as on individual human lives, especially of the most vulnerable participants, of the various alternatives available to migrants are matters for analysis and debate. The mobility of financial capital is typically much greater than the mobility of labor. It is true that advances in information technology have benefited both workers and investors.

Opportunities for both jobs and investments are more widely and rapidly disseminated. Nevertheless, in the increasingly efficient global financial markets, the opportunities and instruments available to investors seeking the most lucrative investment possibilities surely exceed the opportunities available to migrant workers, especially those with the fewest marketable skills. Hence, consistent with the fundamental priority of the option for the poor in the Aparecida documents, they call attention simply to the immediate needs of migrants themselves. In doing so, the Aparecida documents reflect the discretion of the authors and acknowledge the complexity of the larger economic and political issues by refraining from specific proposals to resolve those issues.

Conclusion

The principal focus of the documents issued by the bishops at Aparecida is clearly upon the overall pastoral mission of the Church in Latin America, in which economic life is only one of many issues. Therefore, it is not surprising that the updated preferential option for the poor grounds the relatively limited economic portion of the document. Against the background of over two centuries of universal Catholic social teaching, as well as the checkered history of capitalist and socialist regimes and policies in Latin America, the generalized economic observations and recommendations of the bishops at Aparecida may appear somewhat low-keyed. There are no calls for a new "third way" between the poles of extreme capitalist and socialist economic models such as those that characterized sectors of Catholic social thought in the industrial countries of Europe and North America in the last century. Nor are there calls for radical, even revolutionary, overhauls of existing economic systems, such as those proposed by representatives of both the political left and right, which have characterized much of political life in Latin America as well.

Instead, in the pastoral spirit of the Aparecida documents, the general but firm observations, descriptions, and prescriptions of moral priorities in economic and political life are offered as measured challenges. No specific economic actors are singled out and targeted as villains, not the multinational corporations targeted by social activists on the left during the middle of the last century nor the inefficient state enterprises targeted more recently by non-governmental agencies like the International Monetary Fund, along with neo-liberal critics.

Nor are simplistic redistributive "tax and transfer" silver bullets or calls for massive shifts in ownership and control of productive assets offered as quick fixes to market limitations, biases, failures, and imperfections. In so doing the Aparecida documents acknowledge the need for constructive proposals and action by people of faith and of good will in both public and private sectors. The larger priority of human dignity and development in the objectives of the Aparecida documents leaves the door open to a broad range of policy proposals, from policies for improvements in access and quality of long-term investment in human capital through health and education at every stage of life to public and private vehicles for ameliorating short-term human needs resulting from natural disasters, economic dislocation, and other unanticipated circumstances.

The bishops also implicitly acknowledge the inevitability of globalized markets that reach the diverse economies of Latin America. They focus their broad challenges for social justice on the distribution of the fruits of global economic life within and among the populations encompassed by global markets with all their analytic and ethical imperfections and failures. And they do so with special emphasis on an expansive appreciation of the option for the poor that extends not only to the economically poorest, but to all those marginalized in market-driven economic life, including migrants and victims of gender discrimination, human trafficking, and social exclusion, especially within indigenous populations. They do so not to propose solutions or pass judgments, but to challenge and exhort all who have responsibilities that influence global economic life.

Theirs is a bold challenge modestly proposed.

Left to right:
Monsignor Carlos Quintana,
Bishop Ricardo Ramirez, C.S.B.,
Bishop William S. Skylstad,
and Bishop Jaime Soto.

GLOBALIZATION AND ECONOMICS AT APARECIDA

Javier Maria Iguiñiz Echeverria[104]

In the approved final document of Aparecida, the section with the most economic content is concerned primarily with the effects of globalization. Globalization establishes more clearly than ever the broad responsibility that Christians must assume. As Benedict XVI emphasized in his inaugural address, the brotherhood of man today includes "a network of relationships extending over the whole planet" that "benefits the great family of humanity" and expresses "its profound aspirations towards unity."

It is impossible not to be part of globalization. (60) Yet these relationships, benefits, and aspirations have often turned out for to be unfair, deadly, and frustrating, given the characteristics that globalization has acquired today. The final document provides an analysis of these characteristics. It proposes, I would argue, a choice showing a preference for those most in need of support rather than for those who are already safe.

ECONOMICS: HIGHEST IN THE HIERARCHY

Section 61 goes to the heart of the analytical focus of this theme. For the bishops, "Globalization is a complex phenomenon that has diverse dimensions (economic, political, cultural, communications-related, etc.)." Therefore, "to evaluate it fairly, we need a comprehensive, differentiated analysis that allows us to detect both its positive and negative aspects." In practice, however—and this is the main point of the emphasis chosen— these dimensions are not sufficiently independent of each other, nor similar

---

[104] Chair of the Dept. of Economics, Pontifical Catholic University of Peru.

in hierarchy. "Unfortunately, the most extensive and successful face of globalization is its economic dimension, which places itself above and determines the other dimensions of human life." In reality, economics is not just another dimension of globalization since, "in globalization, the dynamic of the market quickly makes efficiency and productivity the most important values for regulating human relations. This peculiar aspect makes globalization a process that promotes multiple inequities and injustices."

This reality obliges us to announce the Gospel in response to a serious distortion of values and priorities. "Globalization as it is now configured cannot interpret and react to objective values which go beyond the market and constitute what is most important about human life: truth, justice, love and most of all, the dignity and rights of all people, even those who live at the margin of the market itself."

In the next section, the bishops highlight and explain a broadly recognized aspect of globalization: the exceptional inequality of income and wealth in Latin America. The distortion of priorities leads to exclusion.

From the Distortion of Priorities to Exclusion and Poverty

Essentially, the Latin American bishops begin section 62 by indicating their awareness that the structural problem is found on many levels. Among these is the hierarchy of values, the priority given to profit as a goal and the secondary place given to life in relation to profit, and the main rule of the game in human economic relations: competition. Later, they state that the operation of these values and rules leads to inequality of access to knowledge and information. Here it is worthwhile to quote the document at length, in order to anchor my interpretation in the text itself:

> Driven by a tendency to place profit above all else and to stimulate competition, globalization follows a dynamic that concentrates power and wealth in the hands of a few, not only in relation to physical and monetary resources but also information and human resources. This causes the exclusion of all those who are not sufficiently trained and informed: it increases the inequalities which sadly mark our continent and which keep a multitude of people in poverty. Poverty today is poverty of knowledge, and of the use of and access to new technologies. Therefore, business-people must take responsibility for creating more sources of employment and for investing in the elimination of this new poverty.

Thus, the distortion of priorities leads to unjust rules for human relations, to an enormously unequal distribution of the factors of power, and to poverty. In a region where poverty is associated in large part with the proliferation of family-run initiatives and very small businesses, this reference to the structure of production is very pertinent.

Moreover, one of the most typical and universally recognized traits of this poverty is its concentration in those enormous activities that are most vulnerable to competition. As the Aparecida document states:

> It is undeniable that the predominance of this tendency does not eliminate the possibility of forming small and large businesses, which are associated with the dynamic export sector of the economy, provide it with collateral services or take advantage of specific niches in the internal market. Nevertheless, their economic and financial fragility and the small scale in which they operate make them extremely vulnerable to interest rates, exchange rate fluctuations, provisional costs and variations in the costs of inputs. The weakness of these businesses is associated with precariousness of employment that they are able to offer. Without a specific state policy of protection from these forces, there is a risk that the economies of scale of large consortia end up imposing themselves as the only determining force for economic dynamism. (63)

The panorama of human suffering cannot be reduced to that which derives from human economic relations. In Aparecida, there was a renewed attempt to incorporate the multiplicity of suffering faces that have impressed pastoral ministers and bishops since Medellín.

> This should lead us to contemplate the faces of those who suffer. Among them are the indigenous and Afro-descendant communities, which in many cases are not treated with dignity and equality of conditions; many women who are excluded, because of their sex, race or socioeconomic situation; young people who receive a low quality education and lack opportunities to progress in their studies or to enter the workforce and develop as people and create families; the many who are poor, unemployed, migrants, displaced, landless peasants and who attempt to survive in the informal economy; boys and girls forced into child prostitution, many times linked to sexual tourism; also those children who are victims of abortion. Many people and families live in misery and suffer from hunger. We are also concerned with those who are addicted to drugs; those with disabilities; carriers and victims of serious diseases such as

malaria, tuberculosis, and HIV-AIDS, who suffer loneliness and exclusion from family and social life. Nor do we forget those who have been kidnapped and who are victims of violence, terrorism, armed conflict and daily insecurity. We also remember the elderly, who, in addition to being excluded from productive systems are often rejected by their families as useless and inconvenient. Finally, we are pained by the inhuman situation in which the vast majority of prisoners live, though they also need our solidarity and fraternal support. Globalization without solidarity negatively affects the poorest sectors. It is no longer simply a phenomenon of exploitation and oppression, but something new: social exclusion. This has a deep impact on one's sense of belonging to the society in which one lives, since one is no longer on the bottom, on the periphery or powerless, but rather on the outside. The excluded are not only "exploited," but also "surplus" and "disposable." (65)

Once again in the documents of the Church, the perverse mechanisms that John Paul II denounced are present. This time, they are mentioned along with labor relations and the various losses of freedom to fight for life implicit in discrimination, disposability, and insignificance. The problem is not a simple one. The document insists on the predominance of unjust social structures of sin (92, 532), death (95, 112), and violence (546).

An Invitation to Search

Following their denunciation, the bishops list the spheres of action for confronting human suffering. A plan is offered, in the sense that suffering is not seen as inevitable but rather as an exercise of free choice. In the spirit of a proposal, the bishops suggest several spheres of action with various levels of scope and specificity.

A Different Type of Globalization

How can there be hope if there are so many expressions of indifference that make Latin America the most unequal continent in the world? Another type of globalization is needed. "Therefore, in the face of this form of globalization, we feel a strong call to promote a different kind of globalization that is marked by solidarity, justice, and respect for human rights, making Latin America and the Caribbean not only the continent of hope but also the continent of love, as His Holiness Benedict XVI proposed in the inaugural address to this conference." (64)

Economic power and the forces that drive it stand in the way. Despite the undeniable advances that set globalization apart from other eras, the Pope also states that it "brings with it the risk of vast monopolies and of treating profit as the supreme value." Therefore, Benedict XVI emphasizes that "as in all areas of human activity, globalization too must be led by ethics, placing everything at the service of the human person, created in the image and likeness of God" (60). The radical nature of this proposal is proportionate to the indignation it must provoke. "The Holy Father has reminded us that the Church is convened to be 'an advocate of justice and defender of the people' before 'intolerable social and economic inequalities' that 'cry to the heavens.'" (295). The corresponding challenge is not to focus on the care of the sheep that are already safe and congratulate them for the progress that they have made, but instead to go out in search of the faces highlighted in the aforementioned list.

This was the proposal of Medellin and now, forty years later, in the context of deeper globalization, it is the proposal of the final document from Aparecida. It is a tradition that sets the standard for choosing preferred themes and subjects.

AGAINST THE ENCOURAGEMENT OF MORAL SMALLNESS

Is this task too broad and deep? Do we have a moral responsibility to set the goal of committing to the poor individually and, at the same time, to a new kind of globalization? The usual neo-liberal argument against changing human relations beyond their current state is based on the difficulty of obtaining all the information needed to be effective. This was the basis of the critique of attempts at centralized Socialist planning. The theme of information in Aparecida is crucial and deserves a separate analysis. "When people perceive this fragmentation and limitation, they usually feel frustrated, anxious, and upset. The social reality is too vast for a consciousness that, given its lack of knowledge and information, can easily believe itself to be insignificant and without any impact on events, even when it adds its voice to other voices that seek to help." (36)

The ignorance and the supposed human smallness that comes with it is the vehicle for rejecting the relevance of any ethical questioning of the current international order and social situation. Hayek maintains that because no person can ever have all the information he needs about others, he should not take on tasks beyond his immediate sphere.[105] Contrary to this argument, the final document proposes a vision that does not paralyze public action and even less so, of course, private action.

The recognition of the complexity of human phenomenon (34), of the acceptance of the need for differentiated analyses by sphere (61), of the opaqueness this complexity causes and of the value of avoiding simplistic visions (36) and unilateralism (41) should not render people powerless before such phenomena as globalization and the reality of the market. Along with the analysis outlined in many sections of the text, there is another constant theme that relates to the responsibility of the authors of the document: faith as the source of the unitary meaning of life. (37, 38) This, once again, is a theme beyond the scope of this chapter but which can be expressed in the following quote: "In Christ the Word and Wisdom of God (Corinthians 1:30), culture can return to find its center and depth, from which we can view reality in the context of all its factors, discerning these in light of the Gospel and giving each one its appropriate place and dimension." (41)

Any knowledge that is acquired should be for freedom and social responsibility. (42) "Therefore, it is not enough to suppose that the mere diversity of points of view, options and finally, information—which is usually given the name multi-culturalism—will make up for the absence of a unitary meaning for everything which exists. The human person is, in essence, that place in nature where the variety of meanings converges in a single vocation of meaning. People do not fear diversity. What they fear more is not being able to bring together all the meanings of reality in a unified understanding that allows them to exercise their freedom with discernment and responsibility. A person always searches for the truth of his being, since it is this truth that illuminates reality in a way that allows him to develop with freedom and happiness, with enjoyment and hope."

---

[105] "La Fatal Arrogancia: los errors del socialismo." Madrid: Unión Editorial. "El orden extensor nunca habría a surgir si no hubiese sido ignorado la recomendación de que todo semejante sea tratado con el mismo espiritu de solidaridad que se dedica a quien habita el entramo más próximo . . . integrados en el orden extensor salimos beneficiados de que no se trate a todos con idéntico espíritu de solidaridad."

(42) Just as we need not know someone completely to have a relationship with him or her, we need not have perfect knowledge of human relations to change what seems to be inadequate.

PUBLIC POLITICAL TASKS

In the context of globalization, the commitment to building a just order at every level of human, family, local, national, and global relations becomes more imperative than ever:

> The disciples and missionaries of Christ must illuminate every sphere of social life with the light of the Gospel. The preferential option for the poor, which has Gospel roots, demands close pastoral attention to the building blocks of society. If many of the current structures cause poverty, it is in part due to the lack of fidelity to Gospel commitments on the part of many Christians, who have special political, economic, and cultural responsibilities. (501)

Similarly, the document continues:

> The preferential option for the poor demands that we pay special attention to those Catholic professionals who are responsible for the nation's finances, or encourage employment, and to the politicians who must create the conditions for economic development in each country, to give them an ethical orientation which is consistent with their faith. (395)

The call to public responsibility and, in this sense, to political action, is direct. Today more than ever, this action includes interacting with the globalized world and taking advantage of its possibilities for communication.

The bishops do not avoid giving specific guidelines for commitment. They offer multiple, specific possibilities since so many aspects are in need of change: care for the environment in the face of extractive activities (66); the autonomy of local economies (66); the strengthening of the State vis-à-vis business (76); the "illicit intellectual appropriation" of knowledge stemming from biodiversity through patents (83, 67); a warning against the establishment of commercial treaties without considering that economic relations are asymmetrical (67); the questioning of lax regulation of financial institutions and of speculative capital that concentrates profit and wealth (69); the excessive burden of service to the external debt (68); the creation of more efficient tax systems (68); the warning against public and private corruption, including drug trafficking, the lack of transparency and accountability to civil society (70); the denunciation of underemployment, unemployment, and lack of protection for workers in the informal sector, of the precariousness of work conditions, of outsourcing, and of the weakening of labor unions (71); the damage to poor peasants caused by the lack of access to land, by the existence of large estates, by international competition and the manipulation by the drug traders (72); the migration and forced displacement that result from the economic situation, poverty and violence; the lack of opportunities for professional development and support for research (73); the scandal of human trafficking, prostitution, slavery and the exploitation of workers (73). It is an agenda that calls for all of us to reflect on the moral problems that emerge by omission rather than wrongdoing. In the list, we find a combination of causes and effects that concern the Latin American bishops, which form the backdrop behind the many faces described in the final document.

SIGNS OF HOPE

In response to these realities, which are so resistant to doctrine, the bishops place before us the challenge of generating hope—which is possible only with specific action. Doctrines that do not lead to action are discredited; they fail to awaken interest and, in many cases, are abandoned. This is the challenge of the Church's social doctrine: to spur action in the spheres mentioned above and in many other realms that the document was not able to mention. "We have much to offer, since 'there is no doubt that the Church's Social Doctrine (CSD) is capable of reviving hope in the face of the most difficult circumstances because if there is no hope for the poor, there is no hope for anyone, not even for the so-called rich." (395) As the bishops have understood it, from speaking to many Catholics in Latin America and the Caribbean, the challenge is not the lack of capacity, but rather of exercising this capacity in service of the poor. This leads to the long list of options for action summarized above.

The final document from Aparecida tells us that the conditions that CSD puts forth in order for the economy to fulfill its function are not being fulfilled in Latin America and the Caribbean. Globalization as it occurs in reality—and more specifically, the creation of wealth—are not morally correct, although as Catholic social doctrine recognizes, they could be so in principle under certain conditions that unfortunately are not present. The message seems to be that today's values, institutions, and economic practices are not on the morally correct side because the economic process "is not oriented toward global development and toward solidarity with men and the society in which they live and work." (69)[106]

The effort by many to legitimize current economic activity based on the way it should be carried out, putting forward the conditions necessary for it to be compatible with Catholic doctrine, conflicts with a reality that cannot easily be sugarcoated and from which the bishops do not flee. The limited dissemination of the Aparecida proposals by the mass media is a result of the bishops' refusal to turn their backs on the unnecessary suffering of millions of Latin Americans.

We have the problem that economic well-being comes at a cost that is morally unacceptable, unfair, and unnecessary. Economic well-being is just one dimension of human activity among many that should be encouraged, but often cannot be, because of the dominance of economic rationality and the power behind it in more and more spheres of life including, we fear, the religious sphere. For this last reason, the bishops insist in Aparecida that the subordination of multiple spheres of human activity to economic criteria is unacceptable. For this reason also, they defend a religion that refuses to be subordinated to the power and rules of economics and to lose its authority before them.

As they state, "Development cannot be reduced to a mere process of accumulation of goods and services; even if this favors the common good, it is not enough for the realization of authentic human happiness (CSDI, 334)." Even a new economic order would never equal the richness of human beings themselves. The authority of the Church's Social Doctrine is betting on this autonomy and richness of humanity, which in Aparecida showed itself to be vivid and questioning.

---

[106] This is not to ignore the existence of very valuable efforts in the other direction such as, for example, micro-finance, local and sustainable economies, and fair trade (71, 97, 98).

AN ANALYSIS OF THE APARECIDA DOCUMENT IN TERMS OF STRUCTURAL SIN

Margaret R. Pfeil, Ph.D.

When the Second General Conference of Latin American Bishops met in Medellín in 1968, they embraced terms like "sinful situation" and "institutionalized violence" to name the *systemic* roots of poverty and oppression that marked the social reality enveloping their peoples.[107] Over the course of the next thirty years, the language of social sin appeared in official teaching texts with increasing frequency and clarity, particularly in the documents of John Paul II. He first invoked the language of social sin in an address given in 1979 at the Basilica of Our Lady of Zapopán in Guadalajara, Mexico, in preparation for the Third General Conference of the Latin American Bishops in Puebla. Affirming the significance of Mary for Mexico and for the entire continent, he observed that as the refuge of sinners, she "enables us to overcome the multiple 'structures of sin' in which our personal, family, and social life is wrapped."[108] The final Puebla document followed the pope's lead in calling attention to the structures of

---

[107] See, e.g.; "Justice" paragraphs 2 and 3; "Peace" paragraphs 1 and 16; and, "Poverty" paragraph 5 in *Second General Conference of Latin American Bishops. The Church in the Present-Day Transformation, Volume II: Conclusions*, Official English Edition, ed. Louis M Colonnese (Washington and Bogotá: USCC and CELAM, 1968). Unless otherwise noted, all references to Catholic Social Teaching texts will be parenthetically cited by paragraph number.

[108] John Paul II, "Responsible for One Another," (Address at the Basilica of Our Lady of Zapopán, Guadalajara, 30 January 1979). *L'Osservatore Romano*, 19 February 1979.

sin threatening their continent, bearing lethal consequences for the poor in particular.[109]

In his 1987 encyclical, *Sollicitudo rei socialis,* John Paul II deliberately invoked the language of social sin to address development, particularly the gross disparities dividing the Northern and Southern Hemispheres. " 'Sin' and 'structures of sin' are categories which are seldom applied to the situation of the contemporary world. However, one cannot easily gain a profound understanding of the reality that confronts us unless we give a name to the root of the evils which afflict us."[110] He appealed to the concept of structural sin precisely to emphasize the moral quality of the systemic disorders that he observed throughout the world and to suggest corresponding paths of transformation: "[I]t is a question of a *moral evil,* the fruit of *many sins* which lead to 'structures of sin.' To diagnose the evil in this way is to identify precisely, on the level of human conduct, *the path to be followed* in order *to overcome it.*" (37)[111]

John Paul II's ethical method of naming structural sin as part of a process of social transformation proves quite useful in interpreting the text issued by the Fifth General Conference of Latin American Bishops (CELAM V) following their meeting in Aparecida, Brazil, in May 2007. How could the concept of structural sin illuminate some of the most urgent and pervasive injustices identified there? First, the concept of structural sin brings epistemological considerations to the surface, for example, who is absent from ecclesial and societal discussions of the moral evil of structural sin and how might the text's description of reality benefit from their perspective?

---

[109] See CELAM, *Evangelization in Latin America's Present and Future. Final Document of the Third General Conference of the Latin American Episcopate* (Puebla de los Angeles, Mexico. 27 January–13 February 1979), in *Puebla and Beyond,* ed. John Eagleson and Philip Scharper, trans. John Drury. (Maryknoll: Orbis Books, 1979), paragraph 28. See also paragraphs 73, 281, 482, 487, 1032.

[110] John Paul II, *Sollicitudo rei socialis (On Social Concern,* 1987), in *Catholic Social Thought. The Documentary Heritage,* ed. David J. O'Brien and Thomas A. Shannon (Maryknoll: Orbis Books. 1992), 36.

[111] Emphasis in the original.

Secondly, the language of structural sin helps form consciences sensitive to various degrees of complicity in systemic moral evil. This is especially important because social manifestations of sin can entail an unconscious or non-voluntary dimension. Gregory Baum characterizes this phenomenon as a sort of "blindness produced in persons by the dominant culture, blindness that prevents them from recognizing the evil dimension of their social reality."[112] Explicit invocation of the language of structural sin helps to dispel such blindness by attempting to name the "root of the evils which afflict us," as John Paul II put it.

Thirdly, structural sin provides a necessary correlate for structural transformation. If the initial analysis of a situation of sin neglects structural dynamics and emphasizes the role of personal sin alone, it becomes much more likely that the recommended solutions will take the shape of parenesis, or moral exhortation, rather than genuine structural alternatives for organizing society in a manner that better serves the common good.

Finally, and in a related way, the deliberate correlation of structural sin with structural transformation offers the institutional church a way to hold itself accountable. As the 1971 Synod of Bishops courageously proclaimed, this sort of integrity represents the *sine qua non* of credible evangelization, the essence of the church's mission.[113]

Mindful of these attributes, I suggest in this essay that while the Aparecida text takes up an impressive array of pressing social justice concerns in sometimes prophetic tones, more frequent and careful use of the language of structural sin would greatly enhance its analysis of systemic moral disorder. Among many possible examples, I will focus on four: the historical consciousness of colonization, cultures, and race; globalization; ecology; and finally, the ecclesial challenge of evangelizing with integrity.

---

[112] Gregory Baum, "Structures of Sin," in *The Logic of Solidarity*, ed. Gregory Baum and Robert Ellsberg (Maryknoll: Orbis Books, 1989), 113. For a careful account of the dynamics of social sin, see Gregory Baum, "Critical Theology," in *Religion and Alienation: A Theological Reading of Sociology* (New York: Paulist Press, 1975), 200–204.

[113] See Synod of Bishops, "Justice in the World" ("Justitia in mundo"), in *Catholic Social Thought*, pp. 288–300.

HISTORICAL CONSCIOUSNESS OF COLONIZATION, CULTURES, AND RACE

Recalling the tumultuous process of conquest and colonization that shaped the Church's evangelizing efforts in the Americas, the final document acknowledges:

> The Gospel arrived to our lands in the midst of a dramatic and unequal encounter of peoples and cultures. . . . From the first evangelization up to recent times, the church has experienced light and shadows. It wrote pages of our history of great wisdom and holiness. It also suffered difficult times, in the form of harassment and persecution, as well as weaknesses, worldly compromises and inconsistencies, in other words, the sin of the church's sons and daughters, that blurred the novelty of the Gospel, the luminosity of the truth and the practice of justice and charity.[114]

Invoking light and shadows, this passage echoes Benedict XVI's remarks at a general audience on May 23, 2007, shortly after he returned from Brazil. On that occasion, the pope chose to dwell on the shadows cast by the conquest of the Americas, in part to compensate for having neglected to acknowledge in his Inaugural Address the often-violent methods of evangelization in the colonial context. As CELAM V began, he asserted, "In effect, the proclamation of Jesus and of His Gospel did not suppose, at any time, the alienation of pre-Columbian cultures, nor was it an imposition of a foreign culture."[115] Upon returning to Rome, though, he offered this correction: "Certainly, the memory of a glorious past cannot ignore the shadows that accompany the work of evangelization of the Latin American Continent: it is not possible, in fact, to forget the suffering and the injustice inflicted by colonizers on the indigenous populations, whose fundamental

---

[114] "Discípulos y Misioneros de Jesucristo," *Documento Conclusivo de Aparecida* (Bogotá: CELAM, 2007, 2nd Edition), paragraphs 4–5. Unless otherwise noted, all translations in this essay are my own.

[115] "Discurso Inaugural de su Santidad Benedicto XVI," (May 13, 2007), in *Discípulos y Misioneros de Jesucristo. Docuniento Conclusivo deAparecida* (Bogota: CELAM, 2007, 2nd Edition), p. 8, available from http://wwwcelam. infoldownloadlDocumento_Conclusivo_Apareci da.pdf.

human rights were often trampled upon."[116] The pope's further reflection paved the way for the reference in the final document to the "sin of the church's sons and daughters." His initial stance, however, reveals an operative epistemology that does not take into account the fact that the violent conquest and colonization of the Americas was structurally mediated through institutions and *systemic patterns of behavior* that manifested moral evil, or structural sin.

This same epistemology seems to have shaped paragraph 96 and its editorial journey. This passage addresses the historical reality of the social subordination of indigenous peoples and African Americans. In the first version approved by CELAM V, the corresponding section (paragraph 118) stated, "There still remain in the collective imagination a colonial mentality and gaze with regard to native peoples and African Americans." This was revised to read, "In some cases there remain a mentality and a certain gaze of diminished respect for the indigenous and African Americans."[117]

As Ronaldo Muñoz has insightfully noted, this change downplays "Western ethnocentrism." The shift in language from "collective imagination" to merely "some cases" represents a retreat from acknowledging the sinfulness of structures and practices that guided the process of colonization historically and still reverberate through the matrices of societal interrelationship and institutional life today. The phrase, "some cases," implies that the moral disorder at stake could well be confined to personal behavior and attitudes. The language of "a colonial mentality" shaping "the collective imagination," on the other hand, conveys the pivotal point that racial and ethnic discrimination against indigenous peoples and African Americans has been mediated from generation to generation through structured patterns of behavior and institutions systematically oriented toward the exclusion of whole categories of human beings from full participation in society.

To its credit, the first part of the Aparecida text does appeal to the language of structural sin in relation to systematically marginalized peoples

---

[116] May 23, 2007, General Audience, available from http://www.vatican.valholy_fathctBenedictxvi/audiences/2007/documents/hfben-xviaud20070523en.html.

[117] Ronaldo Muñoz, "Los cambios al documento de Aparecida," in *Aparecida. Renacer de una esperanza Fundación Amerindia*, 2007), 185. Note: I am using the final version, which is different from the one that Muñoz refers to as the "official" version. Changes were made, apparently, even after the "official" version.

of Latin America: "Our pastoral service to the full life of the indigenous peoples demands the annunciation of Jesus Christ and the Good News of the Reign of God, denunciation of situations of sin, structures of death, violence and internal and external injustices, [and] encouragement of intercultural, interreligious, and ecumenical dialogue." (95) The Aparecida document also quotes Santo Domingo 243 in two different sections, remembering the affirmation of the Fourth CELAM General Conference that the Church defends the authentic cultural values of all peoples, especially the oppressed and marginalized "against the overwhelming force of structures of sin manifested in modern society." (92 and 532)

The bishops' efforts to address racial and ethnic identity at Aparecida are commendable. But, overall it seems that the document uses the language of structural sin superficially, without embracing its epistemological implications. As paragraph 89 illustrates, the text still reflects the perspective of those exercising dominant power: "The indigenous and African Americans are, above all, different 'others' who demand respect and recognition." The terms "different" and "other" presume a standard of measurement that functions normatively but goes unnamed.

Precisely at this point, a deeper analysis of structural sin could help the bishops cultivate an awareness of the systemic dynamics of racism. As race theorists have established, race-based privilege engenders an epistemological blindness on the part of those who derive advantage from structures of racial dominance[118]. Often unconsciously, they become the dominant center around which all 'others" are assigned relatively less value.

This point takes on salience when considering the bishops' positive affirmation of black racial identity. Paragraph 97 reads, "Movements for the recovery of identities, of civil rights, and against racism, alternative communities of economic solidarity, make black men and women subjective builders of their own history, of a new history that is being drawn in the

---

[118] I have developed this point further in "The Transformative Power of the Periphery: Can a White U.S. Catholic Opt for the Poor?" in *Interrupting White Privilege: Catholic Theologians Break the Silence*, ed. Laurie Cassidy and Alex Mikulich (Maryknoll: Orbis Books, 2007) 127–146. On the issue of epistemological blindness as a function of the standpoint of the dominant center, see Sandra Harding, "Rethinking Standpoint Epistemology: What Is 'Strong Objectivity'?" in *Feminist Episteinologies*, ed. Linda Alcoff and Elizabeth Potter. New York: Routledge, 1993.

Latin American and Caribbean reality." Pastorally, this passage represents a significant contribution to Catholic social teaching on race, but it does not mention a crucial correlative point: the work of recovering racial and cultural identity as part of social solidarity is also a necessary task for those groups that have occupied social locations of racial dominance. Indeed, recent Catholic social teaching on racism as well as the growing body of scholarly literature on white privilege would suggest that particularly those benefiting from race-based privilege stand most in need of moral conversion if they are to contribute to social transformation.[119]

GLOBALIZATION

Before addressing the treatment of globalization in the Aparecida text, it is worth attending to some preliminary considerations offered by Benedict XVI regarding the concept of social structures, particularly in relation to the relative responsibilities assigned to church and state. The pope specifically addressed the significance of social structures in his Inaugural Address. "Just structures are, as I have said, an indispensable condition for a just society, but they neither are born nor do they function without a moral consensus in society about fundamental values and the necessity of living these values with the necessary renunciation, including acting against personal interest."[120] Using this measure, he notes the existence in Latin America of unjust structures, but he stops short of calling them sinful. Whereas John Paul II referred frequently to structures of sin, particularly when engaging Latin America and the Global South, Benedict XVI

---

[119] See, for example, Francis Cardinal George, "Dwell in My Love: A Pastoral Letter on Racism" (2001), available from http://www.archchicago.orglcardina Udwellinmyloveldwellinmylove.shtm; Bishop Dale Melczek, "Created in God's Image: A Pastoral Letter on the Sin of Racism and a Call to Conversion" (2003), available from http://www.dcgary.orglbishop/CreatedInGodslmage. pdf: James Baldwin, "White Racism or World Community?" in *The Price of the Ticket. Collected Nonfiction 1948–1985*. New York: St. Martin's/Marek, 1985), 440; and Janet Helms, *A Race Is a Nice Thing to Have*. Topeka, Kansas: Content Communications, 1992.

[120] *Discurso Inaugural*, p. 17.

mentions his predecessor only once in this address and does not appeal to the concept of structural sin.

The Aparecida text follows the pope's lead. It establishes the transformative reality of the Reign of God made present in Jesus as the horizon orienting the lives of his disciples in mission. (382)[121] This evangelizing work entails both merciful actions to meet urgent basic needs as well as collaboration with institutions in civil society to develop more just social structures at the national and international levels. (384) The love of divine mercy "urges the creation of structures that consolidate a social, economic, and political order in which there is no inequity and there are possibilities for everyone." (384)

Fleshing out this vision further, the document adopts an understanding of the respective responsibilities of church and state that cites and builds on that of Benedict XVI's first encyclical, *Deus caritas est*. The just ordering of society is a principal concern of the political sphere, and the church supports this task through its sacramental and catechetical work in service of integral liberation. In particular, it seeks to cultivate spiritual tools for the development of social values in society. "Only in this way will structures really become more just and able to be effective and sustain themselves over time. Without values, there is no future, and there will not be salvific structures because human fragility always underlies them." (385)

These preliminary considerations establish the theoretical context within which Benedict XVI offers a vision of globalization in his Inaugural Address as "a framework of relations at the planetary level." Adverting to the risk that large monopolies might turn financial gain into a "supreme value," he insisted that the dynamics of globalization be subject to ethical regulation, "putting everything at the service of the human person, created in the image and likeness of God."[122]

In similar fashion, the final document sets forth an ethical framework to evaluate globalization and offers an assessment (60–73): "Globalization, as it is actually configured, is not capable of interpreting and reacting according to objective values beyond those of the market and that constitute what is most important in human life: truth, justice, love, and especially,

---

[121] Cf. *Discurso Inaugural*. section 3.
[122] *Discurso Inaugural*, p. 10.

the dignity and rights of all, even of those who live on the margins of the market itself." (6l; cf. 64)

Using the method of "see, judge, and act" (19) the Aparecida text begins by contemplating the faces of those who suffer in Latin America and the Caribbean, bearing the scars of a globalization devoid of solidarity. The bishops also detect a new phenomenon of social exclusion, not merely marginalization on the periphery of society. "The excluded are not only 'exploited' but 'superfluous' and 'expendable'." (65) These disposable human beings include victims of inequitable free trade agreements (67), unmanageable external debt (68), systemic corruption (70, 77), drug trafficking (70, 78, 81), human trafficking (73), multivalent violence (78, 81), economic and natural exploitation of the Amazonian region (83–86), exploitation of indigenous lands and cultures (83, 86, 90), and unemployment as well as underemployment. (71)

With the eyes of "missionary disciples," the bishops discern that these signs of the times have taken on a global character (33–34), and the phenomenon of globalization affects Latin America above all in terms of culture. (43) In particular, the document laments the lack of cultural synthesis of the multivalent diversity among their peoples with a view toward a "common historical destiny." (43) Instead, the bishops notice a countervailing tendency to emphasize individualism at the expense of the common good, culminating in a new sort of "cultural colonization." (44–47) In other words, they are noticing institutionalized patterns of behavior that constitute a moral evil. This description encompasses what is meant by the term "structural sin," but the bishops do not appeal to the concept of structural sin in their moral analysis of globalization.

Among the "suffering faces that cause us pain," (407–430) the bishops contemplate the situation of the homeless, the vast numbers of migrants throughout the Americas, the sick, those addicted to drugs, and those imprisoned. Repeatedly, the text emphasizes the role of the state in redressing the systemic injustice incarnated in these human beings. (423, 425, 428) It assigns to the Church, by contrast, a role more personalist and pastoral than systemic.

The one exception to this trend occurs in the paragraphs dealing with migration, in which the bishops acknowledge a key difference between a statist and an ecclesial approach to this pan-American problem: the mission of the church transcends the borders established by nation-states. Thus, the vision of social transformation offered on this issue takes on the structural dimension that has been relegated to the state in other matters. In dealing with migration, the text urges,

> The Church, as a Mother, should understand itself as a Church without borders, a family Church, attentive to the growing phenomenon of human mobility in diverse sectors. It considers indispensable the development of a mentality and spirituality of pastoral service to brothers in mobility, establishing appropriate national and diocesan structures that facilitate the encounter between the foreigner and the particular local Church that offers hospitality. Episcopal Conferences and Dioceses should prophetically assume this specific pastoral work through a process that unites criteria and actions that facilitate sustained attention devoted to migrants, who also should become disciples and missionaries. (412)

Two paragraphs later, the bishops offer a radical proposal, suggesting that the Church "deepen its pastoral and theological efforts to promote a universal citizenship in which there is no distinction among persons." (414) To follow their guidance in this respect would entail nothing less than a transformation of the nation-state system, a truly revolutionary concept. They do not elaborate upon the details of their vision, but it is a remarkably prophetic response to one of the most urgent and life threatening signs of the times affecting their peoples and "relations at the planetary level."

Ultimately, though, the church-state framework established in the Aparecida text cannot accommodate the realization of such radical structural transformation. Their justifiable and repeated condemnations of financial and political corruption notwithstanding, the bishops place a good deal of responsibility upon the state to curb the practices of dehumanization they have insightfully traced through contemplating the faces of the suffering majority who pay a bloody price for the prosperity of the global elites. In response to a process of globalization that concentrates power and wealth in the hands of very few, (62, 69, 72) they warn against a growing economic and political juggernaut driven by transnational corporations and recommend political forms of protection, including a robust role for the state within the limits of subsidiarity. (63; cf. 76, 539)

They do emphasize the importance of social participation of those excluded from society, (407, 454–456, 528) and particularly the significance of solidarity among poor people. (416) But, without significant structural transformation, those who have been systematically excluded from the societal decision-making process will not find ready access. If the bishops had invoked the language of structural sin, perhaps they would have been able to make a stronger ethical case for the imperative of structural transformation.

ECOLOGY

The absence of the language of structural sin is particularly noticeable in Aparecida's treatment of the interrelationship between the dynamics of economic globalization and environmental degradation. Noting the tendency of financial institutions and transnational corporations to overpower state and local governments' efforts to sustain local economies and conceptions of the common good, the bishops observe that international extraction enterprises and agro-business often "subordinate natural preservation to economic development, resulting in harm to biodiversity, depletion of water supplies and other natural resources, pollution, and climate change" (66). Though Latin America is home to the world's largest number of aquifers, as well as forests and jungles that serve as the "lungs of humanity," these ecological goods are not valued on the terms of the market economy. Moreover, "the region finds itself affected by global warming and climate change precipitated principally by the unsustainable lifestyles of industrialized countries." (66; cf. 87)

Absent an appeal to the concept of structural sin, the bishops' assessment of the situation again takes on the quality of parenesis rather than offering substantive alternative models of structural transformation. ". . . As prophets of life, we want to insist that in matters involving natural resources, the interests of economic groups that irrationally destroy the sources of life, at the expense of entire nations and of humanity itself, ought not to predominate." (471) They recognize that a large part of the moral responsibility for the "irrational devastation" of the natural wealth of Latin America and the Caribbean lies with

> the actual economic model that privileges the disproportionate urge for wealth over the lives of human beings and peoples and rational respect for nature. The devastation of our forests and biodiversity through an egotistical and predatory attitude involves the moral responsibility of those who promote it because they are jeopardizing the lives of millions of people and especially the habitat of rural and indigenous peoples who have

been expelled toward the mountains or the large cities to live piled up in the beltways of misery. (473)[123]

The prophetic nature of the bishops' account of the urgency of the ecological crisis facing their people cannot be overemphasized. Their treatment here marks a significant contribution to the surprisingly small body of Catholic social teaching texts that address environmental concerns. However, their approach also reveals a tension between precisely identifying an entire economic system as the driving force behind the environmental degradation they describe, on one hand, and attributing moral responsibility merely to individuals who have adopted greedy, predatory attitudes, on the other hand. When ecological devastation takes on planetary proportions, it becomes clear that institutionalized patterns of decision-making and patently unsustainable lifestyles on the part of whole cultures, not a few individuals, lie "at the root of the evils that afflict us." Having pointed to an ethically disordered economic model as the principal structure leading to this situation, the bishops could readily have described it as a moral evil, or structural sin. Instead, they retreat to the level of individual attitudes, making it difficult for them to propose necessary structural changes with any moral force.

So, they proceed to suggest an approach to evangelization that emphasizes the value of contemplating nature and the importance of developing sustainable living practices (474), as well as an alternative model of integral development rooted in solidarity, justice, and the universal destination of created goods. It would respect the relationship between "natural and human ecology" (474) as well as "privilege the poor and serve the common good." (475)[124] But it is not apparent from the text how a given society might move from the personal moral task of changing ecologically destructive attitudes to this national and international challenge of effecting new structures of alternative development.

EVANGELIZING WITH INTEGRITY

Toward the end of the document, the bishops write, "An evangelization that puts Redemption at the center, born of a crucified love, is capable

---

[123] Cf. Aparecida 510.

[124] Invoking the concept of human ecology in paragraphs 472 and 474, they cite *Centesimus annus* 38.

of purifying the structures of violent society and of generating new ones. The radical nature of violence is only resolved with the radical nature of redemptive love." (543) Wisely, the bishops perceive that this dictum applies to the institutional life of the Church itself when they propose a "Solidarity Fund' to allow the Church as a whole to take responsibility for promoting pastoral efforts in places where a local ecclesial community may lack the necessary resources. (545)

Given this remarkably forward-thinking vision of redistributing ecclesial goods as one facet of communal accountability, the bishops' treatment of clericalism in the church seems decidedly incongruous. In the original version, they identified clericalism as a systemic issue adversely affecting the life of the Church, and they even lamented evidence of discrimination against women, particularly their exclusion from pastoral participation in the ecclesial community. The final text, however, invokes the subjunctive tense to speak of "some attempts to return to a certain type of ecclesiology and spirituality contrary to the renovation of Vatican II.[125] The tone has shifted from a declarative observation about the fact of clericalism in the Church to a much more ambiguous statement regarding not structures but rather theological perspectives or attitudes. Gone is the reference to women. The concept of structural sin as it applies to the institutional church is also absent.

Yet, in order to "purify structures," the bishops would first need to offer an honest account of the structural disorders at stake, both within the church and in society. John Paul II's explanation of the significance of "naming the evils which afflict us" finds resonance here. Only by doing so in its own institutional life will the Church be able to evangelize with any credibility, witnessing to the sort of moral conversion and social transformation that it upholds as a model for attaining the common good in society.

Toward the end of the document, the bishops articulate a disturbing truth: "In effect, it is a painful contradiction that the continent with the largest number of Catholics also has the greatest social inequity." (527) Much evangelization remains to he done, beginning with the Church's own sons and daughters. Parenesis will not be sufficient for this task, but as previous CELAM texts and John Paul II have taught, the concept of

---

[125] Muñoz, 188, citing original version of the Aparecida text, corresponding to 100b in the final version.

structural sin provides a useful ethical tool for forming consciences, both personal and social, that are capable of choosing courses of action, shaping institutions, and nurturing cultures oriented toward social solidarity rather than exploitation. These are the seeds of the sort of social transformation that the Aparecida text recommends.

AMERINDIA: RETURN FROM INTERNAL EXILE

Sergio Torres

The title of this chapter is provocative. Normally, the word "exile" applies to people who find themselves forced to leave their country, often against their will. They return from abroad, from a place where they have lived that is far away from their beloved country. For this reason, it seems strange for the members of a group to be exiled within their own family, within their own common milieu.

Nevertheless, the title is correct and it rings true. Amerindia is the name of a group of liberation theologians, some of whom, after participating actively in the Church, particularly in the 1968 Medellín Conference, were marginalized and exiled for varied and complex reasons. As the title indicates, at Aparecida they felt they had justly returned home.

In the following pages, I will attempt to explain this strange paradox. I wish to do so in an objective way, although the aforementioned marginalization caused great suffering and in my view, serious damage to the Church itself. The occurrence of these painful events can be seen as an existential experience that sometimes took on dramatic characteristics. Yet this was not a symbolic representation played out on some imaginary, open-air stage, but instead a true story, marked by the cross and the hope of a group of visionary, committed, and persistent men and women. They are and were, like all of us, weak and susceptible to errors and missteps, but at the same time capable of conversion and correction, as they have demonstrated in recent years.

At the outset, it is worth clarifying Amerindia's relationship to liberation theology. First, Amerindia is a Latin American network not limited to theologians alone. All the identities and ministries of the people of God are represented. Within the organization, theologians comprise only a small group of the members. It is a small but very representative group.

137

When someone refers to Amerindia they are speaking about liberation theologians. Over the last 30 years, the organization has come to be recognized as an expression of liberation theology. For this reason, when I speak of Amerindia here, it should be understood that I am referring to the story of a group of people who are identified with liberation theology in Latin America and the Caribbean.

Among us, the word "theology" is understood in the broad sense. According to Greek etymology, "theology" means a word (logos) or knowledge of God. Any Christian who believes in and knows God can reflect upon God and share this experience. It can be said, then, that we are all theologians. In Bethlehem, the shepherds were the first to receive the news of the incarnation. Today it is the poor who are most prepared to continue receiving this message and to transmit it to others. Latin American liberation theologians recognize that they are indebted to the experiences of thousands of poor people who live their faith through oppression, suffering, and hope. They know that those who can best speak about God are those who are marginalized and who struggle for their liberation, as well as the martyrs who have given their lives in love of Jesus Christ. With this perspective, they recognize a fundamental debt to the poor and they feel they are their interpreters.

Throughout this chapter, I will speak repeatedly of liberation theology. It is important to remember always that these theologians neither consider themselves to be the protagonists nor wish to appropriate the merits of the leading actors in the liberation story—this role belongs to the forgotten ones, as I have said. To tell this story I have chosen the model of a play, lived out passionately in real life over the last 40 years. The story can be described as having three time periods or three acts.

Act One: Medellín (1968), Foundations and Anticipation of Liberation Theology

It is worth remembering that in 1968, the name "liberation theology" did not yet exist.[126] During that period, however, its foundations were laid. The content was taking shape and the themes that would later characterize this type of theological reflection were beginning to be formulated. As proof of this assertion, we can point to two aspects of the Medellín Conference

---

[126] Gustavo Guitièrrez published his definitive book, *Liberation Theology Perspectives* in 1972.

that showed the influence of liberation theology: the actors involved and the themes proposed for discussion.

At Medellín, 249 people were gathered, including 145 bishops, 70 priests and religious brothers, six sisters, 19 laypeople, and nine non-Catholic observers. Among both the bishops and their advisors were leading personalities who already identified themselves with the experiences, methodologies, and theological content that would later be translated into liberation theology. Among the bishops were Samuel Ruiz, Leonidas Proaño, Cândido Padin, José Dammert, Gerardo Valencia Caro, José Mada Fires, Juan Sinforiano Bogarin, and others. Among the advisors were Gustavo Gutiérrez, founder and father of liberation theology, Lucio Gera, Luis Patiño, José Marins, Pedro Velásquez, Alvarez Icaza, Pablo Latapi, Cecilio de Lora, Marina Bandeira and Sister Irany Bastos. More broadly, it can also be said that Bishops Marcos McGrath and Eduardo Pironio, who gave magnificent speeches in the first week of the conference, shared an affinity with the liberation theology current, as they would later demonstrate.

These bishops and theologians defined and positively influenced this great event. For this reason, it is unjust, and can even be considered a desecration of ecclesial memory, to affirm, as some have boldly done, that Medellín was the work of theologians and not of bishops. It is customary for the two groups to work together, but always—as at the Second Vatican Council, the Rome synods and the Latin American Bishops' Conferences—it is the bishops who are aided by the Holy Spirit and, consequently, who vote on and approve the final documents.

Here we have the first application of the general principle proposed earlier in this chapter. At the 1968 conference, the bishops and theologians present in Medellín expressed the great processes of transformation occurring throughout the region in the 1960s and 1970s. They were the visible face of a of longing and hope that included millions of people who were crying out for liberation in their respective countries.

Analyzing the Medellín documents, we discover several theological and pastoral constants and themes that continued in the years ahead.

THE THEME OF LIBERATION

As noted, the name "liberation theology" did not yet exist in 1968. Nevertheless, in Medellín there were strong and frequent references to a reality experienced throughout the continent: the yearning and hope for liberation. Document Number 14 reads as follows: "A deafening cry pours from the throats of millions of men, asking their pastors for a liberation that reaches them from nowhere else." Facing this situation, the Church has a message. The God of creation is "the same God who, in the fullness of time, sends his Son in the flesh, so that he might come to liberate everyone from the slavery to which sin has subjected them: hunger, misery, all oppression and ignorance, in a word, that injustice and hatred which have their origin in human selfishness."[127]

In these documents, we find more than an analysis of reality. The bishops had already begun to explore the theological dimension of liberation. In Document Number 1, they reflect on this aspect: "In the history of salvation, divine work is an action of integral human development and liberation, which has love for its sole motive." They speak similarly of education: "Since all liberation is an anticipation of Christ's full redemption, the Church in Latin America feels particular solidarity with all efforts to liberate our people through education."

In Medellín, the bishops also invited the Church as a whole to experience a deep conversion, a change in social position, and a coming together with the poor. In the Document on "Youth" they request "that the face of an authentically poor, missionary, and paschal Church define itself ever more sharply in Latin America, separated from all temporal power and boldly committed to the liberation of each and every man."[128]

These texts reveal a change in the bishops' analysis of reality. They leave aside explanations that view underdevelopment and development as two phases of the same process, and use a more structural scheme of analysis that includes the explanation of unjust dependency and the resulting need for liberation. This departure was the first step toward the "See-Judge-Act" approach that was utilized in Medellín and that became a key element of theological reflection and pastoral planning in Latin America.

THE OPTION FOR THE POOR

This formulation also came after Medellín, but its content was present in the majority of the final conference documents. One of these reads as

---

[127] Document No. 1, Justice, Section 3.
[128] Document No. 5, Youth, Section 15a.

follows: "The Latin American bishops cannot remain indifferent in the face of the tremendous social injustices existent in Latin America, which keep the majority of our peoples in dismal poverty that in many cases becomes inhuman wretchedness."[129] Next, they propose a real commitment: 'We wish the Latin American Church to be the evangelizer of the poor and one with them."[130] Moreover, they suggest a preferential dedication to the poor: "The Lord's distinct commandment to 'evangelize the poor' ought to bring us to a distribution of resources and apostolic personnel that effectively gives preference to the poorest and most needy sectors."[131] The broad theme of the "option for the poor" is already implicit in these affirmations.

CHRISTIAN BASE COMMUNITIES

This expression, of major theological and pastoral importance, arises for the first time in Medellín. The document on Joint Pastoral Action indicates: "The life of communion to which Christians have been called must be found in base communities."[132] Soon after, there is a description of the nature of these communities that has not been improved upon: "The Christian base community is the first and fundamental ecclesial nucleus that must, on its own level, be responsible for the richness and expression of the faith as well as for the worship that is its expression. The base community is the first cell of ecclesial structure and the focus of evangelization, as well as the primary factor for promoting human welfare and development today."[133]

This does not mean that the themes noted here were the only ones developed during the conference. They are the merely most emblematic. The bishops undertook a complete evaluation of the spirituality and pastoral practice of the Church during this period and underwent a profound spiritual and ecclesial experience along with Pope Paul VI. The conference led to the proposal of guidelines and action plans that produced a new model for the Church.

---

[129] Document No. 5, Poverty of the Church, Section 1.
[130] Document No. 14, Poverty of the Church, Section 9.
[131] Document No. 14, Poverty of the Church, Section 9.
[132] Document #15. *Joint Pastoral Action*, Section 10.
[133] Document #15. *Joint Pastoral Action*, Section 10.

Medellín's influence on Latin America was enormous. It signaled the beginning of a new era in the Church's history throughout the continent. Facing the challenges of that decade, the Church responded with an evangelical, radical, and encouraging message. It helped to transform old ecclesiastical structures and ensured a vigorous ecclesial and evangelizing presence in every realm of Latin America that lasted approximately 20 years. This presence was vigorously influenced by liberation theology—a current assumed and represented directly by the bishops and theologians in Medellín, and indirectly by the many men and women who lived out their faith in the form of their hopes and struggles for full liberation.

Following our literary analogy, we can say that the first act of our story closed with a happy ending. Liberation theology constituted a precious contribution to traditional theology. It brought Christians closer to the person of Jesus and gave the poor of our time greater hope in their suffering and oppression. Liberation theologians were at home within the Church, and nothing foretold the grave difficulties that would follow in the future.

This theological current gave the Latin American Church a new identity. After centuries of "copying" and "translating" European theology, the lands that were far from the center had produced a theological school of thought that reflected their own context. The Latin American Church grew up and reached the age of majority.

Act Two: Puebla (1979), Official Exclusion of Liberation Theology

The impulse for renewal that began in Medellín continued strongly for 20 years. The majority of the region's bishops welcomed its conclusions and guidelines happily and hopefully, and applied them in their respective dioceses. Many remember this era as a springtime for the Church and Medellín as a true Pentecost.

Nevertheless, in the Church's blue sky, large black clouds began to appear and foreshadowed threatening storms. These were timid at the beginning but gathered strength over the years, as certain people acquired power and raised discordant voices. Rich and powerful Catholic laypeople who felt their interests were threatened, priests and bishops who were their allies, conservative theologians, and businessmen raised their voices to criticize, question, demand explanations, and often condemn some aspects of Medellín.

It should be noted that not everything that happened in Medellín was positive or perfect. The bishops certainly did not have time to address every theme. For example, some rightfully regret that they did not speak of the Virgin Mary.[134]

Within the Church itself, opposition forces developed that cast doubts upon and questioned some of the conference's principal directions after it took place. One of the people leading this "anti-Medellín" current was a Colombian bishop who was later elected Secretary General of CELAM in Sucre in 1972, and who exercised a great deal of influence (many would say negative influence) until very recently. His election marked the beginning of an internal division between the majority of the Church which accepted and applied Medellín and an unfortunately increasing minority which questioned such essential elements as the option for the poor and the base communities. This minority received support and legitimacy from some sectors of the Roman Curia, allowing it to increase its influence.

In hindsight, it is disconcerting to understand the reasons why a negative attitude could develop within the Church in opposition to the majority opinion of the bishops who approved Medellín. Various explanations have been proposed, but these are unsatisfactory. An in-depth study of the process is still needed. Some say that overall, Medellín proposed a radical evangelical utopia that would be too difficult to carry out in this world. Powerful sectors within our countries felt displaced and cast aside.

From the United States came accusations that liberation theology favored revolutionary movements against the North American empire. The development of this theological current coincided with the expansion of Marxist thought, which led to complications and confusion. There were also exaggerations and errors by some who spoke, supposedly, in the name of liberation theology. Moreover, in some European countries, another current was emerging that reinterpreted the Second Vatican Council and accused the Council's supporters of exaggerating and distorting its conclusions. The questioning of the Council reinforced criticism of Medellín.

---

[134] By way of illustration, we recall a text in the introduction to Section 8: "At this general conference of Latin American bishops, the mystery of the Pentecost has been renewed. Through Mary, Mother of the Church, whose patronage has helped this continent from the time of its first evangelization, we have asked for the light of the Holy Spirit . . ."

Whatever the explanation for this strange behavior to reinterpret Medellín, we must remember that the Council of Latin American Bishops itself began a campaign to promote a different reading of the conference, to promote new recommendations on the mission of the Church, and to exclude those involved in Medellín from CELAM institutions and departments.

The 1979 Puebla Conference

The announcement of plans to hold a conference in Puebla, Mexico from 27 January to 13 February 1979 came in this context. The social situation in the region had worsened and many countries were governed by harsh and cruel military dictatorships that violated fundamental human rights. When the plans for the Puebla conference were announced, a great uncertainty arose. Given the previous direction taken by the Council of Latin American Bishops, which would organize this major ecclesial event, many asked themselves whether its purpose would be to reaffirm Medellín or correct it.

The first steps were not very encouraging. Preliminary documents confirmed the suspicion that something different from Medellín would be sought. The central focus of the conference was to be changed. In Medellín, it was forcefully asserted that the greatest challenge to the Church's mission in Latin America was the "inhuman situation of poverty" of the majority of the region's inhabitants. The actions and commitments of Medellín derived from this conviction.

CELAM's proposal for the Puebla conference was different. The working document stated that the greatest challenge to the Church was not poverty but "the emerging new culture"—that is, the urban, learned, and secular culture of the big cities that had grown spectacularly in recent years. Implicitly, priority was given to the evangelization of the culture of the middle class and of the more comfortable classes, leaving behind a central concern for the poor. There was a return to the old custom of attending to the poor purely out of charity.

It must be recognized that "the emerging new culture" is a widespread and evident reality that affects everyone, not just the rich and the middle class. It also changes, manipulates, and alienates the culture of the poor. Accordingly, it was necessary to propose the "evangelization of culture" as an important objective for the mission of the Church. Yet what displeased many was the attempt to displace the priority given to evangelization of the poor, leaving aside the fundamental proposal of Medellín that had revived the hope of millions of people across the region.

Along with this change in the central objective came a questioning of the option for the poor, which was labeled as a Marxist inspiration that promoted class struggle. The base communities were said to be, in many cases, independent and autonomous vis-à-vis the church hierarchy, constituting the seeds of a popular Church that was different from the official Church. There were attacks on the Confederation of Latin American Religious (CLAR), which was accused of exercising a magisterium that was parallel to the Church's own. It was said that the cause of all these errors was the new reading of the Bible and the theological reflection proposed by liberation theology. This campaign against the supposed errors of liberation theology was not only expressed in documents. It also manifested itself in the exclusion and persecution of individuals. Although CELAM at first invited a few liberation theologians to participate in the preparatory meetings for Puebla, this attitude of tolerance did not last.

When the time came to designate experts or theological "specialists" who would accompany the bishops in Puebla, something surprising and unexpected occurred. Liberation theologians were systematically excluded; not even one was designated. The protests and complaints of many bishops were useless, especially those who had been in Medellín and who asked for the theologians who had advised them in the previous conference to be present at the next one.

With this decision, what I have called the second act of our story, the official exclusion of liberation theology, was complete. It was an arbitrary and unfair decision, based solely on the power exercised by the group that controlled the conference planning, which did not respect the beautiful tradition of Medellín that had produced so much positive fruit in the Church throughout the region.

In contrast to the happy ending to the first act of our story, what prevailed this time was the intolerant attitude of a minority who—in my opinion—failed to interpret the signs of the times and who were sadly mistaken in attributing objectives and pretensions to the liberation theologians that these theologians never intended. And so, the curtain slowly fell on the events of this second period in our story, with the momentary frustration of a great dream and a radiant hope.

Nevertheless, this exclusion was not the last word in this second act. Unforeseen by CELAM, two important new events transpired to change the path that the organizers desired. One of these was the indirect participation in Puebla of the excluded theologians. The other, more transcendent event was the positive result of the Puebla conference, which surpassed and left aside earlier proposals by the organizing committee and reaffirmed the major decisions of Medellín.

The first of these events was the positive and humble attitude of the excluded theologians. When their exclusion was made known publicly, many bishops did not accept this arbitrary measure. Each decided to invite a well-known and trustworthy theologian as a personal, external advisor with whom to consult during the planning phase of the conference. (It is commonly known that every bishop has the right to invite, and to ask for guidance from, a specific theologian with whom he shares a pastoral and theological affinity.) With these invitations, the excluded theologians organized themselves, obtained resources, and moved to the city of Puebla. They set up a workplace a short distance from the Palafox Seminary, where the conference was taking place.

During the day, in their free moments, a significant number of bishops left the conference to work with these advisors. Moreover, CLAR convened another group of religious theologians to respond to requests for advisement from the religious brothers and sisters who were official participants at the conference. Overall, these two groups constituted a large and important nucleus of *extra muros* theologians, sociologists, and pastoral ministers who provided valuable contributions to those who had requested their service.

The second positive result of Puebla surprised and pleased the great majority. The general theme of the conference was "evangelization in Latin America's present and future," taking into account Vatican II (1965), Medellín (1968) and Paul VI's apostolic exhortation *Evangelli Nuntiandi* (1975). The bishops wrote a final document that was very appropriate to the times. It publicly denounced the National Security Doctrine proposed by the dictatorships and made a strong call for a return to democracy in every country in the region. The Puebla conference utilized the new "See-Judge-Act" approach and reaffirmed the major proposals of Medellín, such as the option for the poor, the base communities, the utopia of liberation, and the new lay ministries. Moreover, it added new options appropriate to the situation in 1979, which was distinct from the time of Medellín, such as the option for the young and the programmatic proposal to live and act in communion and participation.

Before and during the conference, different people brought up the theme of liberation theology. Some had attempted to have it condemned during the conference. In contrast, others had asked for explicit support for this theological and pastoral current in preliminary drafts. A Chilean bishop, Monsignor Bernardino Piñero, proposed that a public debate be held during the conference that would include the *extra muros* theologians who represented the tendency and were publicly known to be contributing to the development of the debates. The request was denied, but the conference did not condemn liberation theology as some had proposed it do.

The minority attempting to reinterpret Medellín was not successful in Puebla, and it can be said that they were defeated, albeit momentarily. Their campaign continued in other spheres and institutions. The attitude of persecution found unexpected support from within the highest ranks in Rome. In 1984 and 1986, the Congregation for Doctrine of the Faith published two instructions that contained serious criticisms of "certain aspects of liberation theology." In practice, many considered these documents to be an explicit condemnation not only of "certain aspects" of liberation theology but of the field as a whole. Many bishops and Catholic conservatives throughout the world understood it this way, despite the fact that the theologians did not recognize themselves in these condemnatory documents and did not feel questioned directly since some of the accusations seemed more like a caricature than a real interpretation. Unfortunately, there was no time or space for dialogue, clarification, or justification, either before or after these instructions.

Yet there is a presence of the Spirit in the Medellín tradition and a great strength in liberation theology. That same year, 1986, John Paul II sent a letter to the Brazilian bishops with words of praise for liberation theology. In the letter, he clarifies the true meaning of this theological reflection. In one of the most significant paragraphs, he writes, "We are convinced—we and you—that liberation theology is not only timely, but useful and necessary." Coming from such a high authority, these words should have had a major impact, and might have mitigated the critical and persecutory attitude toward liberation theology. Unfortunately, this was not the case and history followed its course.

THE 1992 SANTO DOMINGO CONFERENCE

In the following years, another event again demonstrated the strength of the Medellín and Puebla tradition: the Latin American Bishops' Conference in Santo Domingo. This time, the Council of Latin American Bishops, with the decisive support of some sectors of the Roman Curia, attempted to control and definitively change the liberation orientation of the Latin American and Caribbean Church. To accomplish this, they took all the measures that they considered necessary. They corrected the working document; they left out the traditional "See-Judge-Act" methodology; they changed CELAM directives and brought theologians and specialists of a clearly conservative orientation from Rome and Chile to influence the development of the debates.

This new effort also failed to have the expected results. The bishops, including conservative sectors, reacted negatively to these attempts to impose excessive control and managed to save the conference, which was on the brink of failure several times. All the participants emotionally remember the figure of a Brazilian bishop, Dom Luciano Méndes de Almeyda, who contributed powerfully to building a consensus that enabled the writing of a final document containing many positive elements. Santo Domingo reaffirmed—although less strongly—some of the options from Medellín and Puebla, and added new ones such as the option for indigenous and Afro-American peoples. Liberation theologians, now calling themselves Amerindia, were present on the island of Hispaniola and made a discreet but useful contribution. Another group participated from Mexico by telephone and through an incipient Internet service.

Perhaps because of the difficult circumstances surrounding the Santo Domingo conference, its final document contains many positive elements but had very little dissemination and relevance in the region. The fourth conference took place almost without notice and left a bitter taste among many of the participants.

Act Three: Aparecida (2007), Return from Internal Exile

Thus, we reach the third act of our play, in which the theologians begin returning to the home that they never should have left. This return took place around the preparation and implementation of the Aparecida conference, convened by John Paul II and confirmed by Benedict XVI following his predecessor's death. Among the many events related to their return, both before and during the major ecclesial landmark in Aparecida, it is worth highlighting the following:

ELECTION OF A NEW PRESIDENT OF CELAM

In July 2003, delegates from each country elected a new Council of Latin American Bishops at a meeting held in Paraguay. The principal leadership positions went to Cardinal Francisco Javier Errázuriz, Archbishop of Santiago, Chile, who was elected President; and to Bishop Andrés Stanovnik of Reconquista, Argentina, who was elected Secretary General. Both were new to CELAM and their election signified a break with the tradition of criticizing Medellín, criticism that had been supported by the majority of previous administrations with the exception of the presidency of Monsignor Oscar Rodríguez Maradiaga (1995–1999).

One of the first tasks of the new administration was to ask the Pope to convene a general conference of bishops. The new presidential administration, however, did not draw upon the Medellín and Puebla traditions. The first preliminary document, called the Document of Participation, reflected this vacuum. For example, it did not include the "See-Judge-Act" methodology. For this reason, it was criticized broadly throughout the region. Later on, the Synthesis Document corrected this deficiency. Nevertheless, there was unanimous recognition that this presidential administration achieved a major task that ended up being overshadowed by external interference in the final document for which it was in no way responsible.

DIFFICULTIES WITH THE CONFERENCE

CELAM's request met with resistance from some sectors who had a negative experience in Santo Domingo and did not want to expose themselves again to questioning. Apparently, they did not want general conferences to continue to be held, and preferred that these be replaced by a Latin American synod. There is a vast difference between a conference and a synod. A conference is a solemn act of the magisterium of Latin American bishops, which concludes with a unique document containing clear, defined conclusions and pastoral guidelines. At a synod, always held in Rome, the bishops finish their reflections and turn in their work to the Holy Father, who later publishes a personal document under his authority.

The CELAM President's Office, after several attempts and efforts, convinced John Paul II and later Benedict XVI to convene a general conference rather than a synod, to be held in Brazil and not Rome. These decisions were very positive initiatives by the new leadership and gave CELAM the independence and legitimate autonomy it needed to organize the next conference.

DIALOGUE BETWEEN CELAM AND AMERINDIA

In the course of preparations for Aparecida, a happy coincidence took place that turned out to be providential for Amerindia. In July 2006, Amerindia gathered in Bogota for its regional meeting, held every two years with delegates from national groups. At the same time, CELAM was holding a broad meeting in Bogota to prepare for its upcoming conference.

On this occasion, the President of CELAM invited two Amerindia representatives to participate in a working group of the bishops who had also gathered in Bogota. Pablo Bonavia, Uruguayan theologian and the coordinator of Amerindia, attended along with Sergio Torres, a Chilean theologian, founder of Amerindia, and its former coordinator for several years. Sixteen bishops participated from CELAM, including five cardinals and several priests from the CELAM Secretariat.

The Amerindia delegates were given a chance to speak openly. They expressed their happiness and gratitude for the opportunity offered to them, and with simplicity and frankness, made their opinions known, reflecting Amerindia's positive attitude, and collaborative spirit toward the conference preparations. They expressed their reservations with regard to the Document of Participation, offered some suggestions for the methodology and content of the next draft, and expressed criticism of the continental mission, which had been proposed as one of the most important objectives for the upcoming conference.

Most important for Amerindia, however, was the chance to express concern about the unfair situation of marginalization in which many liberation theologians found and continue to find themselves, as well as the widespread prejudice and ignorance of the ecclesiastical sectors with regard to this theological current. They expressed their opinion that the Aparecida conference could provide an auspicious opportunity to begin a process of rapprochement and mutual learning among diverse sectors of the Church, as well as a space for evangelical reconciliation.

Finally and emotionally, they asked CELAM to convene a dialogue between bishops and liberation theologians that would be clarifying, constructive, and deep. This request impressed the participating bishops as something unexpected, but at the same time, encouraging. Their faces revealed an attitude of sympathy and positive response. Naturally, it was not the time to give an immediate answer, but the request went straight to God's heart and there was a murmur of happiness and acceptance in the air.

DIALOGUE BETWEEN LATIN AMERICAN LIBERATION THEOLOGY AND THE CONGREGATION FOR THE DOCTRINE OF THE FAITH

Among the precedents presented by Amerindia in its request for dialogue was a similar experience that took place in Germany from 23–25 September 1996. On this occasion, the President of CELAM, Monsignor Oscar Andrés Rodriguez Maradiaga, facilitated a dialogue between the Congregation for the Doctrine of the Faith and representatives of the Latin American theologians.

Participants from the Congregation included Cardinal Joseph Ratzinger, prefect; Monsignor Tarcisio Bertone, secretary; and Father Benoit Duroux, OP, consultant. The Latin American participants were Monsignor Luciano Mendes de Almeida (Brazil), Juan Noemí (Chile), Enrique Iglesias (Uruguay), Gustavo Gutiérrez (Perú), Ricardo Antoncich (Perú), Juan Carlos Scannone (Argentina) and Carlos María Galli (Argentina). Several CELAM board members also participated.

The goal of the meeting was to present four theological perspectives that have dominated Latin American thought and pastoral work since Vatican II: a theological interpretation of comunitarianism (Scannone), culture (Galli), the Church's Social Doctrine (Antoncich) and liberation (Gutiérrez). In addition to the lectures, there was time for prayer and for a free and fraternal dialogue. At the conclusion of the meeting, the participants wrote a document entitled *Projections for a Latin American Theological Reflection.* All the lectures and the final document were published by CELAM with the title, *The Future of Theological Reflection in Latin America.*

Undoubtedly, this meeting was valuable both for the quality of the lectures given and for the symbolic importance of this coming together by the Congregation for the Doctrine of the Faith and the Latin American theologians. Cardinal Ratzinger was the most significant figure present.

Certainly this precedent was a powerful motivator for the CELAM President's Office to accept Amerindia's petition and promote a similar dialogue in March 2007.

DIALOGUE BETWEEN CELAM AND LIBERATION THEOLOGIANS

As in the Gospel parable, the seed fell on good earth. Amerindia's proposal was accepted and a dialogue was planned between CELAM and several liberation theologians. It took place in Bogota on 29–30 March 2007. The following bishops participated from CELAM: Cardinal Oscar Andrés Rodríguez, Archbishop of Tegucigalpa, as moderator; Monsignor Andrés Stanovnik, Bishop of Reconquista and CELAM Secretary General; Monsignor Mario Cargnello, Archbishop of Salta and President of the Department of Mission and Spirituality at CELAM; Monsignor Santiago Silva, Auxiliary Bishop of Valparaiso and head of CEBIPAL (Centre Biblique Pastoral pour l'Amérique Latine); and Monsignor José Luis Lacunza, Bishop of David, Panama and President of the Family, Life, and Culture Department at CELAM. The theologians present were Pablo Bonavía from Uruguay; Gustavo Gutiérrez from Peru; and Maria Clara Luchetti Bingemer, Carlos Mesters and José Oscar Beozzo from Brazil.

This dialogue was of a private nature and not an official event; at the same time, it was neither secret nor clandestine. Still, there was no public information about the fact that the dialogue took place. It fell to the CELAM President's Office, which convened the event, to make an official announcement. Given the urgency of the upcoming conference in Aparecida, there was not time to do so. Amerindia did not feel authorized to publicize the meeting, although it was not restricted from doing so. In any case, it preferred to wait with prudence and discretion.

The lack of coverage was unfortunate, because the dialogue was truly of historical significance. Nothing like it had been seen in Latin America since Medellín—that is, for forty years. The prodigal sons and daughters had begun to return to their father's house. The theologians were affectionately welcomed back to their own home, the CELAM offices, by the bishops who had succeeded those who had marginalized them.

Aware of the importance of the gathering, the participants experienced those two days with a profound awareness that they were actors and protagonists in a transcendent event that held symbolism and positive expectations for the future.

On the first day, before starting, the participants gave a presentation. With gratitude and emotion, each person made his or her expectations and hopes known. The presentations permitted the creation of an atmosphere of mutual sympathy and a strong sense of communion. These were not two groups facing off against each other. Rather, they were brothers and sisters who stood ready to listen to what the Spirit wished to say to the Church about a conflict that had gone on for too many years.

Monsignor Andrés Stanovnik, the CELAM Secretary, spoke of the origin of the initiative for dialogue with Amerindia that had begun in July 2006. He eloquently stated that the true objective of the dialogue "was to return the initiative to God so that the entire Church could become a disciple that is ready to listen."

What is known about the program schedule for those two days is essentially the following. Monsignor José Luis Lacunza, "Liberation Theology: History of a Rupture, Contributions, and Absences." Maria Clara Luchetti: "Theology and its Contexts: Yesterday and Today." Monsignor Mario Cargnello: "Continuity From the General Conferences to the Fifth Conference." Gustavo Gutiérrez: "Following Jesus and the Option for the Poor."

From the titles of the lectures and the names of those presenting the topics, it is apparent that the participants had a unique opportunity to review and clarify historical aspects of the conflict with liberation theology. Several of the participants, especially younger members of the group, expressed happiness and gratitude for the opportunity to meet Gustavo Gutiérrez, whose work they had read and studied since their college days.

At the end of the meeting, there was another opportunity to evaluate the shared experience. Everyone agreed that the initiative provided a valuable chance for dialogue on a topic that formerly had almost felt "banned." They thanked God and the CELAM President's Office for convening the gathering.

The CELAM Secretary also informed the participants that, at a meeting held in Bogotá with all the presidents of the region's 22 Episcopal conferences, it was announced that the Aparecida conference would include groups of advisors, that Amerindia would be present, and that the conference participants would have complete liberty to consult and ask for advisors. Pablo Bonavía announced that Amerindia was indeed preparing to travel to Aparecida and would provide advisement and support services to anyone who requested these. He stated that his group "feels indebted to a spiritual, theological, and pastoral tradition in Latin America and the Caribbean that is considered a gift of the Spirit for the whole Church and for this reason, believed it was appropriate to maintain and enrich it forever."

Reflecting upon what transpired during this dialogue between CELAM and the liberation theologians, it seems timely to offer the following reflections. It must be clearly stated that this "authorization" was not an official act to recognize liberation theology. CELAM made no such decision, nor was it able to do so. On the contrary, the interpretation of many people is that the President's Office no longer wished to continue the persecutory attitude of the past and instead wanted to include the liberation theology current within the region's broad ecclesial and theological pluralism.

At first, many wanted to have more information and details about this new and encouraging dialogue, which was the first of its kind in many years. Thinking it over, however, perhaps this is not necessary. The value and importance of this event are mainly symbolic. It was enough for it to have occurred, for the historical circumstances that made it possible to have presented themselves. Time stood still; the wounds began to heal and those who had been distanced reached out their hands to begin a process of reconciliation.

God's ways are not our ways, says Isaiah. The dialogue in Bogotá happened in an instant, but its echoes will last in time. It fulfilled its goal. It was a sowing of utopia, fidelity, commitment, and hope that will bear fruit at the right moment. St. Paul says that some of us sow; some water; and some reap the harvest. In the words of the psalm, the Bogota participants sowed "between tears and laughter." The fruit will be harvested when God wishes.

The Wisdom of Gustavo Gutiérrez

Liberation theology is a reflection on the experience of faith of a people who seek their salvation and liberation in Jesus Christ. The first person to truly formulate this theology was the Peruvian priest Gustavo Gutiérrez in 1972. He is also the most representative figure in the story summarized here in three acts: participation, exclusion, and recovery.

Gustavo is one of the few survivors of those present in Medellín. Of the group of Amerindia theologians, he is the only one. He played a very important role as a theological advisor at the conference. Afterward, he was not invited as an "expert" to any of the four conferences that followed. Yet he was always present, nearby or at a distance, as an advisor to several bishops and making substantive contributions.

In 1983, the Peruvian Episcopal Conference received a communication from the Congregation for the Doctrine of the Faith, requesting that a critical examination of the theological positions of Gustavo Gutiérrez be carried out and indicating ten serious accusations related to its doctrinal orthodoxy. This served to deepen his exclusion. From that time until 2007—that is, for 24 years—he was questioned and put under suspicion. He showed a deep ecclesial sensibility; he responded to and refuted all the accusations in a timely fashion. Nevertheless, time passed without any definitive response from the Congregation. On the other hand, since this intervention did not carry any sanctions with it, Gutiérrez continued to write books, to give classes and lectures in various countries, and to receive recognition and distinction from theologians and universities.

The Congregation's response came only recently. In July and September of 2007, the very same Congregation for the Doctrine of the Faith—but with other people in charge—sent two communications to the Peruvian Episcopal Conference stating that its questions about Gutiérrez's orthodoxy had been cleared up and that the case was closed. It was a much-needed, albeit late, clarification.

The doctrinal clarification of the theology of Gustavo Gutiérrez is not only a personal matter. His theology was precisely what was questioned. The decision to exempt it from suspicion thus benefits all liberation theologians. For this reason, Gustavo's situation is emblematic. As a person, he embodies the story that I have sought to chronicle in this chapter.

Amerindia in Aparecida

This was the final step of Act Three. Isaiah tells us, "The people who walked in darkness have seen a great light." Something similar happened to the theologians. Finally, after a long walk, they arrived in Aparecida. They stayed in an exercise center a short distance from the sanctuary where the conference took place and prepared the spiritual and technical conditions for their work. They reestablished contact with the bishops and other participants they had contacted in the months before, and with humility and prayerfulness waited for the Spirit to come upon this great ecclesial gathering. In contrast to Puebla (1979) and Santo Domingo (1992), for the first time the group had visibility and the legitimacy to be present. Although they were not official members of the conference, their presence was recognized and they could work without difficulty.

And this is what took place. Everything that happened in Aparecida is past and known. In summary, it can be said that despite some early difficulties, Aparecida surpassed expectations and retook the path that was lost after Puebla, taking on once again some of the fundamental orientations of Medellín and welcoming other perspectives and orientations from the present day.

Aparecida was mainly an action of the Spirit. No one can truthfully and honestly evaluate the merit of the final result. All the participants contributed to creating the climate that prevailed during the conference. The CELAM President's Office must be remembered as having played an appropriate role. It created the conditions for openness, prayer and mutual welcome that helped to generate a profound experience of communion, which facilitated a Gospel response that was appropriate to the region's current challenges.

Amerindia fulfilled its role. A group of theologians and social scientists from the Medellín and Puebla tradition, inspired by a renewed and timely liberation theology, worked with a significant group of bishops and other participants, and contributed to the preparation of the final document.

LOOKING TO THE FUTURE

It is difficult to predict the future. Many have asserted that Aparecida is not the final word, but instead a new point of departure. Doors were opened for us to enter and travel through. It is a new beginning, but only a beginning; time will be needed to reestablish trust, closeness, and communication. May the barriers and prejudices fall away so we can face the new challenges together.

Some argue that the times require a different set of tasks. One of the most important is to recover the fundamental elements of Vatican II: to return to a sense of collegiality, reciprocity and communion; to feel that we are all members of the People of God, with a common dignity and vocation but with different charisms and ministries for serving the community; to live and express authority as a service and not an imposition; to encourage decentralization, subsidiarity and participation; to leave aside the centralism that tries to make everything uniform and instead encourage local experiences and inculturation which do not undermine but enrich the universal communion that Jesus wanted for his Church.

In Latin America and the Caribbean after Aparecida, the conditions must be created for a "true reception" of the event itself and its final document. This reception will not be easy. Each sector, with its own theology and spirituality, tends to seek what reinforces its own positions in the final document. There are many priests and young pastoral ministers who are unfamiliar with the recent history of the Church and do not identify themselves with Medellín and Puebla. There are middle-aged and older bishops and priests who absorbed the prejudices against liberation theology uncritically as they came of age, failing to seize its capacity for self-criticism and renewal.

Some members of new movements and communities—who constitute large groups in every country in the region—are living an important faith experience and cultivating a profound spirituality. However, many of them do not feel a part of the Latin American tradition and are not motivated by the new theology of our continent; nor do they take on the personal commitment demanded by the option for the poor.

Liberation theologians and all those who identify with this type of theological reflection must take on a great responsibility. They cannot ignore that because of what happened in the past, a large number of bishops, laypeople, religious, and priests were left with a very negative interpretation of liberation theology. They have the duty, therefore, to explain what happened, clear up prejudices, and respond to accusations.

Some individuals, especially the followers of these theologians, failed to interpret their teachings correctly and committed errors and exaggerations. Some were not sufficiently critical of socialist projects and were careless about distinguishing themselves from Marxist atheism. The distinction they made between Marxism as a philosophy and as a tool for analysis was not well understood. Others showed a very critical attitude toward the Church hierarchy and contributed, in some cases, to divisions in the Christian community. Later events revealed these mistakes.

In light of these experiences, liberation theologians have carried out an evaluation and self-criticism in recent years. The crisis of real socialism has served to highlight the evangelical originality of this theology and to distinguish it from social and political projects, without taking away its social and historical impact. It seems necessary to share this evaluation publicly as well as the connections that have been proposed.

Finally, it will be necessary to reestablish a new dialogue between Rome and all of the theological-pastoral currents of the region, without exclusion. We must all come together around the great tradition of the universal Church, the magisterium of the recent Popes, and the Latin American tradition of Medellín and Puebla. With the help of the Spirit, may we be able to discern the "signs of the times" of this era and to respond to those challenges. The general theme of Aparecida, "Disciples and Missionaries of Jesus Christ," can be the element that unifies and enlivens each and every one of us.

Aparecida made possible the first steps in a long process of evaluation, self-criticism, and reconciliation. The CELAM President's Office gave the initial impetus. Amerindia, on behalf of the liberation theologians, made its own contribution. Some voices have yet to be heard, for example, those from some sectors who have shown little respect for the legitimate pluralism of the children of God and have supported conservative individuals and proposals, causing serious damage to the Church's vitality in the region.

Conclusion

Finally, the curtain falls on the three-act play presented here, and on the story of the protagonists and circumstances they lived, suffered through, and hoped for. It can be said that liberation theologians have begun to return slowly to their paternal and maternal home. These are emotional times of gratitude and hope. Many tears have been wiped away, but we have not forgotten those who fell in the road. The privileged group that has "returned" cannot forget its predecessors, especially the martyrs among them. The Jesuit martyrs of the University of Central America in El Salvador have a place of honor. They were cruelly murdered for defending causes and people in the conflictive context of Central America that defined them as liberation theologians.

This is the cross and resurrection of their martyrdom. Accordingly, they are honored patrons of those who are attempting to follow and live liberation theology as a way of reflection.

The present day is a time of transition. The future may be as beautiful as a spring morning, but nothing is guaranteed. Amerindia puts all of its faith in the Spirit of Jesus of Nazareth. With the Seer of Patmos we repeat and pray, "Come, Lord Jesus!"

APARECIDA AND PENTECOSTALISM IN LATIN AMERICA

Edward L. Cleary, O.P.

When Pope Benedict was preparing for his journey to Brazil to inaugurate the Aparecida Conference, international media gave most of its attention to what they called the Evangelical or Pentecostal challenge to the Catholic Church in Latin America,[135] as well they might since both Catholics and mainline Protestants had lost more than twenty-five million adherents to this twentieth-century challenger.

Pentecostals are now a global force, numbering by Vatican estimates some 600 million worldwide, second to the Catholic Church's one billion. Rome has been tracking this phenomenon for a long time, especially through an extended formal Dialogue with Classical Pentecostals.[136] On the 100th anniversary of the Pentecostal movement (which the Vatican describes as Pentecostal/Charismatic) in 2006 the Vatican held a special meeting at Rome with Pentecostal leaders, such as Stanley Burgess, to increase mutual understanding within both traditions.

The following account delineates the essential background for understanding Latin American Pentecostalism and the CELAM V response to this challenge. For purposes of simplicity in their reporting, journalists and some scholars conflated the complex religious world of Latin America. This is especially unfortunate since the response of CELAM V to its religious

---

[135] In reporting on Latin America journalists often used Evangelicals and Pentecostals as interchangeable terms. While any Protestant may be called *evangélico* in Spanish, the term among scholars is typically reserved to a Billy Grahamlike person and group, among whom Baptists in Latin America would be typical.

[136] See for example Walter J. Hollenweger, "Roman Catholics and Pentecostals in Dialogue," *Ecumenical Review* (April 1999).

competitors would have to be determined by the religious nature (as Christian or not) of the group.

PENTECOSTALS, OBSERVERS, AND THE CONTINENTAL RELIGIOUS REVIVAL

Pentecostal Juan Sepúlveda of Chile was chosen by the bishops and approved by the Vatican to be an observer at CELAM V. Pastor Sepúlveda obtained a doctorate in theology at Birmingham University, has written (with the present author) an account of Chilean Pentecostalism,[137] and has taken part in the Vatican-sponsored dialogue between Catholics and Pentecostals. Sepúlveda expressed publicly his gratitude at being chosen to participate in the conference. As an expression of his gratitude in the conference's early phase, he offered a written reflection on Latin American Pentecostalism for conference participants.[138] What he wrote was a measured history, largely of the older and more tolerant version of Pentecostalism.

This was in contrast to the somewhat sensationalist tomes that stirred the world of Latin American religious scholarship and the international media in the 1990s. After David Martin published *Tongues of Fire: The Explosion of Pentecostalism in Latin America* and David Stoll wrote his *Is Latin America Turning Protestant?*[139] in 1990, major print media issued many articles, with increasingly negative assessments of the Catholic Church. One might presume from their one-sided approaches that the Catholic Church was greatly diminished.

While the Church did lose millions of indifferent members, the effects of its own reform are noteworthy, for a religious revival has been taking place in Latin America, in which the Catholic Church and Pentecostal

---

[137] Edward L. Cleary and Juan Sepúlveda, "Chilean Pentecostalism: Coming of Age," in Cleary and Hannah Stewart-Gambino, eds. *Power, Politics, and Pentecostals in Latin America* (Boulder, CO: Westview, 1997, pp. 97–121).

[138] Juan Sepúlveda, "Algunas notas sobre el pentecostalismo en Amèrica Latina," available at www.celam.info at the time of the meeting.

[139] David Martin, *Tongues of Fire: The Explosion of Protestantism in Latin America* (Oxford: Blackwell, 1990); and David Stoll, *Is Latin America Turning Protestant? The Politics of Evangelical Growth* (Berkeley, Calif.: University of California Press, 1990).

churches shared abundantly. This shared religious resurgence, the author contends[140], is the proper starting-point for delineating the religious situation in Latin America. The numbers of Latin Americans entering the priesthood and religious life, the quality of laity participating in the church, and the reformed orientation of the church shown in the Medellín and Puebla documents demonstrated a Catholic institutional vitality that was exemplary, worthy of global leadership.

Religious Challengers

This vitality, the author believes, derives partly from facing up to competition from non-Christian and Christian groups. In contrast to Pentecostals and many Protestant groups in Latin America, the Catholic Church has been in contact in Latin America with non-Christian indigenous and African-based religion for centuries. These religions and their Catholic hybrids have also been part of the religious resurgence in the region. While African religions found acceptance among middle-class Brazilians and spread to white, mulatto and mestizo practitioners in Uruguay and Argentina, Indian religion gained the most regional attention, in part because Indians greatly outnumbered those who identified themselves as Afro-Latin American or black. These challengers come from non-Christian religions, and Catholic relations with them follow different inter-religious dynamics, commonly called *missio ad gentes,* in contrast to relations with sister Christian churches.

Clearly, the Catholic Church is occupied on several fronts in relating to religious rivals, but its main challenge is from Christian Pentecostals. The prospects of engagement are inherently easier because of many shared beliefs, but organizationally and culturally more problematic because of the fragmented structures, the non-theological character of Pentecostalism, and the belligerency of newer variants, the Neo-Pentecostals.

Only a small percentage of even the older Pentecostals tolerate ecumenism. In the United States, an Assembly of God participant in the Vatican-Classical Pentecostal Dialogue found himself alienated from his denomination because of ecumenism. In Brazil, the Assemblies of God

---

[140] See Edward Cleary and Timothy Steigenga, eds., *Resurgent Voices in Latin America* (New Brunswick, NJ: Rutgers University Press, 2005), and John Burdick, *Legacies of Liberation* (Burlington, VT: Ashgate, 2004).

has even less tolerance for inter-religious dialogue. In a word, only a small number of Pentecostals cooperate in ecumenical encounter with other Protestants and perhaps with Catholics. The groups can often be identified by membership in the World Council of Churches.

PROTESTANT PRESENCE AND PENTECOSTAL BEGINNINGS

By mid-twentieth century, Protestant churches had gained a small but well-established presence in Latin America. With about five per cent of the Latin American population, the Protestant sector was probably divided evenly among historical Protestants and Pentecostals. The historical Protestants and interdenominational missionary churches became more accepted in Catholic Latin America through establishing first-rate American and British secondary schools that trained students in English and led to higher education overseas. Middle-class Latin American students, some Protestant but mostly Catholic, who attended these schools often went on to prominent positions in public life.

These churches drew into their membership talented young men and women, who increasingly furnished Latin American leadership for their churches. Several of them were thrust onto the world stage. Orlando Costas became head of the of the World Council of Churches; José Míguez Bonino developed into a major liberation theologian; and Samuel Escobar and others assumed leadership in missionary theology.

Latin Americans thus furnished the intellectual leadership necessary for Latin American Protestantism to assume its own identity apart from foreign parent churches. This leadership found a home in several seminaries spread through Latin America, such as the Evangelical Seminary in Puerto Rico. the Instituto Superior de Estudios Teológicos (ISEDET) in Buenos Aires and the Department of Ecumenical Investigations at the National University in San José, Costa Rica. These religious studies centers were cooperative efforts of various Protestant denominations and included Roman Catholics students, as well as a few Catholic faculty. From these academic quarters, theologians as José Míguez Bonino, Elsa Tamez and others published works that increasingly gained world attention.

Despite increased institutional consolidation and intellectual vigor among historical Protestants, by far the greatest religious growth of the latter half of the century occurred in Pentecostalism, a largely twentieth century variant of Protestantism. Historical Protestants lost large numbers of their members to Pentecostalism. Nonetheless Historical Protestant leaders remained important voices in Latin America at the end of the millennium.

One should understand that the Latin American versions of Pentecostalism started about 1909 within Latin America and were not carried there by missionaries. Pentecost-like events occurred in Chile, Brazil, and Central America. Missionaries from Sweden, Italy, and the United States were present at these events but Latin Americans were far greater in number at the inception of the Pentecostal movement. They quickly assumed most of the pastoral responsibilities for spreading the movement. Unlike mainstream Protestantism, Pentecostalism grew largely on the margins of society, so much so that some who studied the movement referred to it as a "haven for the masses." By the 1960s, a small number of social scientists took note of the movement. Foreign social scientists, Christian Lalive d' Epinay and Emilio Willems, published pioneering studies, now largely supplanted by more sophisticated analyses by Latin American academics.[141] Nonetheless, important aspects of Pentecostalism, as retention rates and the role of women, lacked comprehensive research.

One foreign anthropologist's views from mid-century remained prescient. Eugene A. Nida pointed out the indigenous character of Latin American Pentecostalism.[142] Unlike historical Protestantism, born in the European Reformation, or unlike religions, as Adventism, Jehovah's Witnesses, and Mormonism, created in the United States, Pentecostalism assumed from the beginning a Latin American character. It was *criollo* whereas the other religious groups were not. Latin Americans with little theological education took over as pastors. They learned on the job, proving themselves by probity of life and success in extending the movement through drawing in members.

Responsibility for church growth also fell to all church members who drew and kept new members through warm welcome, shared tasks, and promise of divine healing and miracles. While some groups, as the Assemblies of God and Church of God (Cleveland, Tennessee), had fairly strong

---

[141] Noteworthy in this regard were the efforts of Social Scientists of Religion of the Southern Cone Region who met regularly and issued periodical bulletins.

[142] Eugene A. Nida, "The Relationship of Social Structure to the Problems of Evangelism in Latin America," *Practical Anthropology* 5 (1958), pp. 101–123.

organizational unity, many Pentecostal congregations remained independent. The unifying spirit behind the amoeba-like growth was a belief that
an occurrence like that mentioned in Acts 2 on the day of Pentecost took
place in their midst and was an experience available to all believers.

While some groups had strong organizational structures and a
centrally imposed discipline, many churches fragmented, resulting in a
wide array of pastoral tendencies, a zeal to add new members, and an
independence of Biblical interpretations. Census-takers found hundreds of
different church names among Pentecostal groups.

Another strain of Christianity, Neo-Pentecostalism, appeared in the
1970s and 1980s and gained many followers. Neo-Pentecostalism looked
like a variant of Pentecostalism in its emphasis on the Holy Spirit, but it also
emphasized that true believers could expect wealth and good health from
faith in God and the practice of their religion. As with the Elím church in
Guatemala, this strain often had connections to groups in the United States.
However, Latin American Neo-Pentecostal churches were more like borrow-
ers and adapters than franchises of North America. Several of the more prominent churches of this type, for example, those in Guatemala and especially
the Church of the Universal Kingdom of Bishop Edir Machedo of Brazil,
were Latin American based, middle-class in membership or aspiration, and
more politically active than the earlier and more numerous classical Pentecostals. Edir Machedo and former Guatemalan general and president Efraín
Ríos Montt thrust themselves, along with some followers, into national politics in marked contrast to the more quiescent Pentecostals.

In general, the earlier generation commonly called classical Pentecostals
differs considerably from Neo-Pentecostals who are aggressively and sometimes openly anti-Catholic in their sermons, television programming, and
on-the-street recruiting. Bishop Sergio Von Helder of the Universal Church
of the Kingdom of God (IURD), the very fast growing Brazilian church of
the "Prosperity Gospel," kicked a statute of Mary, the Mother of Jesus, during
a publicly televised segment of his tirade against Catholic practices.

Cardinal Walter Kasper, who heads the Vatican Council for Christian
Unity, has kept a close watch on the Neo-Pentecostal groups such as IURD.
He characterized these newer groups as using instruments and having objec-
tives that are not purely spiritual nor are Christian in nature.[143] The church

---

[143] "Los grupos pentecostales son el nuevo desafío para la Iglesia," La Naciûn
[Buenos Aires] (Sept. 21, 2007).

has spread to Europe and the United States. Everywhere it travels, it brings controversy, especially for its emphasis on giving money to the church. Virginia Garrard Burnett of the University of Texas says: This formula for earthly salvation, which IURD founder Obispo (Bishop) Edir Macedo has referred to as "the miracle of the tithe" or "putting God to the test," is as much sympathetic magic "essence for essence, money for money" as it is an article of faith. According to the church, the giving of money in larger and larger amounts is both a test of faith and an act of obedience. As Macedo phrases it: "God orders us to test Him so that blessing can descend upon us."[144]

Proselytism, defined as defaming rival religions in order to gain adherents, is commonly practiced by these newer groups. Pastor Manuel Alvarez has written that Pentecostals feel the need to "unveil the truth to those who have remained deceived or neglected by an obsolete religious system."[145] He states that, "The Catholic Church represents, in their minds, an agent of alienation, oppression, and compromise with the demonic powers of the world."[146] Hence, the continuing use especially by younger Catholic bishops of depictions of these groups as "sects" and "ravenous wolves." This phrasing, commonly used by Catholic leaders in the 1990s,[147] was repeated by Pope John Paul II at CELAM IV (Santo Domingo, 1992). After criticisms of that characterization, the Vatican made clear to its dialogue partners that classical Pentecostal churches were not considered sects. However, many other groups were still considered hostile and abusive.

By 2000 Pentecostals and Neo-Pentecostals—often bunched together for census purposes, to the chagrin of older Pentecostals—had achieved a remarkable place in Latin American society. Protestants accounted for about 40 million Latin Americans, with Pentecostals comprising generally 75 to 90 per cent of Protestants, depending on the country. The magnitude

---

[144] Virgina Garrard Burnett, "Stop Suffering: The Universal Church of the Kingdom of God in the United States," in Timothy Steigenga and Edward L. Cleary, eds., *Conversion of a Continent* (New Brunswick, N.J.: Rutgers University Press, 2007, p. 221.

[145] Manuel Alvarez, "El Sur y el paradigma del movimiento pentecostal latinoamericano," www.pentecostalidad.com viewed Sept. 23, 2007.

[146] Manuel Alvarez, "El Sur y el paradigma del movimiento pentecostal latinoamericano," www.pentecostalidad.com viewed Sept. 23, 2007.

[147] In the Working Document for the earlier CELAM IV (Numbers 294 and 295) the authors described "a fanatic and growing proselytism" against a "defenseless people."

of growth in Latin America was illustrated by what took place in Brazil between 1990 and 2000 when the number of Protestants (mostly Pentecostal ones) almost doubled from 13 to 25 million. This alone was enough to alarm the Vatican, as well as Brazilian church officials, years before CELAM V was to take place.

Half of Latin American Protestants were in Brazil, accounting for about 15 per cent of the population. There classical Pentecostals outnumber Neo-Pentecostals about two to one.[148] In terms of national percentage within a country, the highest, 25 per cent was in Guatemala.[149] While Pentecostals and other Protestants could be found throughout Latin America, their presence in some countries remained small.

Despite the uneven spread of Pentecostalism, its influence on style of worship and prayer and on missionary zeal for other churches was so great that both scholars and journalists described Pentecostalization as a major trend of the 21st century for Latin America and other regions.[150] Catholic Charismatics, frequently called Catholic Pentecostals, are numerous and are the fastest growing movement in the Latin American Church. This movement was not started in Latin America as a conscious copy of a major challenger but was sparked by missionaries from Canada and the United States.[151] Nonetheless to superficial observers, at least, it seems like the whole region is replicating the events of Acts 2.

Two aspects of Pentecostalism became apparent only during the 1990s. First, studies in Chile and later in Central America and Mexico revealed that large numbers of Protestants, most of them presumably Pentecostals, were not very observant. Less than half attended church weekly, even though Pentecostal pastors and congregations emphasized much more frequent attendance. Second, the apostasy rate among Pente-

---

[148] Everett Wilson, "Brazil," in Stanley Burgess and Eduard M. Van Der Maas, eds., *The New International Dictionary of Pentecostal and Charismatic Movements* (Grand Rapids, MI: Zondervan, 2003), p. 38.

[149] The Guatemalan percentages were highly contested until the 2000 census and numerous Gallup polls in the 1990s.

[150] See among many sources the Pew Forum on Religion's Ten Country Survey of Pentecostals and Charismatics, online.

[151] Edward L. Cleary, "The Catholic Charismatic Renewal: Revitalization Movements and Conversion," in Timothy Steigenga and Edward Cleary, eds., *Conversion of a Continent: Religious Change in Latin America* (New Brunswick, NJ: Rutgers University Press, 2007), pp. 153–172.

costals appeared to be very high. Kurt Bowen found that 68 per cent of those baptized in Protestant churches in Mexico in the 1980s had left by 1990. Hence, while they entered Pentecostal churches, very large numbers left after a few years. Bowen and others attribute the high dropout rate to the perfectionist character of Pentecostalism. The 2000 Mexican census showed a small percentage increase in Protestants in the ten years from 1990–2000.

Thus at the millennium, a relatively new category of "no religion" grew from insignificance (one to two per cent) to 12 percent in Guatemala, 8 per cent in Chile and 7 per cent in Brazil. In the state of Río de Janeiro, more than 15 per cent, some 2.2 million Brazilians, list themselves as having no religion. However, belief in God continues at a very high rate. About 99 per cent of Brazilians and the vast majority of Latin Americans persisted in their faith in God.

RELIGION AND POLITICS

Persons from the sector of non-religiously affiliated joined Protestants and other non-Catholic groups in political conflicts with the Catholic Church. With growth in numbers, Protestant and Pentecostal groups increasingly entered the political arena in the late 1980s and 1990s. Largely quiescent politically prior to that time, Protestants in countries as Chile, Guatemala, and Brazil felt that they had an assured place in society and became more assertive in the public sphere. One of their targets was the privilege enjoyed by the Catholic Church and the effective legal restrictions placed on other churches in some countries. The privileges of the Catholic Church were less than those enjoyed by the state churches of Great Britain and Scandinavia but nonetheless rankled some Protestants.

Both Pentecostals and the religiously non-affiliated exerted pressures on lawmakers. Three issues were of special concern: the vestiges of Catholic privilege that existed in law, the explicit mention of Catholicism in national constitutions, and the teaching of Catholic doctrine and morals in public schools.[152] In a few countries Protestants argued that they had

---

[152] Brian H. Smith, "Pentecostalism and Catholicism in Contemporary Latin America," paper prepared with support of National Endowment for the Humanities, Sept. 1996, p. 53.

secondary legal status and were required to register as civic associations, not churches. In general, though, Pentecostals "have a great deal of freedom to practice their faith," as Pentecostal writer Miguel Alvarez has noted.[153]

While a formal dialogue between classical Pentecostals, including some from Latin American countries, and the Vatican took place for twenty-five years, little dialogue occurred in Latin America between Catholics and Pentecostals at the end of the millennium. On the other hand, creative dialogue between Catholics and historical Protestants did take place, especially in the 1970s, following a worldwide pattern.

With the ecumenical opening of the Catholic Church at Vatican II, extraordinary levels of cooperation between Catholic and Protestant groups took place in Latin America especially during the military period (1964–1990). Catholics, Presbyterians, and the Protestant World Council of Churches brought forth the heroically published *Brazil: Never Again.* Lutheran Bishop Medardo Gómez stood up as fearlessly as did Catholic Archbishop Oscar Romero in El Salvador. Catholics and Protestants cooperated in numerous human rights efforts from Paraguay through Guatemala.

Nonetheless, the vast majority of Latin American Pentecostals and especially Neo-Pentecostals shunned ecumenical dialogue and Catholic bishops did not have dialogue with Pentecostals as a high priority. Aside from grassroots ecumenism, especially through inter-marriage, the day-by-day realities of Catholic and non-Catholic relations were determined in politics. The conflicts were kept within tolerable limits of national democratic arenas that grew since the 1980s.

APARECIDA

A long preparation that included grassroots discussions throughout Latin America preceded Aparecida. A task force of theologians and pastoral care experts produced a "Synthesis" of responses to the initial working document. The Synthesis document had in the words of Bishop Ricardo Ramírez of the United States, "very limited acknowledgment of ecumenism, which is totally subsumed under the 'challenge of the sects,' the term used in Latin America for proselytizing Christian groups."[154]

---

[153] Miguel Alvarez, "El Sur y el paradigma del movimiento pentecostal latinoamericano," www.pentecostalidad.com.

[154] Ricardo Ramírez, "The Pope in Brazil," *America* (May 14, 2007), pp. 9–11.

The differences between Catholics in the United States and Latin America on ecumenism are acute. Dr. Jeffrey Gros, a Christian Brother who had the unique experience of working both at the (Protestant) National Council of Churches and the U.S. Conference of Catholic Bishops, explained that cultural differences aided or hindered the teaching of Vatican II. The reception of *Dignitatis Humanae,* Vatican II's *Declaration on Religious Liberty,* he believes: "differs according to the culture in which it was received."[155]

In his view of Latin America: "It may be impossible for the ecumenical project of the Council to be realized in cultures where the Roman Catholic Church predominates, at least until there is an understanding of religious liberty, religious pluralism, and the difference between religious liberty and tolerance . . . This is a particularly sensitive problem in the Western Hemisphere."[156]

For an important sector of mainline Protestant or Pentecostal churches on Latin America and around the world, the selection of observers to the CELAM V Conference was watched with close attention, believing that the selection would signal a continuation or an end to ecumenical relations between church bodies. One of the key invitations went to Néstor Míguez, a New Testament professor at ISEDET seminary in Buenos Aires. His father, José, was extraordinarily important for the change in Catholic-Protestant relations in Latin America. José Míguez Bonino attended Vatican Council II and wrote a book interpreting the council for non-Catholics that allowed them to view substantial changes in the church they had considered to be a monolithic medieval institution.[157] Nestor Míguez had expertise in his own right, being an acknowledged scholar in Biblical understandings of the economic order.

Other Protestant observers in addition to Sepúlveda and Miguez were Orfelia Ortega, Co-President of the World Council of Churches; Walter Altman, president of the Lutheran Church in Brazil; and Harold Segura, a

---

[155] Jeffrey Gros, "Dignitatis Humanae and Ecumenism: A Foundation and a Promise," Symposium on Religious Liberty: Paul VI and Dignitatis Humanae (Brescia: Istituto Paulo VI, 1995), p. 43.

[156] Jeffrey Gros, "Dignitatis Humanae and Ecumenism: A Foundation and a Promise," Symposium on Religious Liberty: Paul VI and Dignitatis Humanae (Brescia: Istituto Paulo VI, 1995), p. 145.

[157] José Míguez Bonino, *Concilio Abierto: Una interpretaciûn protestante del Concilo Vaticano II* (Buenos Aires: Editorial La Aurora, 1967).

Baptist pastor. As far as could be determined, no Catholic Charismatics— bridges to Pentecostals—were invited to Aparecida.

Pastor Míguez was called upon to address an early session of the Aparecida CELAM Conference. In the name of the other Protestant observers he thanked publicly the conference organizers and, presumably, hoped for the best. Unfortunately the best did not occur. Some bishops, apparently stung by accusations from Neo-Pentecostals and other religious rivals that they were the whores of Babylon,[158] repeated what Pope John Paul II had said: sect leaders [code words for aggressive and theologically weak rivals] are ravenous wolves, stealing our sheep. A Catholic laywoman approached Segura and Míguez during a break in the meeting to apologize for the "anti-sectarian avalanche," as Harold Segura described it. Cardinal Francisco Javier Errázuriz of Santiago, when the next session started, clarified that when the word "sects" had been used, it did not refer to historical Protestants or to those Evangelicals present or to Pentecostals.

Non-Catholics who were not present at the conference could follow on the Internet comments by a Colombian Baptist observer, Harold Segura. His credentials were uncommonly broad and include his working for a doctorate in theology from a prominent Catholic university, Pontficia Javieriana Universidad in Bogotá. His almost daily comments were posted through the Brazilian Catholic Frei Tito website and elsewhere. In his blogs, he expressed his relief at the Cardinal's explanation and continued to hope until the end of the conference for an ecumenically improved situation.

In general, the sessions had a more ecumenical tone than was sometimes the case in previous conferences. "The participants," wrote John Allen at the end of the meeting, recognized "that in the light of secularization and a sometimes hostile political climate, the various Christian need to stand together." Rolando Muñoz, a noted Catholic ecumenist and liberation theologian, and Pastor Segura agreed that Protestant observers through their dialogue with Aparecida participants promoted hope of ecumenism for the continent.[159]

Applause was technically a breach of conference protocol as was extension of time for floor speeches but both were granted to Pastor Miguez

---

[158] Other expressions used by the bishops included: "anti-Catholic Protestantism," "the advance of evangelical proselytism," and "the attractive offer of the sects."

[159] Harold Segura, "Desde Aparecida, un Pastor en el CELAM," Commentary posted on web September 11, 2007 at www.desdeaparecida.blogspot.com.

as he urged that "a diverse Christian presence in Latin America not be marked by confrontation and competition" but "by the common vocation to be disciples and missionaries of Our Lord Jesus Christ."[160]

The bishops affirmed that ecumenism is the "*camino irrenuenciable*." They wrote that the Church was committed to following that pathway established clearly at Vatican Council II. Clerical and lay members were encouraged to prepare themselves (no small task) to join ecumenical organizations. In this endeavor, they should follow the norms of the Magisterium for dialogue. Catholics looking at other groups were advised not to stereotype Protestants or Pentecostals by bunching the myriad groups into one category of analysis. The bishops also acknowledged that some former Catholics may have aligned themselves with other Christian churches because some did not find adequate pastoral care due to lack of priests and similar causes. Unspoken in the document but frequently heard among theologians and bishops through decades of interviews was the attraction for former Catholics to groups that promised relief from the pathogens of illness and poverty, as Andrew Chesnut has described their appeal.[161]

The bishops emphasized that not merely cooperation with other Christian churches was sought, but ultimately unity of the churches into one Christian body. With communion as a main theme of the document, the bishops especially stressed that this communion resulted from the common bond of Baptism among Christians, leading to dialogue and reconciliation of differences.

At the end of conference meetings, Segura noted regretfully that little had changed in terms of a wider ecumenism. He believed that ecumenical encounter goes well at the grassroots level. However, in the national bishops' conferences of Latin America and the Caribbean, ecumenical relations are suffering from a "new cold." He summarized the results of Aparecida in terms of ecumenical relations: "the traffic light of official ecumenism is an intermittent yellow." At least there were continued good relations with classical Pentecostals like Sepúlveda, Evangelicals like Segura, and historical Protestants like Miguez. This, indeed, was a major re-affirmation of cooperation with major Christian bodies, but no breakthroughs occurred

---

[160] John Allen, Jr., "Sorting Out the Results of the Latin American Bishops' Meeting," *National Catholic Reporter* (June 1, 2007).

[161] R. Andrew Chesnut, *Born Again in Brazil: The Pentecostal Boom and the Pathogens of Poverty* (New Brunswick, NJ: Rutgers University Press, 1997).

with the rapidly spreading Neo-Pentecostals and very numerous non-ecumenical Pentecostals.

The conference generated a heightened urgency about Pentecostal-Catholic relations. The Argentine Bishops Conference and the Pontifical Council for Christian Unity held a workshop for bishops of the Southern Cone with the ecumenically minded Cardinal Walter Kasper acting as keynote speaker. Church leaders from other denominations participated in the September 2007 meeting in Buenos Aires, a month after the final Aparecida document appeared.

THE FUTURE AS SEEN FROM APARECIDA[162]

Daniel H. Levine, Ph.D.

When Latin America's Catholic bishops met in Aparecida, Brazil (May 13–31, 2007) their goal was to preserve, enrich, and extend the Catholic faith of the region's peoples, a long tradition acknowledged to be "a fundamental source of the identity, originality, and unity of Latin America and the Caribbean,"(8) "among its greatest riches."(7) The gift of this rich tradition of faith sets the context for developing the bishops' overall theme of the meetings, which was the identity of the church and faithful as missionary disciples, a theme echoed by the Pope in his opening speech and underscored throughout the documents.

To be a missionary disciple in Latin America today means striving to bring the good news (the original meaning of Gospel or *Evangelios*) and to do so joyfully and with hope, but also in a way that resonates with the realities of daily life in the region. How the Church, through its leaders gathered at Aparecida, understands itself and the situation of faith in the social, economic, cultural, and political world of Latin America, is the central factor that structures the way in which the message is presented and carried forward. Is it joyful, optimistic, and open to change—a genuine *Kairos* or propitious moment of grace in which commitments and solidarities can be

---

[162] I acknowledge with gratitude helpful comments and reactions to an early draft of this chapter by Edward Cleary and Frances Hagopian.

173

reaffirmed, or is this instead a defensive moment, concerned to preserve, protect, and reinforce what exists?[163]

There are many ways to read the documents of Aparecida and the process and debates surrounding them. They may be seen in terms of continuities with a line of significant conferences of the region's Catholic bishops (Medellín in 1968, Puebla in 1979, Santo Domingo 1992) that set an agenda for Latin American Catholicism, and provided a new moral vocabulary with which activists and believers could understand the world. (Cf. Gutiérrez, 2007, Tovar, 2007) One need only remember the impact of such phrases as "institutionalized violence" (Medellín) or "preferential option for the poor" (Puebla) to grasp the salience and potential impact of such meetings. Aparecida can also be understood as an effort by Pope Benedict XVI to continue the policies of his predecessor John Paul II, while placing his own mark on them, and becoming acquainted with and open to what is, after all, the major Catholic region of the world.

This chapter tackles the matter from a different angle. I look at Aparecida in terms of the vision of the future embedded in the documents, debates, and "between the lines" and set that against an understanding of what the present is like, how it got that way, and of likely and possible futures both for the Church and for society as a whole. If we ask how the future looks as seen from Aparecida, a short answer is *dangerous and filled with threat and peril*. There are dangers from cultural inroads to Catholic ideas of a proper moral sphere (concern about the decay of traditional gender roles is prominent) and to the role of the Church in ordering that moral sphere. There is the related peril of dissolution of a worldview once united around the Catholic faith and guided by its official leaders. There is the threat from competition by other churches (above all, "sects," meaning Neo-Pentecostal churches) along with the danger posed by indifference, apathy, and a tendency of many to see themselves as *católico a mi manera*, (Catholic in my own way), disengaged from Church supervision and discipline (Cf. Parker, 2005).[164] All

---

[163] The concept of *Kairos* denotes to a right or opportune moment, a historical crisis, which is also an opportunity for change, an appointed time in which a document can resonate. In South Africa, the 1985 *Kairos* document identified just such a moment, and called the churches to be present in the struggles that brought an end to apartheid.

[164] Parker Gumucio, Cristián. "¿América Latina ya no es católico? Pluralismo cultural religioso creciente." *America Latina Hoy Revista de Ciencias Sociales*, Vol. 41, diciembre 2005. Pp. 35–56.

these perils are exacerbated by a context of accelerated social dissolution brought about by poverty, violence, and drugs.

A simple listing of threats, perils, dangers, and decay does not, of course, exhaust the agenda of Aparecida: these are balanced by nuanced recognition of progress in politics (with democracy), education, ecological concerns, rights, and recognition and dignification of excluded groups, especially indigenous communities and those of African descent. Nevertheless, the predominant note is fear, above all fear of loss. The collection of fears scattered through the documents rests on a particular understanding of change in contemporary Latin America that warrants a closer look. What is the motive force of this change, who are its agents, and what does it mean for the Church as an institution and collection of faithful?

The answer given at Aparecida is that change is impelled by global forces (economic and cultural) that together undermine cultural unity, reorder social roles, and undercut important values and authority. Facing a situation that is perceived as challenging in these ways, an institution like the Catholic Church has several options: it can simply adapt and go with the flow; it can engage as a participant in the process with its own message and with enthusiasm; or it can resist by consolidating its forces and rebuilding around a common purpose and leadership. The position taken at Aparecida lies somewhere between the second and third option, with the weight on the latter. As we shall see, final revisions put in place by the Vatican heightened salience of fear and the insistence on control. Whether or not this vision of the world will work, and what specific policies it may produce, will depend on how accurate the underlying analysis of reality turns out to be. The next section outlines the main parameters of the current situation and identifies the forces and trends that have made it the way it is.

THE PRESENT STATE OF RELIGION, SOCIETY, AND CULTURE AND HOW IT GOT THIS WAY[165]

In the run up to Aparecida, the world that Catholic leaders saw around them was like night and day compared to the one in which most had been born and raised. The unquestioned monopoly of the Catholic Church as *the*

---

[165] This section draws freely on my *The Future of Christianity in Latin America*, University of Notre Dame, Kellogg Institute Working Paper 340, August 2007.

church had eroded, replaced by a plurality of churches and a new presence of religious competition (for members, space, public sanction, and goods) throughout the region. Statistical reports (including national census data and a series of surveys and studies) confirmed what they could see every day. The numbers of men and women identifying themselves as "Catholic" was in steady decline, while those declaring affiliation to Protestant (especially Pentecostal and Neo-Pentecostal churches) had grown, along with a smaller, but still notable segment that affirmed no connection to any church or religion. Surveys also regularly report a substantial sector that declares itself *católico en mi manera*, (or as Mallimaci and Villa put it, *cuenta propista*, on ones own) picking and choosing the kinds of issues on which they adhere, or even listen to "official teachings."

The erosion of monopoly is not limited to statistics of membership or church attendance. The Catholic Church no longer monopolizes the moral sphere in the name of religion: its leaders and official voices must share the airwaves, TV screens, public platforms, and arenas of power with representatives of these other churches. Even within the admittedly broad net that the Catholic Church casts, there is growing diversity of opinion visible in publications, schools, and group positions, leading Catalina Romero (2008) to speak of the development of public space and civil society *within the Church*. She writes, "Through these different forms of association and the construction of new spaces for encounter and interaction, the church has renovated itself and infused religious meaning in everyday life problems. In the last decade, this space has begun to close once again due to the intervention of a number of bishops who are trying to take back control of public space in the church itself and in the way the church expresses itself and is represented in civil society, political society, and the state." (2008, 22)

The trend that Romero identifies for Peru is visible throughout the region: groups proliferate while many prelates, fearing division and loss of control, have tried to rein them in by cutting funds to dissident groups and striving for greater control over schools, universities, and publications. (Drogus and Stewart-Gambino)

The decay of Catholic monopoly and the growing pluralism of religious expression and organization are accompanied by processes that have moved religious groups, issues, and leaders off center stage of public debate, contestation, coalition formation, and political discussion. This is an inevitable consequence of important currents of pluralism that have come with the democratization of civil society and politics of the last two decades.

There are many more options and vehicles for expression now than in the past; Church leaders can no longer monopolize the public expression of religious comment, nor can they count on being king makers or critical veto players. The effort is bound to run into multiple figures working the territory. There is simply a lot of competition out there.

The convergence of these multiple pluralisms means that simple references to church and state, much less exclusive attention to the institutional Catholic Church (or to the statements of its official leaders and spokespersons) no longer suffices as a guide to understanding religion or its place in society and politics in Latin America today.

Detailed examination of the organizations and vehicles of mobilization that the Church presumably "controls" and could use to further its agenda (Hagopian), reveals that the bishops' capacity to manage groups and members is much weaker than they would like or that they often imagine. Many of the "resources" that prelates commonly list or rely upon turn out on closer inspection to be hollow shells, groups that exist more on paper than in reality. Even where groups as such do survive, members prove much less malleable than the evidence of formal ties and documents might indicate. In any case, the effort to ensure loyalty by insisting on separate groups with built-in clerical supervision runs into the problem of control in a world where citizens have too many skills, connections, and possibilities to engage to be treated as sheep by a shepherd, or to be controlled or moved en bloc in traditional ways. In this world, loyalty is more likely to be secured through provision of spaces and engagement, not by demarcation of boundaries.[166] For their part, explicitly religious ties to political parties, be they Catholic for Christian Democrats or specifically Protestant parties or candidacies, have weakened substantially. (Freston) There have also been notable cuts in Church sponsorship of social movements (Drogus and Stewart-Gambino, Ottmann) along with a return to more traditional lobbying on a core group of conventional issues surrounding subsidies, education, sexuality and reproductive issues, and public morality and thus away from the social justice issues that dominated public debates in the 1980s and 1990s.

---

[166] Romero (2008) argues that the public space emerging within the church is a space of liberty where believers encounter others (both believers and non believers) in voluntary associations, social movements, personal development courses, as well as arts, music, expressive mobilizations, the internet and mass media.

Taken together, these changes have altered the public face of religion and transformed the ways in which religion is present in the public sphere. The past was marked in many countries by multiple images and symbols of religious-civic fusion such as *Te Deums* with the presence of political and ecclesiastical "authorities" at the highest level, or the repeated joint presence of politicians, clergy, and military officers at the inauguration of public works, the opening of stores or factories, and a wide range of events. This omnipresent triad offered a public affirmation of the identification of "the church" (only one was recognized) with political and economic power and social hierarchy.

The public face of religion now is quite another matter: street preachers abound, men (mostly men) working public spaces with a Bible, a loudspeaker, and something to stand on. New churches proliferate, and new voices jostle for space and attention. Where there was once monopoly there is now pluralism and where a limited number of spaces were once officially reserved for religious practice (with a limited number of authorized practitioners) there is now a rich profusion of churches, chapels, and mass media programming, not to mention campaigns and crusades that carry the message to hitherto "profane" spaces like streets and squares, and to beaches, sports stadiums, jails, bars, and nightclubs.

This new landscape challenges the traditional role of the Catholic Church as *the church*—officially acknowledged wielder of moral and social authority within the boundaries of a defined national territory. In Casanova's terms, the church is no longer *church*—religious institution with an official or semiofficial monopoly in a given territory—but rather one actor among many in an open civil society. Casanova argues that only when religions abandon the status of "church" and the privileges that come with it can they be fully compatible with a modern society. "The conception of modern public religion that is consistent with liberal freedoms and modern structural and cultural differentiations," he writes, "is one that builds on notions of civil society." (Casanova, 1994, 217)

But making this change work is no easy task, and learning to live in a world that no longer can be defined by *one church* in mutual alliance with *one state* can be unsettling. Institutions long accustomed to public support may find competition and cultural openness to be less opportunities for growth than signs of decay and disintegration. Although the rhetoric has cooled in recent years, and one hears less often about the 'invasion of the sects" who are described as "rapacious wolves" preying on the (Catholic) flock, caution, fear, and suspicion remain central themes when the Catholic hierarchy faces Pentecostal and Neo-Pentecostal Churches.[167]

If the last half century has witnessed dynamic and far-reaching transformations in what religion means in Latin America, these changes were all the more startling coming from Latin America itself, a part of the globe where for so long the monopoly of the Catholic church seemed secure, if never wholly unchallenged. Change arising from within religion (any religion) was in any event a surprise to most social scientists, who remained firmly in the grip of theories of secularization (and related ideas about of modernization) according to which the progressive spread of science, education, industrialization and urban life would cut the ground out from under religion. In this view, religion would simply fade away, disengaging from state institutions, fading from public life and becoming a matter of scattered, and declining, personal devotions or ritualized markers of the passage of life stages.[168]

Such theories provided the underpinning for enduring academic fashions that pushed enterprising researchers to topics other than religion in search of a meaningful research pay off and an effective career boost. The power of academic fashion and intellectual blinders cannot be denied, but there are also *facts* that break through our concepts, inconvenient facts that force themselves on us and make us re-consider the foundations of our approaches. What are the facts that have broken through in Latin America to remind us of the power of religion, not just to sustain itself but also to change itself as part of a changing world? A brief list, in no particular order, makes the point.

The explosion of multiple churches and religious spaces is a prime fact. It is not that Latin America is "becoming Protestant" to cite the title of David Stoll's important early book. (Stoll 1990) It is rather becoming pluralist for the first time in its entire 500-year history. (Levine, 2008) In

---

[167] Cleary quotes one Protestant observer of the meetings to the effect that "the traffic light of official ecumenism is an intermittent yellow light." (Cleary, 2007, p. 15).

[168] All that remained of religion would be perhaps some lovely buildings, music, and works of art. As Tocqueville once wrote, "Eighteenth century philosophers had a very simple explanation for the general weakening of beliefs. Religious zeal, they said, was bound to die down as enlightenment and freedom spread. It is tiresome that the facts do not fit this theory at all."

social and political terms, although the orientations and connections of the churches range across the ideological spectrum and up and down the social hierarchy, a fact that presses itself on our attention is that with rare exceptions all the churches now support some form of political democracy and open civil society.

This is a cultural shift of prime significance, with roots in debates within the churches as well as in the end of the global cold war which loosened once immutable religio-political alliances. The relation of churches to civil society (both the idea and the reality of independent groups) is a third fact. Catholic and later Protestant churches played a key role in sponsoring and protecting a wide range of social movements—land leagues, housing coalitions, neighborhood groups, or human rights organizations to name a few. This sponsorship entailed serving as a conduit for resources and information, training leaders, bringing church-inspired activists together with grass roots groups, and providing legal defense if needed. With the restoration of democracy and the declining status of many of these movements, churches continue to shape civil society through less mobilizational civic networks along with institutions such as schools, new media outlets, cooperatives, and health centers.

Much as I dislike stratigraphic metaphors, it is worth noting that these new facts and the eye-catching change in religion's public faces are undergirded by "deeper" long-term social, cultural, and political transformations that provide the raw materials and the dynamic of the process. A brief list, once again in no particular order, suggests the dimensions of the process. These fifty years have seen significant migration, mostly rural to urban but also intra-rural, accelerated in cases like Peru or Central America by extremes of civil war and violence but present everywhere. Cities have grown and bigger cities have everywhere grown faster than smaller cities.[169] I have already pointed to the important political fact of democratization, which has brought with it an end to civil wars and massive political violence. Two related facts are expanded literacy and access to mass media along with drastically reduced barriers to organization and public participation. Together with the growth of cities, these facts set the scene for competition among churches and between churches and other groups, and provide both means and targets for those seeking to gain or hold members, acquire resources, and get a

---

[169] The importance of city life and the need for an urban pastoral strategy get detailed attention in the Aparecida documents (10.4).

public hearing. The preceding lays out what are, in my view, the bare bones that define the situation of religion in Latin America today. These "facts" that together broke through the intellectual blinders of ideas about secularization also provide the context for the reflections undertaken at Aparecida, and for the kind of planning and actions that flow from them.

THE VIEW FROM APARECIDA

All Church documents are the creation of many hands, and undergo much editing and many revisions before a final version is approved and made public. The meeting at Aparecida was preceded by a lengthy preparatory process throughout the region that produced consultations and pre-documents, all put together into working documents for conference discussion. After a "final" version was passed at the conference and submitted to the Vatican for approval, a series of changes—some of considerable moment—were made before a definitive text was released. (Anonymous, de la Serna) I go through this well-known process to underscore the point that although the document, like the conference, has a unifying theme (*Discípulos Misioneros,* or missionary disciples, Matthew 28:18–20) the text itself incorporates multiple views and like any collective document, responds to different constituencies all at once. Although I will cite passages in support of my interpretations, I acknowledge that citations with varying if not opposed emphasis can easily be found.

As noted earlier, from the vantage point of Aparecida the present and future of the Church in Latin America embody notable values (including a rich and vital tradition of Catholic values and practice) but there is also significant danger and numerous threats that are likely to grow in the future. There is the threat of inroads to Catholic ideas of a proper moral sphere and of the Church's unique orienting role in that sphere. There is the threat of losing members and social position as a result of competition from other churches (above all, "sects" meaning Pentecostal and Neo-Pentecostal churches). The peril arising from competition is compounded by the decay of discipline and loyalty within the church. In a world where secularization is seen to erode the hold that religion, any religion, has on cultural norms in the traditional European heartland, the perception that Latin America is a Catholic reserve for the whole world heightens the sense of potential loss (Jenkins). All these threats gain a sharper edge given fears of cultural disintegration (brought by globalization of cultural imagery that undermines norms in critical areas such as gender) along with the danger of social disintegration flowing from continued and heightened poverty, violence, and exposure to drugs.

The general theme of missionary disciples of course comes from the text in Matthew widely known as the Great Commission, to "go therefore and make disciples of all nations."[170] At Aparecida this provides a charter for evangelization in and through existing institutions, for re-emphasizing the role Catholic groups can play as sources of clergy and sisters, for insisting on close ties between any Catholic group and the institutional church (bishops, clergy, parishes), and for working for closer control of Church educational institutions (especially secondary schools and universities).[171] Given the dangers facing the Church and its missionary disciples, several steps are evidently required: understand the situation; reinforce existing Catholic institutions and groups; strengthen their ties with core leadership (through appropriate supervision); rejuvenate educational and other institutions; reach into new areas including mass media; and move carefully but with a clear bias in favor of democracy in the newly consolidating plural environment of the region.

To understand the situation, the documents affirm the value of the See-Judge-Act method, legitimized in previous conferences of the region's bishops. The use of this method has often been linked with a turn to the social sciences for analytical tools, and to the position that the

---

[170] Mt. 28:18–20 "And Jesus came and said to them, 'All authority in heaven and on earth has been given to me. Go therefore and make disciples of all nations, baptizing them in the name of the Father and of the Son and of the Holy Spirit, teaching them to observe all that I have commanded you. And behold, I am with you always, to the end of the Age.'"

[171] Limitations of time and space preclude a complete review of the documents. My concern with perceptions of danger and threat in the Church's present and future situation in Latin America means that I will draw primarily from three chapters (2 La Mirada de los Discípulos sobre la realidad, (Disciples Look at Reality), 5 La Comunión de los Discípulos Misioneros en la Iglesia (The Communion of Missionary Disciples within the Church) and 8 Reino de Dios y Promoción de la Dignidad Humana, (The Kingdom of God and the Promotion of Human Dignity). I also draw some material from Chapter 6, on Formation, in particular concerning the role of schools, seminaries, and universities.

commitments of the institutional Church must begin with understanding and participating in reality: drawing from the world, not only applying derived principles to it. As Gutiérrez puts it, this is the place where theology is made out of experience illuminated by faith.[172] This method is endorsed at Aparecida (19–35) but emphasis is placed throughout on the need to bind the use of this methodology to authorized expressions of Catholic Social Doctrine and practice, and thus to clerical supervision. Using this methodology, what do the documents see, what strikes them about today's Latin America? A predominant note in the texts is growing cultural upset and confusion or *desconcierto* (10) that undermine the unifying legacy of the faith and the normative guidelines it provides. Such confusion is nowhere more evident than in an "ideology of gender" (40) brought to the region and diffused by global cultural forces, which undermine family, community solidarity, and unleash an uncontrolled individualism. (36, 47, 51, 503)

Gender images and gender roles are of course highly sensitive issues in all religions, given the role of the family as primary social unit. In the specific case of Latin America, the erosion of proper gender images, and by extension of the family, is attributed to a situation in which the church and Christians have become the objects of culture, and no longer its producers. (509) This "lamentable situation" is exacerbated by the multiplication of new sources and new cultural arbiters (the Greek term *areópagos* or judges is used in the text) and points of decision" in cultural life, (10.4) and by the absence of firmly and explicitly Catholic figures in prominent public positions which is repeatedly noted as regrettable.

The peril of cultural disintegration gets extensive attention in Chapter 10, which is entitled "Our Peoples and Culture." Despite the region's rich Catholic heritage and the inculturation of the faith in norms and institutions, hostile cultural forces are present, deriving strength from the power of globalizing media. Individuals, families, and communities are left to orient themselves alone, given "the dissolution of a single unified image of the world that gave orientation to daily life." (479) This kind of lament over loss of unity, a unity rooted in common religious identity, is of course not unique to Catholic leaders. It appears regularly in the most varied faiths and

---

[172] Gutiérrez, 2007 finds in Aparecida a continued commitment to understanding that "the site of theology is at the same time an ecclesial and social site, from which a discourse on faith can be elaborated. The firm foundation of this is the biblical fact of the presence of God in history."

social contexts, often linked with concerns about secularization, or some-times simply with the loss of a single standard presumed to have existed in a past golden age which is itself identified with culture. (Cf. Bellah) The notion that cultural norms could be changing, or perhaps be diverse within an overall framework of unity, is excluded from this view. The extent to which this sense of disintegration and lack of order hinges on issues of gender (as opposed, for example, to hierarchy) will vary among traditions but there is no denying the importance of gender in Catholic discourse and debates, and its salience at Aparecida.

The concern with loss expressed at Aparecida has several very spe-cific referents: a growth rate (of members and especially clergy) that lags behind population increase; (100) inadequate numbers of clergy and sisters; the direct defection of Catholics either to other faiths (notably Pentecostal or Neo-Pentecostal Protestant) or to indifference; and the loss of status as unique arbiter of morality in the public sphere. Why do growing numbers loosen their ties with the Church or simply leave? The bishops' answer falls in the line already noted of the impacts of a hostile or indifferent culture exacerbated by inadequate attention to the faithful. Hence the need for more clergy. The relevant text was changed by late Vatican editing to underscore the perils to the faithful. The text approved at Aparecida stated that "the truth is that many of those who pass to other religious groups are not so much looking to leave our Church, as they are sincerely searching for God." (241) The final version is less sympathetic and more wary: "They hope to find responses to their concerns. They search, not without incur-ring serious dangers, to find responses to some hopes that have not been provided (as they should have been) in the Church." (225) In this vein, a complex distinction is drawn between ecumenism, in principle good, and competition between religions, which is dangerous. (232)

Looking to solutions or means with which to counter these trends, the document examines various organizations and possibilities. Consider-able attention is paid to reinforcing the parishes and schools, and also to Catholic movements including the base ecclesial communities (*comuni-dades eclesiales de base*) or CEBs, which have had so prominent a role in discussion of the church in Latin America. In line with the general trend of Vatican and local church policy in recent years, it is no surprise to find that such communities are praised, but that praise comes along with stress on the need to be closely tied to parishes and to the authority of the bishops. (178) Base communities are admonished that their validity depends always on "Keeping themselves in full communion with their bishop and in the context of the pastoral plan of the diocese." (179)[173] Later in the text, considerable emphasis is given to these communities and other movements, along with schools and universities not as valid expressions per se, but rather as potential sources of clergy and persons choosing a consecrated life. (309, 311)

On the other side of what one might visualize as a ledger of issues, the persistence of grinding poverty and inequality, attention to ecology and biodiversity (2.1.4, *Biodiversidad, ecología, Amazonia y Antártida*) the limited opportunities for ethnic minorities, women, and migrants, prisoners, and the ravages of drugs are all duly noted and put in the context of the "faces" of the faith, faces that underscore a commitment that is central to the faith. This places Aparecida squarely in the tradition of Medellín and Puebla. The continuing force of these and other inequalities and injustices underscores the re-affirmation of the preferential option for the poor as central to a Christological faith. Jesus made himself poor and was friend to the poor, and this model is present not just in policies that do things for others but also in commitment and closeness, ("the closeness that makes us friends,") (398) and in work for social and economic policies of integral promotion to change the situation.

The documents are positive about the emergence and spread of democratic rule in the region but the endorsement of democracy in the final text is notably cautious. The text approved at the meetings spoke openly of acknowledging the strengthening of democracy as a good thing. "We note as a positive fact the strengthening of democratic regimes in many countries of Latin America and the Caribbean as shown by the most recent electoral processes. Nonetheless, we are concerned to see . . . (74) The original goes on to express concerns about corruption and neo-populism. But the final text is much drier and limits itself to, "We note a certain democratic process revealed in various electoral processes." (74) Politics is in any case not the proper mission for the Church, whose role is to serve as an ethical model and provide general orienting norms along with acts of mercy and solidarity and denunciations of injustice when appropriate.

---

[173] This is consonant with general trends throughout the region. One recent, thorough empirical study is Mallimaci and Villa.

Subsidiarity, that is, yielding primary place and role to public officials and lay groups, is enjoined.[174]

Conclusion: The Future as Peril and as Opportunity

The present in Latin America cannot be captured in one phrase, or understood on one dimension alone. There are significant grounds for both optimism and pessimism: political openness is present along with aggravated inequality; political violence has declined but the violence of daily life is, if anything, worse. All aspects of culture are changing so quickly that one sometimes feels like a kid riding on the handlebars of a bicycle careering down hill. The exhilaration of speed comes along with the danger of crashing. I have made fear a central theme of Aparecida, and perhaps this is unfair or exaggerated. But I underscore the sense of threat and fear about the future in order to make a point. The point is that how the future is viewed conditions how the present will be engaged. This present reality of change and competition can be engaged openly and with confidence or defensively and with fear of loss.

At the heart of the fears and concerns that run through the Aparecida documents are fears of loss, decline and decay: loss of the Church's role as sole moral arbiter of the public sphere; potential loss in competition with others; decline of unity around the institutional leadership of the Church (bishops and clergy) and ultimately, loss of a Catholic reserve for the world. Let us consider these fears a little more closely. As a social scientist with enormous respect for the power of religious faith and commitment, I have long been surprised by the fear many church leaders have of competition. This fear is partly compounded of an older tradition that error has no place alongside truth, but more is at issue. There appears to be a conviction that faith and commitment are shallow and that therefore in an open competition will lose unless buttressed and supported by continued official support and extensive clerical advice and supervision. Loss of control seems to be equated with loss.

---

[174] Individual hierarchies continue to take important public stands, for example on issue of poverty or land issues (Brazil) or corruption (Mexico) but in terms of partisan choice, with rare exceptions the norm has been to stay away from this area.

One way to ensure control might be to build a wall and mount a defense, controlling entry to the community and access to its people and resources. Walls can be physical or metaphorical, actual barriers of brick, wood, stone, cement, or steel with doors and checkpoints, or simply a statement of closure. Let us consider this metaphor of the wall for a moment. In several important books on religion, society, and politics in the United States, the legal scholar Stephen L. Carter has argued that religion is trivialized in American public discourse and confined to a marginal role in institutional arrangements. (Carter, 1993, 2006) To assert religious ideas or beliefs as a justification for public policy runs into the "wall of separation between church and state" and the religious element is reduced to insignificance.

In a more recent work, Carter adduces Roger Williams' metaphor of the garden and the wilderness to capture the relation of religion and faith with the world at large. For Williams, he writes,

> The garden was the domain of the church, the gentle fragile region where the people of God would congregate and try to build lives around the Divine Word. The wilderness was the world lying beyond the garden wall, uncivilized and potentially quite threatening to the garden. The wall separated the two and the reason for the wall was not that the wilderness needed protection from the garden-the wall was there to protect the garden from the wilderness. (Carter, 2006, 75)

This metaphor evokes a garden that is ordered and tranquil, a secure space in which "the people who joined in community within it would be free to come to their understanding of God's will, safe from the coercions of a society that might disagree." (Carter, 2006, 76)

Carter develops this garden/wall/wilderness metaphor at some length, and he argues, "the survival of a religion rests on its ability to avoid being overwhelmed by the secularity of the wilderness." (76) Protected by the garden wall, religions can freely do what he argues is their work of cultural formation and cultural dissent. But walls are fragile, and "The culture will find a way in, no matter how far away a religionist may burrow. When the breach occurs, as Williams argued, the religionist must leave the garden and go out into the wilderness prepared once more to do battle. (Carter, 2006, 117)

This extended metaphor of garden/wall/wilderness as articulated by Carter evokes many of the fears visible at Aparecida and shares the sense of danger stemming from uncontrolled change. But although the fear is real, the metaphor of gardens and walls does not quite capture the situation. The effort to build a wall, or retreat into a protected garden, runs up against some defining characteristics of Catholicism itself, and does not in any case square well with the particular realities of Latin America. McBrien reminds us that if anything characterizes Catholic tradition over two millennia, it is its very *catholicity,* its breadth and persistence over time, "characterized by a *both/and* rather than an *either/or* approach to nature and grace, reason and faith, law and Gospel, scripture and tradition, faith and works, authority and freedom, past and present, stability and change, unity and diversity." (McBrien 1981, p. 1184) In the experience of Latin America, elements of Catholicism surely straddle all sides of any such barrier, if indeed, it ever existed, and the Catholic community has itself been enriched by interchange of models and forms of action across the porous line that marks the religious community off from the community as a whole.

Many are familiar with the first and last lines of Robert Frost's celebrated poem, *Mending Wall.* "Something there is that does not love a wall" and "Good fences make good neighbors" have entered into our common vocabulary,[175] but fewer recall a later stanza where the poet expresses his doubts: "Before I built a wall, I'd ask to know/What I was walling in or walling out/And to whom I was likely to give offense. Something there is that doesn't love a wall/That wants it down!"

Indeed, there is something that does not love a wall. Nothing flourishes for too long behind a wall, however strong or imposing it may be. Walls also need constant attention and repair, absorbing energies that might be used in other ways. Additionally, as Frost reminds us, walls exclude as much as they protect. One wants to know what is being kept out, who might be offended, and what might be lost by building a wall and staying behind it.

Walls and related barriers are means and metaphors of control, keeping things and people out or in, controlling access or exit and monitoring traffic. They are all about control. But why should there be such concern with control, and why should loss of control be taken as loss in the first place? Control is essential to continuity only if control is built into the very definition of what is being continued, in this case "the Church" and the Catholic community conceived in hierarchically dependent terms. To

---

[175] In the poem, "good fences make good neighbors" is a quote from Frost's neighbor, a view the poet clearly questions.

be sure, much of Catholic tradition is indeed built around hierarchy and a top-down concept of authority, with power and knowledge descending across a large number of levels in complex social settings. However, this is not the only Catholic model available on which to build. Romero states it forcefully: "Understanding persons as friends of God is quite different than looking upon them as serfs, in the same way that inviting them to follow God's project is different than ordering them to follow the law." (2007, 41) The seemingly sudden shift to openness and open competition seems to preoccupy the bishops, but it is also a source of potential energy and commitment in yet unknown forms. In Latin America today, religion is a buzzing, blooming confusion of possibilities, full of innovation and charged with social and cultural energies.[176]

Although fear is clearly a key element in the tone of the Aparecida documents, there are also contrary tendencies, tendencies that respond to other traditions and to a sympathetic understanding of the realities of the region. The ultimate result is mixed, if pessimistic in its overall thrust. To use Berryman's comment on the 1979 Puebla Conference, one might say that Aparecida produced a tie for those committed to the ecclesial and social vision articulated at Medellin and Puebla (preferential option for the poor along with a concern for seeing the church in the faces of the excluded) and to a kind of theology that draws strength and inspiration from the world of which it is an integral part rather than seeking separation in a garden.

In more general terms, although interchurch competition remains intense, the diffusion of evangelicals and their institutions throughout the society has also dampened the hard edge of hostility and difference between Catholics and Protestants, particularly in large urban areas where most Latin Americans live. Most of the empirical work of which I am aware affirms that evangelicals (the preferred umbrella term for Protestants in Latin America) are much like their Catholic neighbors in everything but churchgoing—they participate in organizations in similar ways, they live in the same neighborhoods and they consume in comparable patterns. These are concrete changes that lay a basis for cooperation in meeting the ordinary needs of community life.

---

[176] The success of innovations like the Catholic Charismatic Movement is a case in point. Cf. Chesnut, chapter 4.

What will the future look like in Latin America? What will its religious life and identity be like? It seems clear that despite a growing edge of secularization and disconnect from the churches visible in many countries (e.g. Parker, 2005).[177] Christianity will remain dominant, but the Christianity in question will clearly be very different from the past. There will be continuity, not least in the continued presence of the Catholic Church, which remains everywhere the single largest and most powerfully institutionalized religion. But the pluralization of religious options, the spreading Pentecostalization of religious experience[178] the prominent role of mass media, and intensifying competition among religious groups for legitimate access to public space suggest a dynamic and open future. Latin America is not so much "turning Pentecostal" or even "turning Protestant" as it is "turning pluralist" for the first time in modern history. Expectations of a thoroughgoing transformation of Latin American societies stemming from religion—something like a new Reformation—may be premature, but the reality of change is there to be embraced and worked with.

---

[177] Parker Gumucio, Cristián. "¿América Latina ya no es católico? Pluralismo cultural religioso creciente," *America Latina Hoy Revista de Ciencias Sociales*, Vol. 41, diciembre 2005. Pp. 35–56.

[178] Steigenga (2001. 44–48) speaks of a general pentecostalization of religious experience and practice as elements once limited to Pentecostal churches (direct experience of the Holy Spirit, divine healing speaking in tongues etc) have diffused more widely.

CONTRIBUTORS

Pope Benedict XVI, born Joseph Alois Ratzinger, is the 265th and reigning pontiff of the Roman Catholic Church.

Rev. Ernest Bartell, C.S.C., Ph.D. is a former chair of the Department of Economics at the University of Notre Dame. Father Bartell also served as president of Stonehill College, and as Director of the U.S. Department of Health, Education, and Welfare's Fund for the Improvement of Post Secondary Education. His current research interests include economic development of Latin America, economics of education, and Catholic social teaching.

Rev. Edward L. Cleary, O.P., Ph.D. is Professor of Political Science and Director of the Latin American Studies Program at Providence College. Father Cleary's major interests as a teacher, researcher, and writer include: Latin American society, Latin American government and politics, human rights in Latin America, and the methodology of mobilization of human rights movements. Since the conference of Latin American Bishops in Puebla, Mexico in 1979, he has been an outstanding commentator on the role of the Catholic Church in Latin America.

Rev. Virgilio Elizondo, Ph.D. is Professor of Pastoral and Hispanic Theology at the University of Notre Dame. One of the Catholic Church's foremost Hispanic theologians, Father Elizondo was named by *TIME* magazine as one of our most innovative spiritual leaders, was the co-recipient of the 2007 Community of Christ International Peace Award, and received the University of Notre Dame's most prestigious award, the Laetare Medal. The author of many books and journal articles, he is perhaps best known for *Galilean*

Journey: The Mexican-American Promise, which examines the similarities between Christ's Galilean background and the mestizo experience.

The Rev. Gustavo Gutiérrez, O.P., Ph.D. is widely regarded as the founder of liberation theology. He is the author of the watershed book, *A Theology of Liberation: History, Politics, Salvation.* In addition to spending much of his life working among the poor people of Lima, Peru, and being awarded the Legion of Honor by the French government in 1993, Father Gutiérrez holds the John Cardinal O'Hara Professorship of Theology at the University of Notre Dame. He has been professor at the Pontifical Catholic University of Peru and a visiting professor at many major universities in North America and Europe.

Javier Maria Iguiñiz Echeverria, Ph.D. is Professor of Economics at the Catholic University of Peru. Professor Iguiñiz is widely regarded as one of the world's foremost experts on the economic development of Latin America and on economic ethics. He was the primary Latin American consultant when the United States Catholic Bishops prepared their Pastoral Message on Catholic Social Teaching and the U.S. Economy, *Economic Justice for All.*

Daniel H. Levine, Ph.D. is Professor of Political Science at the University of Michigan, and has served as the chair of graduate studies in political science. Professor Levine's principal research interests are political development and comparative government. His research and publication in recent years focused primarily on three issues: the relationship between religion and socio-political change, issues of democratization, and state-society relations with emphasis on the evolution of civil society.

Rev. Jose Marins was one of the official experts at CELAM II in Medellín in 1968. He is the foremost spokesman for the Basic Ecclesial Communities of Latin America.

Rev. Robert Pelton, C.S.C., Ph.D. is Concurrent Professor of Theology, Fellow of the Helen Kellogg Institute for International Studies, and Director of Latin American/North American Church Concerns at the University of Notre Dame. One of the nation's foremost Latin Americanists, Father Pelton's major areas of expertise include the Catholic Church of the Americas, Small Christian Communities (CEBs), liberation theology, and the Cuban Church.

Margaret Pfeil, Ph.D. is Assistant Professor of Theology at the University of Notre Dame, and a founder and resident of the St. Peter Claver Catholic Worker House in South Bend, Indiana. Professor Pfeil specializes in Catholic social thought, peace and justice issues, and the development of moral doctrine. She has been published in many prominent theological, sociological, and academic journals, and is currently completing a book about social sin and social reconciliation.

The Most Reverend Ricardo Ramirez, C.S.B. is the first and current Bishop of Las Cruces, New Mexico. Within the United States Conference of Catholic Bishops, Monsignor Ramirez sits on the International Policy Committee, Committee on the Liturgy, Committee on the Catholic Common Ground Initiative, and Committee on Hispanic Affairs. He formerly chaired the Committee on the Church in Latin America and the Catholic Campaign for Human Development. He was the bishop chosen to represent the United States at CELAM V, where he collaborated with the Latin American bishops in the planning of the conference at Aparecida.

Rev. Sergio Torres, Ph.D., a Chilean diocesan priest, is a leading voice for the Amerindian theologians. He was instrumental in bringing about the constructive dialogue between Amerindian theologians and CELAM officials prior to and during the Aparecida Conference. English translations of his writings have been published by Orbis Books.

APPENDIX

CELAM
Latin American Episcopal Council

The Continental Mission:

Toward a Missionary Church

Introduction

The purifying and renewing fire of the Holy Spirit that moved us in Aparecida as the Church of Latin America and the Caribbean, wants to extend itself to the particular Churches by way of a CONTINENTAL MISSION.

The main subject carrying the mission is, of course, each diocese, where the Aparecida orientations want to impregnate the Church of which we are part. The mission wants to be CONTINENTAL, in a way that at some shared times and signs, it may express and enrich the communion of all the pilgrim Churches walking together in Latin America and the Caribbean, and that we may mutually animate each other in a renewal effort toward a missionary Church.

Here we present a document that has emerged from many successive contributions that were finally approved by the Presidents of the Episcopal Conferences as a minimal orientation and synchronization for this great missionary impulse of the Spirit. The document brings together the spirit, goals and a minimal plan for the visible effect of communion.

Praying is being open to the Spirit, so that He may renew in each disciple of the Lord, the permanent spirit of the mission. May Mary, Mother and Model of all the disciples of Jesus, implore this commotion in the Spirit, a new Pentecost. Let us pray with Her.

> Bishop Víctor Sánchez Espinosa
> Auxiliary Bishop of the Archdiocese of Mexico
> CELAM Secretary General
>
> March 25, 2008
> Annunciation of the Lord

PRAYER FOR THE CONTINENTAL MISSION

Stay with us, Lord,
Keeping us company, although
We have to not always recognized you.

You are the Light of our hearts,
And your give us your fire with the certainty of Easter.
You comfort us at the breaking of the bread,
To announce to our fellow Christians
That You are truly risen
And have given us the mission to be witnesses
To your victory.

Stay with us, Lord,
You are Truth itself,
You reveal the Father.
Illumine our minds with your Word,
Help us feel the beauty of belief in you.

You who are the Life,
Stay in our homes,
That they may walk united,
And in them human life may grow generously.

Jesus, stay with our children
And call our youth
To build a new world with you.

Stay, Lord, with those
To whom our society
Denies justice and freedom.
Stay with the poor and the humble
With the aged and the infirm.
Strengthen our faith as disciples
Always attentive to the voice of the Good Shepherd.
Send us as your joyful missionaries,
That our people
May adore the Father in You, through the Holy Spirit.

To Mary, your Mother and our Mother,
Our Lady of Guadalupe, the woman clothed with the sun,
We entrust the pilgrim People of God,
In the beginning of the third Christian millennium.
Amen.

(Taken from the magisterium of Benedict XVI in Aparecida)

I

A MISSIONARY CHURCH IN THE CONTINENT

1. THE SPIRIT MOVES US TO THE MISSION

The concluding document of the V Conference of Aparecida, mindful of the Lord's mandate to "go and make disciples of all peoples"[179], wants to spur on a great missionary impulse in the Church in Latin America and the Caribbean. Without doubt, this is one of the main conclusions emanating from this great ecclesial encounter. This missionary impulse can be subdivided into four practical consequences:

- To profit intensely from this time of grace
- To implore and live a New Pentecost in all Christian communities
- To awaken the call and missionary action of the baptized, to encourage all vocations and ministries that the Holy Spirit gives the disciples of Jesus in the living communion of the Church.
- To go out to persons, families, communities and people, in order to proclaim to them and share with them the gift of an encounter with Christ, who has filled our lives with "meaning", truth and love, with joy and hope[180].

The Holy Spirit precedes us in this missionary way. Thus, we trust that this witness to the Good News will constitute, in turn, an impulse toward ecclesial renewal and to the transformation of society.

---

[179] Matthew 28, 20.
[180] Aparecida Document, DA 548.

2. Nature and Goal of the Mission

The mission is a constitutive part of the identity of the Church, called by the Lord to evangelize all peoples. "Its purpose is to act as leaven and soul of society, which should renew itself in Christ to be transformed into God's family."[181] Thus, the mission that will be carried out as a fruit of the Aparecida encounter should, above all, animate the missionary call of Christians, strengthening the roots of their faith and awakening their sense of responsibility, so that all Christian communities get set in a state of permanent mission.

It is a matter of awakening in Christians the happiness and fecundity of being disciples of Jesus Christ, celebrating with true joy "being- with-Him" and "loving- as- He- loved", so as to be sent forth to the mission.

> *We cannot waste this time of grace. We need a new Pentecost! We*
> *need to reach out to persons, families, communities and towns to commu-*
> *nicate and share the gift of the encounter with Christ, who has filled our*
> *lives with "meaning", with truth and love, with happiness and hope!*[182]

In this way, the mission leads us to live the encounter with Jesus as a dynamic of personal, pastoral and ecclesial conversion, which is able to urge the baptized to holiness and the apostolate, and of bringing back those who have left the Church, those who are distant from the influence of the gospel and those who have not yet experienced the gift of faith.

This missionary experience opens up a new horizon for the Church in the whole continent, that wants to "start again in Christ", walking with him along a path of maturity that enables us to go an encounter every person, speaking the familiar language of witness, of fraternity, of solidarity.

3. The Church in a State of Permanent Mission

The Church in Latina America and the Caribbean wants to bring upon itself a "state of permanent mission"[183]. It is a matter of strengthening

---

[181] GS 40.

[182] DA 548.

[183] DA 213 NS 551.

the missionary dimension of the Church in the Continent and from the Continent. This carries with it the decision to walk together on a path of conversion that will lead us to be missionary disciples of Jesus Christ. In fact,

> *Discipleship and mission are like the two sides of a single medal: when the disciple is in love with Christ, he cannot stop announcing to the world that only He can save us (Cf. Acts 4:12)[184]*

The "state of permanent mission" implies inner fire and full trust in the Lord, as well as continuity, firmness and constancy to bring

> *our boats into the open sea, with the powerful breath of the Spirit, without fearing the storms, confident that the Providence of God will bring us great surprises[185]*

The same Spirit will awaken within us the creativity needed to find diverse forms of drawing close, even to the most difficult environments, developing in the missionary the capacity to become a "fisher of men".

In fine, "a state of permanent mission" implies a great willingness to rethink and reform many pastoral structures, having as the constitutive principle the "spirituality of communion"[186] and of missionary audacity. The main thing is personal conversion. There is no doubt[187]. But this should naturally lead us to create open and flexible structures, capable of animating a permanent mission in each particular Church.

---

[184] DI 3.
[185] DA 551.
[186] Cf. John Paul II, NMI 43.
[187] Cf. DA 10.

II

THE CONTINENTAL MISSION

4. A CONTINENTAL MISSIONARY ACTIVITY FOR A CHURCH IN PERMANENT MISSION

To the question "a mission, what for?", we must answer with the faith and hope of the Church: our mission is to share the Life that Christ transmits to us[188].

> It is love that gives life; thus, the Church is sent to spread the charity of Christ in the world, so that men and peoples "may have life in abundance" (John 10:10)[189]

In this way, the Church is

> Missionary, inasmuch as it is a disciple, that is, capable of allowing itself to be ever drawn, with a renewed sense of awe, to God who loved us and loves us first (Cf. 1 Jn. 4:10)[190].

This missionary dynamism happens at a very opportune moment.

> When many of our peoples prepare to celebrate the bicentennial of their independence, we find ourselves before the challenge to revitalize our way of being Catholic and our personal options for the Lord, so that the Christian faith may take deeper root in the hearts of persons and of

---

[188] RMi 11.
[189] Benedict XVI, Homily at the Eucharist in Aparecida. May 13, 2007.
[190] Idem.

> *Latin American people as a founding event and an enlivening encounter with Christ. He manifests Himself as the newness of life and of mission in all the dimensions of personal and social existence. This requires, from the perspective of our Catholic identity, a more missionary evangelization, in dialogue with Christians and in service to all men[191].*

In this matter we get help from the next meeting of the Missionary Latin American Congress–COMLA 8/CAM 3, as well as the Synod on the Word of Life and the Mission of the Church (2008), and the celebration of the Pauline year in 2008–2009.

a. The Mission Is a Constitutive Trait of the Church

An essential goal of the Continental Mission is to awaken awareness that the missionary dimension is a constitutive part of the identity of the Church and of the disciple of the Lord. Thus, starting with the *kerygma,* she tries to vitalize the encounter with the living Christ and to strengthen the sense of belonging to the Church, so that the faithful baptized progress from being evangelized to be evangelizers and, through their witness and evangelizing activity, our Latin American and Caribbean peoples may come to have full life in Him.

Achieving this goal

> All the baptized are called to begin anew in Christ, to acknowledge and follow His presence with the same realism and novelty, the same affective power, persuasion and hope that was experienced by his first disciples at their encounter on the shores of the Jordan River, 2000 years ago, and with the "Juan Diegos" of the New World. Only through this encounter and following, which becomes familiarity and communion, through an outflow of gratitude and joy, are we rescued from our isolated conscience and go out to communicate the true life to all, the happiness and hope that we have been given to experience and enjoy.[192]

---

[191] DA 13.
[192] DA 549.

b. Means for the Mission

1. Drinking from the Word, as a place of encounter with Jesus Christ.

    If the central goal of the Mission is to lead people to an authentic encounter with Jesus Christ, the first room for encounter with Him will be the deep and lived knowledge of the Word of God, of Jesus Christ, alive in the Church, our home.[193]

    The joyful proclamation of Jesus Christ dead and risen, whom we seek, and whom God has constituted as Lord and Messiah (Acts 2:36), is already and encounter with the living Word, with Jesus Himself, the saving Word.

    To enter and remain in this encounter place with Jesus that is the Word, a privileged instrument of the mission, we must underscore five particular goals:

    - The development of a biblical pastoral activity, understood as

        Biblical animation of pastoral work, as a school of interpretation or knowledge of the Word, of communion with Jesus or prayer with the Word, and of inculturated evangelization or proclamation of the Word.[194]

    - The formation in the Lectio Divina, or an exercise of prayerful reading of the Sacred Scriptures,[195] and its ample spreading and promotion;

    - Preaching the Word, in a way that it really leads the disciple to a living encounter, full of awe, with Christ, and to following Him in the actuality of live and of history;

    - The strengthening of the treasure of popular piety of our peoples, in the light of the Word of God.

        So that the precious pearl that is Jesus Christ, may shine ever more in that piety, and so that it will be again an evangelizing in the faith of the Church and through its sacramental life.[196]

---

[193] Cf. DA 246.
[194] DA 247.
[195] DA 248.
[196] DA 549.

- The presentation of the lives of the saints, especially the Virgin Mary, as incarnate pages of the Gospel that touch the heart and motivate the way of the disciple toward Jesus and of the missionary toward the people.

Because of this, the people must be educated in the reading and meditation of the Word: that it becomes its food, and so that, through personal experience, they may see that the words of Jesus are spirit and truth (Cf. John 6:63). Otherwise, how can the people announce a message whose content and spirit they do not know deeply? We must base our missionary commitment and all our life in the rock of the Word of God.[197]

2. Being nourished by the Eucharist

A second means for the Mission is the Sacred Liturgy, especially, the sacraments of Christian Initiation, signs that express and actualize the vocation of the disciples of Jesus, called to follow Him. In a special way, the Eucharist is a privileged place for the encounter between the disciple and Jesus Christ. And it is, at the same time, an unending source of the Christian vocation and of missionary thrust;

> There, the Holy Spirit strengthens the identity of the disciple and awakens in him the resolute will to boldly announce to others what he has heard and lived.[198]

Within this second missionary means, we must point out four particular goals:

- To lead, by means of Christian Initiation, to a living incorporation into community, whose source and peak is the celebration of the Eucharist, and to give time and attention to the follow up of those who become members of the community;

- To underscore the dimension of renewal in the New and Everlasting Covenant in the Eucharistic celebration, a meeting place with the Father, the Son, and the Holy Spirit, with the angels, the saints, and among the brethren;

---

[197] DI 3.
[198] DA 251.

an offering of the life of the disciple, carrying his cross, while at the same time being a missionary sending;

- To encourage the Eucharistic style of Christian life, and to recreate and promote the "Sunday ministry";[199] giving it a special place in ministerial programs,[200] for a new impulse for the evangelization of the People of God;[201]

- In those places where it is not possible to celebrate the Eucharist, to encourage the Sunday celebration of the Word,

that makes present the Paschal Mystery in the love with which it congregates (Cf. 1 Jn. 3:14), in the word received (Cf. Jn. 5:24–25), and in communal prayer (Cf. Mt. 18:20).[202]

3. Building the Church as a home and school of communion

A third necessary meeting place with Jesus Christ is community life,

Jesus is present in the midst of a community alive in the faith and in fraternal love. There He fulfills His promise: "Where two or three are gathered together in my name, there I am in the midst of them" (Mt. 18:20).[203]

To form a community implies embracing Jesus' style of life, to assume his paschal destiny with all its demands, to participate in His mission, to be in an attitude of permanent conversion and to maintain the joy of the missionary disciple in the service of the Kingdom.

Within this third means for the mission, we must underscore five particular goals:

- To encourage the awareness of communion at the family level, so that each home may become a domestic Church, a sanctuary of life, where persons are seen as a gift of God and people are trained in this direction; a true school of faith, a space wherein missionaries of hope and peace grow;

---

[199] Cf. Sacramentum Caritatis.
[200] DI 4.
[201] DA 252.
[202] DA 253.
[203] DA 256.

- To form small Christian communities, open and available, in their diverse forms and expressions. To cultivate in them the ministry of welcoming, so that people will experience their belong to the Church in a personal and familial way;

- To deepen the community dimension at the parish level, so that the parish will truly be a community of communities;[204]

- To animate communities of Consecrated Life, so that they may seek to share their witness of missionary communion with the greater ecclesial community;

- All of this should be geared toward the renewal of pastoral structures, so that we may give impulse to a new way of being Church: more fraternal, an expression of communion, where people participate more, and more missionary.[205]

4. To serve society, and especially, the poor

A fourth means for the encounter with Jesus Christ and for missionary activity is the service to society, so that our people will have life in Christ, and in a special way, service to the poor, to the ill and the afflicted,[206] *"who call for our commitment and give us witness of faith, patience in suffering, and a constant strife to keep on living."*[207]

Within this fourth means for the mission, we must underscore four particular goals:

- Brotherly love for the poorest and afflicted, our brethren in whom we find ourselves and serve the Lord, and the defense of the rights of the excluded,[208] since therein lies the fidelity to the Church of Jesus Christ;[209]

---

[204] Cf. RMi 20.
[205] DA 379.
[206] Cf. Mt. 25, 37–40.
[207] DA 257.
[208] DA 257.
[209] NMI 49.

- The renewal and affirmation of social ministry, so that it may express in concrete signs the preferential option for the poor and the excluded, especially with migrants, the sick, dependent addicts, children in moral risk and those in prison;[210]
- Pastoral attention to the builders of society, who have the mission of creating just structures, at the service of the dignity of persons and their families; also, to the social communicators, so that they may encourage the growth of a culture that is a manifestation of the Kingdom of God;
- The definite backing to all those persons and institutions that "give witness to a search for justice, for peace and for the common good, sometimes even surrendering their own life."[211]

The means of the mission, in their totality, should be a new instrument to achieve a great goal: to give impulse to the execution of the Continental Mission in such a way that the Churches of the continent go into a state of mission. This means that the intensive missionary action be so motivating, as to make us assume the permanent mission as a pastoral plan.

c. Simultaneous and Shared Signs

In order to be *continental*, it needs to make visible the Latin American and Caribbean action in some particular moments of missionary action that is some simultaneity and shared signs:

- The triptych gift by Pope Benedict XVI in Aparecida, along with a simple catechesis on its symbology of faith;
- The prayer proposed by the same Pope to prepare for the V Conference and also the one with which he finished his inaugural speech.
- The logo used in Aparecida can still be the distinctive sign for the missionaries and for the subsidies prepared for this work.

---

[210] Cf. DA 399.430.
[211] DA 256.

- To these signs we can associate other inspired acts, hopefully simultaneously, related to liturgical solemnities, or Marian feasts, especially the titles of Aparecida (Dec 10) and Guadalupe (Dec 12).

5.1 The Pedagogy of the Continental Missionary Activity

Five aspects of an evangelizing process
In the process of formation for the missionary disciples

We point out five fundamental aspects that appear in a different way in each stage of the way, but which are intimately related and are mutually nourishing:

The Encounter with Jesus Christ, Conversion, Discipleship, Communion and Mission.[212]
This implies:

- To know the quests of persons—and peoples—which God entrusts to us, and to lead them to an encounter with the living Jesus Christ,
- Eliciting an attitude of conversion,
- The Decision to follow in the steps of Jesus
- So that, living in comm—union with Christ, as con-voked by Him,[213] within the communion of the Church, there may grow a living and strong sense of ecclesial belonging,
- And a process of holistic formation, kerygmatic, permanent, process oriented, diversified and community minded, that contemplates the spiritual companionship.
- That the baptized assume their missionary commitment and go from being evangelized to being evangelizers, so that the Kingdom of God may become present, and thus, our Latin American and Caribbean people may have life in Him.

---

[212] Cf. DA 278.
[213] Cf. DA 154 and 156.

These dimensions of the way can be explained in the words found in the gospel itself, that describe the process of encounter, formation and sending forth, of those who receive a vocation to be missionary disciples so that the people will have life in Christ;[214]

- It all begins with a question: what are you looking for? (Jn. 1:38). The Aparecida document remarks about this in 279a:

    Those who will be His disciples are already seeking Him. They will discover the deeper meaning of their search, and their encounter with Jesus will be fostered, He who gives origin to Christian initiation (Search).

- The disciples who want to meet Jesus ask Him: "Master, where do you live? (Jn. 1:38) Jesus invites them to live an experience: *Come and see* (Jn. 1:39). I am the Way, the Truth and the Life (Jn. 14:6). (Encounter)
- Finding Philip he said: *Follow me (Mt. 4:19)*, and later on, on the shore of the Lake of Galilee, amazed by the teaching of the Master and the miraculous catch of fish, also Peter, Andrew, James and John, *leaving everything behind, followed Him*. (Conversion and Discipleship).
- He called them *to stay with Him* (Mc. 3:14) to "remain in His love", forming a community of disciples, later known for its solidarity and its unity in prayer, the breaking of the bread and the teaching of the apostles (Cf. Acts 3:42 ff). (Communion).
- But Jesus' call to discipleship is inseparable from the missionary call. Already in the encounter on the shore of the lake he manifests his goal: *I will make you fishers of men*, and when He calls the twelve, He tells them explicitly that they have been called to preach (Mc. 3:14). And before ascending to heaven, He sends them to make disciples of all peoples, baptizing them . . . (Mt. 28:19). (Mission).

To achieve this process and to bring back people who have turned away "we should strengthen four turning points in our Church:

- A personal encounter with Jesus Christ, *a deep and intense religious experience*, a kerygmatic announcement and the personal

---

[214] Cf. DA 244, 245, 276, 278.

witness of the evangelizers, that will lead to personal conversion and to a holistic change of life";

- *Living in community,* thus, our faithful seek communities where they can be fraternally welcome . . .

- It is necessary that our faithful feel they are really members of an ecclesial community and be corresponsible in their own growth";

- "A doctrinal-biblical formation (. . .) markedly experiential and communitarian", which is necessary to mature in the religious experience and is perceived as a "fundamental and necessary tool in spiritual, personal and communal knowledge";

- "The missionary commitment of the whole community . . . comes to meet the fallen away, gets interested in their situation, in order to enkindle in them the love of the Church and to invite them to come back to it".[215]

We must keep in mind that missionary disciples will only come if in the above mentioned process, our communities are committed to the evangelization of the baptized who have no awareness of being disciples, walking with them so that they can live a gradual growth toward willingness to serve, and thus, to respond to the sending forth the Lord gives them by means of the Church.

In this experience, the renewal and personal and pastoral conversion of the shepherds and of all the consecrated is an indispensable element in order that the coherent witness of life become the basic pedagogical foundation.

5.2 Ways to the Encounter with Christ

An authentic offer of encounter with Jesus Christ must keep the following elements in mind:

- An *experience of the presence of Jesus Christ* in the personal and community life of the believer: in the meditated and ecclesial reading of the Sacred Scriptures; in the Eucharistic celebration,

---

[215] Cf. DA 226.

unending source of the Christian vocation and inextinguishable source of the missionary commitment; in the dynamics of community life, which is participatory and fraternal; in the service of the poor and the excluded;

- A new recognition of *popular piety*, which is

> *A legitimate way of living the faith, a way of feeling they are part of the Church and a way of being missionaries, where we find the deepest vibrations of America.*[216]

- A strengthening of the close presence of Mary, "the ultimate and most loyal image of the following of Christ",[217] at once mother and teacher of the missionary disciples of Jesus Christ;[218]
- A rescue of the *Gospel witnesses* in America, men and women who lived their faith heroically in a path of holiness, together with those who shed their blood in martyrdom".[219]

5.3 The Pedagogy of Encounter and Communion

a) The pedagogy of encounter: The mission should be carried out within the dynamics of the pedagogy of encounter that can be found person to person, house to house, community to community.[220] Since every pastor–and this holds also for each missionary- must reflect the Good Shepherd, it is evident that our ministry must be interwoven with encounters, simplicity, cordiality, solicitude, hearing and service to others.

> *In this evangelizing effort, the ecclesial community stands out for its pastoral initiatives, above all among the homes in poor areas of the city and the interior; its lay and religious missionaries, seeking to dialogue with all in the spirit of understanding and delicate charity.*[221]

---

[216] DA 264 The mission of the Church is wider than the "communion among the Churches": this is, resides being a help for the new evangelization, and should have above all an orientation with a specific missionary character.

[217] DA 270.

[218] Cf. DA 267, 270.

[219] Cf. DA 275.

[220] DA 550.

[221] Benedict XVI, Homily to the Bishops of Brazil, 3. May 11, 2007.

b) Pedagogy of communion. It is important to achieve the mission in the continent as a great expression of communion. That the communion with God in unanimous prayer, imploring with Mary, the Mother of Jesus, the Holy Spirit, and the unity with the Pope, between the Episcopal Conferences and among the particular Churches, helping each other reciprocally in their activities, especially through personnel and resources;

> *Every particular Church should open itself generously to the needs of others. The collaboration between the Churches, by means of an authentic reciprocity that will prepare them to give and receive, is also a source of enrichment for all and takes in various sectors of ecclesial life. In this respect, the declaration of the Bishops in Puebla is exemplary: "Finally, the time has come for Latin America . . . to project itself beyond its own frontiers, ad gentes. It is true that we ourselves need missionaries. But we must share even from our poverty . . . The mission of the Church is wider that the "communion between Churches"; this, besides the help it gives for the new evangelization, must above all have an orientation in view of the specific missionary character."[222]*

5.4 THE MISSION, A TASK BY ALL AND FOR ALL

a. Pastoral and Evangelizing Agents

The carrying out of the mission with "require the decisive collaboration between the Episcopal Conferences and of each diocese in particular".[223]

The Bishop is the first one responsible for the mission in each particular Church, and he is the one who ought to invoke all the living powers of the community to this great missionary commitment: "priests, religious men, religious women, and laity who devote themselves, often with immense difficulties, to the spreading of the gospel truth."[224]

> *This firm missionary decision should impregnate all the ecclesial structures and all the diocesan, parish and pastoral plans of any institution in the Church. No community should excuse itself from entering*

---

[222] Redemptoris Missio 64.
[223] DA 551.
[224] Benedict XVI, Homily to the Bishops of Brazil, 3. May 11, 2007.

with decisiveness, with all its strength, in the constant processes of
missionary renewal, and to abandon the outdated structures that no
longer favor the transmission of the faith.[225]

For the Ordained Ministers it is a great moment of grace that asks them to
renew the communion between Presbyters and Deacons with the Bishop,
and among themselves. Just as the enthusiasm and dedication in the service
of the gospel. They are the first carriers of all this missionary impulse and
they ought to be made sensitive especially to the spirit and pastoral conversion of Aparecida.

> *The renewal of the parish demands new attitudes in pastors and in*
> *priests in the service of the parish. The first demand is that the pastor be*
> *an authentic disciple of Jesus Christ, because only a priest who is in love*
> *with the Lord can renew a parish. But, at the same time, he should be an*
> *ardent missionary, who lives the constant desire to seek those who have*
> *fallen back, and is not satisfied merely with administration (DA. 201).*

b. The Privileged Role of the Laity

Any missionary effort demands, in a particular way, active and committed
participation of the lay faithful in all the stages of the process.

> *Nowadays, all the Church in Latin America and the Caribbean wants*
> *to get into a state of mission. The evangelization of the Continent, we were*
> *told by Pope John Paul II, cannot be done today without the collaboration*
> *of the lay people.*[226] *They must be an active and creative agent in the elabo-*
> *ration and carrying out of pastoral projects in favor of the community. This*
> *demands, on the part of pastors, a greater openness in mentality so that*
> *the understand and accept the "being" and "action" of the lay person in*
> *the Church, who in virtue of his Baptism and Confirmation is a missionary*
> *disciple of Jesus Christ. In other words, it is necessary that the lay person*
> *be taken into account in a spirit of communion and participation.*[227]

The Continental Mission should specially reach out to cultural, political and
social sectors that identify our globalized society. For this to be possible,

---

[225] DA 365.
[226] Cf. EAm 44.
[227] DA 213.

we must reaffirm vigorously the peculiar and specific mission of the laity in the secular world,[228] avoiding the temptation motivating the laity more committed to their faith, only to involve themselves in the services needed by the ecclesial community in their formation, sustenance and growth.

c. The Inestimable Mission of the Consecrated Life

The participation of the members of the Institutes of Consecrated Life in the Continental Mission, men and women who are called to bear a convincing witness of joy and of belonging to God as disciples and missionaries of Christ, to devote themselves generously in the service of His children, especially the most marginalized, and to manifest in the Church the multiplicity of the charismatic gifts of the Holy Spirit, as great collaborators of the pastors, will strongly contribute to the missionary awakening of Latin America and the Caribbean.

d. Interlocutors and Addressees

The addressees (or "interlocutors") of the mission are all of us, beginning with the missionary disciples who animate the evangelizing process, but it must especially be directed to the poor, to those who suffer and to those fallen away,[229] and it should encourage the builders of society to their Christian mission of transforming it.

To reach the fallen away should always be one of the goals of the missionary dimension of the Church, using the adequate means for each situation.

> We cannot remain indifferent, passively waiting in our temples. Rather, we are urged to reach out in all directions to proclaim that evil and death do not have the last word, that love is stronger, that we have been liberated and saved through the paschal victory of the Lord of history, that He convokes us to the Church, and that He wants to multiply the number of His disciples and missionaries in the building of His Kingdom in Latin America. We are witnesses and missionaries: in the great cities and in the country, in the mountains and jungles of our America, in all the environments of social coexistence, in the most diverse "areopagi" of the public life of nations, in the extreme situations of existence, assuming ad gentes our readiness for the universal mission of the Church.[230]

---

[228] Cf. DA chapter 10.

[229] DA 550.

[230] DA 550.

6. RESOURCES FOR THE MISSION

a. Communal Convocation

The parish is still a fundamental reference in the evangelizing project, with its base ecclesial communities, its movements and apostolic groups. The mission is called to be a permanent dynamism of great importance in order that the parish be a missionary parish.

The mission demands a calling of the missionary disciples and of ecclesial communities. In the mission, we should profit from the educational potential of the Church, by means of schools and institutes of formation, appreciating the missionary dynamism of the members of the teaching community.

An important phenomenon of our time is the surfacing and growth of diverse forms of missionary volunteers,[231] made up in good part by the young people, who are ready to give time and talent for the mission. A special mention must be given to the groups and associations of missionary children, because this creates a special dynamic in the family. On the other hand, the work of migrants as missionary disciples is considered important, of those

> *Who are called to be a new seed of evangelization, following the example of so many migrant missionaries that brought the Christian faith to our America.*[232]

b. Formation of Missionaries

Aparecida assumed a

> *Clear and decided option for the formation of the members of our communities, for the good of all the baptized, no matter what function they fulfill in the Church.*[233]

---

[231] DA 386.
[232] DA 391.
[233] DA 276.

Formation should be rich in missionary spirituality, which is an impulse of the Spirit that,

> Motivates the areas of existence, penetrates and configures the specific vocation of each one. In this way, the proper spirituality of presbyters, religious men and women, parents, entrepreneurs, catechists, etc. is formed and developed. Each one of the vocations has a concrete and distinctive way of living spirituality that gives depth and enthusiasm to the concrete exercise of their tasks. Thus, the life in the Spirit does not close us off in a complacent intimacy, but converts us into generous and creative persons, happy in the announcement and in missionary service. It makes us become involved with the claims of reality and capable of finding a deep meaning to all that we are meant to do for the Church and for the world.[234]

The Spirit weaves links of communion between the diverse vocations so that they bring about the only mission as complementary members of a single body.

c. Signs and Gestures of Closeness and Dignifying of the Poorest

> Thus, it cannot be separated from solidarity with the needy and their holistic human promotion: "But if the people we find are involved in a situation of poverty—we are told still by the Pope—it is necessary to help them, as did the first Christian communities, practicing solidarity, so that the feel truly loved. The poor people of the urban outskirts or from the country need to feel closeness to the Church, whether it be in terms of help for their more urgent needs, or also in the defense of their rights and in the common promotion of a society based on justice and peace. The poor are the privileged addressees of the Gospel, and a Bishop, modeled after the image of the Good Shepherd, should be particularly attentive in offering the divine balsam of the faith, without forgetting the "material bread."[235]

We ought to live evangelization, as a privileged action toward the poor, conscious of the fact that the most humble evangelize us.

---

[234] DA 285.
[235] DA 550.

7. Criteria for the Mission

a. Pastoral and Personal Conversion

The mission demands an indispensable pastoral conversion, both on the personal level as well as at the level of the very same structures of the Church. Outdates structures should be identified and new forms demanded by change should be sought.

> *The pastoral conversion of our communities demands that we go*
> *from a ministry merely of conservation to a decisively missionary ministry.*
> *This will make possible the "only program of the Gospel be introduced*
> *into the history of each ecclesial community "[236] with new missionary zeal,*
> *making the Church manifest itself as a mother that reaches out, a welcom-*
> *ing house, a permanent school of missionary communion.[237]*

b. Attention to Cultural Signs: Inculturation and Presence in New Areopagi

We must keep in mind the complex and varied reality of our continent, such as the case of the megacities, the ambient of suburban as well as big peripheral areas, the environment of peasants, miners, and seamen, without forgetting hospitals, rehabilitation facilities and jails, as well as the peculiarities of the Churches in the different regions. The mission, being one, must be at the same time diverse. Thus, it is necessary to be attentive to the cultural signs of the time, in such a way that the new expressions and values are enriched with the good news of the Gospel of Jesus Christ, thus trying to "unite faith more with life and contributing this way to a fuller catholicity, not just geographically, but also culturally.[238]

c. In the Context of Normal Pastoral Activity

The carrying out of the continental mission should give dynamic force to contemporary pastoral plans, renewing those structures that are necessary.

---

[236] NMI 12.
[237] DA 370.
[238] DA 479.

This firm missionary decision should fill all ecclesial structures and all pastoral plans of dioceses, parishes, religious communities, movements, and of any institution in the Church. No community should excuse itself decisively, with all its strengths, from the constant processes of missionary renewal, from abandoning outdated structures that do not foster the transmission of the faith.[239]

It would not withstand the impact of time a Catholic faith reduced to luggage, to a list of some norms and prohibitions, to fragmented devotional practices, to selective and partial adhesion to the truths of faith, an occasional participation in some sacraments, the repetition of doctrinal principles that do not bring conversion to the life of the baptized. Our greatest threat is "the gray pragmatism of the daily life of the Church in which, apparently, everything moves normally, but in fact, the faith is wasting away and degenerating into meanness."

We must all begin anew in Christ, recognizing that we do not begin to be Christian through and ethical decision or a great idea, but through the encounter with an event, with a Person, who brings a new horizon to life, and with it, a definitive orientation."[240]

d. With a New Language: Communication

In the mission, it is necessary to keep very much in mind the current culture, which

Should be known, evaluated and in a certain sense, assumed by the Church, in a language comprehensible to our contemporary people. Only thus will the Christian faith appear as a pertinent and meaningful reality of salvation. But, this same faith should engender new alternative cultural models for today's society.[241]

This will help to

Communicate the gospel values in a positive and propositional way. Many claim discontent, not so much with the contents of the doctrine of the Church, but with the way in which this is presented[242] *and lived.*

---

[239] DA 379.
[240] DA 12.
[241] DA 480.
[242] DA 497.

In the mission we must

> *Optimize the use of the Catholic means of communication, making them more active and efficacious, be it for the communication of the faith, as well as for the dialog between the Church and society.*[243]

It will be very important to make present the missionary message in the means of communication in general, as well as in virtual spaces, frequented by the new generations more often. So as in the radio and television there already exist some experiences of training programs in the faith, so also the interactive portal can be a useful option in the development of the mission.

8. Communion Places

The Episcopal Conferences, as places of communion between the local Churches, need to revive their identity and mission, so as to aid especially the Churches with less resources, motivating generosity and openness.

Each diocese needs to strengthen its missionary conscience, going out to the encounter of those who do not yet believe in Christ within the area of their own territory, and to respond adequately to the great problems of the society in which it is present. But also, with maternal spirit, it is called to go out seeking all the baptized who do not participate in the life of the Christian communities.[244]

In the diocese, the central focus should be an organic project of formation, approved by the Bishop and prepared with the competent diocesan bodies, keeping in mind all the living strength of the particular Church. . . We also need formation teams conveniently prepared to ensure the efficacy of the process itself and who will walk along with people with dynamic, active and open pedagogies.[245]

The parish will be the place where Christian initiation is ensured and will have as non negotiable tasks: initiating in the Christian life baptized adults not sufficiently evangelized; to train in the faith baptized

---

[243] DA 497.
[244] DA 168.
[245] DA 281.

children in a process that will lead them to complete their Christian initiation; to initiate the non baptized that, having heard the kerygma, want to embrace the faith. In this task, the study and assimilation of the Ritual for the Christian Initiation of Adults is a necessary reference and a sure support.[246]

The best efforts done in our parishes, in this beginning of the new millennium, should be put into the convocation and formation of lay missionaries.[247]

The renewal of parishes, at the beginning of the Third Millennium, demands reformulating their structures, so that they become a system of communities and groups, capable of articulating themselves making their members feel and really be disciples and missionaries of Jesus Christ in communion.[248]

The missionary renewal of parishes is necessary both in the evangelization of the great cities as well as the rural world of our continent, that is asking us to use our imagination and creativity to reach the multitudes that long for the gospel of Jesus Christ. Particularly, in the urban world, the creation of new pastoral structures is proposed, since many of them were born in different times to respond to the needs of the rural area.[249]

We point out that it is necessary to rekindle the processes of formation of small communities in the continent, for in them we have a certain source of vocations to the priesthood, to religious life, and to lay life specially dedicated to the apostolate. Through the small communities, one could also reach out to the fallen away, the indifferent, and those who feed discontent or resentment toward the Church.[250]

In the life and evangelizing action of the Church, we point to the fact that, in the modern world, we must respond to new situations and needs. The parish does not reach many environments in the big cities. In this context, the movements and new communities are a gift of God for our time, welcoming many fallen away people so that they may have an experience of the vital encounter with Jesus Christ, and thus, they may recuperate their baptismal identity and their active participation in the life of the Church.

---

[246] DA 293.
[247] DA 174.
[248] DA 172.
[249] DA 173.
[250] DA 310.

In them, "we can see the multidimensional presence and sanctifying action of the Spirit."[251]

The option for the Continental Mission and its goal to foster the permanent mission, lends a particularly important responsibility to groups and missionary institutes to give dynamic force to their habitual work and to offer subsidiary support to the different ecclesial levels.

FINAL INVOCATION

We entrust this project into the hands of our Lady, under the titles of Aparecida and Guadalupe, aware that she who opened the way for the Gospel in our Continent be the same one to inspire, help and protect our missionary project. She is not only the first disciple and missionary in the Gospel, but also the one who, with an immensely maternal heart, enjoys more than anyone else when her Son is known and loved, and he hands over to her the new children with the "Here is your son", characteristic of the paschal Hour.

---

[251] DA 312.

III

COMPLEMENTARY SERVICES FOR THE CONTINENTAL MISSION

1. GOALS

1.1 General goal

To be open to the impulse of the Holy Spirit to promote the awareness of and the action of the permanent mission in the disciples, through the Continental Mission.

1.2 Specific goals

1.2.1 To foment a kerygmatic, holistic and permanent formation, of the missionary disciples that, following the Aparecida directives, will foster a spirituality of the missionary action, keeping as the focal point the full life in Jesus Christ.

1.2.2 To promote a deep personal and pastoral conversion of all the pastoral agents and evangelizers, so that, with an attitude of disciples, we can all begin anew in Christ a new life in the Spirit, inserted into the ecclesial community.

1.2.3 To succeed in getting the communities, organizations, associations and ecclesial movements to go into a state of permanent mission, in order to reach even the sectors most distant from the Church, the indifferent and non-believers.

1.2.4 To communicate that the full life in Christ is a gift and a service offered to society and to the persons that configure it so that they may grow and overcome their pains and conflicts with a deep sense of humanity.

2. ITINERARY OF THE MISSION

The mission will be carried out in four stages, following the criteria of simultaneity (they can overlap), flexibility (according to local circumstances), and irradiation (they support each other).

There will be an introductory time to develop the sensitivity and pastoral conversion of the Church, deepening the knowledge of Aparecida so that its contents be studied, thought out and assimilated by all the ecclesial sectors.

Stage 1: Sensitizing the pastoral agents and evangelizers
Stage 2: Going deep with the priority groups.
Stage 3: Sectorial mission
Stage 4: Territorial mission

The missionaries formed in stages 1 and 2 are the evangelizing agents for the Sectorial (Stage 3) and Territorial mission (Stage 4).

3. ADDRESSEES OF THE MISSION

All Christians are at one and the same time both addressees and subjects of the mission. It is necessary to keep in mind that the disciple is formed for the mission and, at the same time, the mission forms the disciple. Thus, in carrying out the missionary activity, at the same time the disciples are renewed in the life of Jesus Christ, they are also being readied for carrying the Good News to all the peoples.

STAGE 1: MISSION WITH PASTORAL AGENTS AND EVANGELIZERS

In order that the pastors, animators and those responsible for the communities be the first ones to assume the challenge of the missionary disciple.

That includes Bishops, Presbyters, Permanent Deacons, Religious and Consecrated Life, including the Monastic and Contemplative Life, Lay People committed with the various areas of pastoral ministry, Leaders of movements and communities, Seminaries and Formation Houses, Pastoral Councils, Group Leaders, organizations, institutions, schools, Catholic Universities.

STAGE 2: MISSION WITH PRIORITY GROUPS

It demands personal and pastoral conversion of the members of groups, movements and associations, so that they then go on to evangelize the different sectors of the community.

Directed to priority pastoral groups: by way of example let us mention some:

Mission in virtual spaces—Catholic Colleges and Universities, Educators, Catechists, Various Pastoral Areas, Catholic Professional Organizations, Pastoral groups dedicated to Indians and Afro-Americans, Confraternities, Brotherhoods, Movements and Communities.

STAGE 3: SECTORIAL MISSION

Directed to the various sectors of society. We name some by way of example: Academicians, Educators and the world of education, Youth, Entrepreneurs and Workers, Communicators in the whole virtual environment, Politicians, the Military, Police, Health Workers, Prison world, Volunteer organizations.

STAGE 4: TERRITORIAL MISSION

Directed to the territorial mission: Parishes, Families, Base Ecclesial Communities, Small Communities, Civil Community Organizations, Neighbor Councils, Sports Clubs, and Non-Governmental Organizations.

In this stage, it is necessary to keep in mind those fallen away, the indifferent and non-believers.

4. SIGNS AND COMMON GESTURES: AN EXPRESSION OF COMMUNITY AND SIMULTANEITY OF THE CHURCH IN THE CONTINENTAL MISSION

4.1 Official opening of the Mission at the CAM 3 (August 17, 2008)
4.2 Distribution of the Bible and the Triptych with a brief catechesis about its meaning, especially as a kind of "Family Altar" for each home.

4.3 Prayer for the Continental Mission

4.4 Logo (Aparecida)

4.5 List of missionary songs and eventually a Hymn based on the official prayer that can be done through national competitions.

4.6 Some celebrations of the great liturgical feasts with a missionary sense:

- Epiphany
- Easter
- Pentecost
- Marian feast in each country

4.7 Production and exchange of the formative missionary subsidies.

4.8 Propaganda material: Mission poster, Radio and TV Spots; Web pages on the mission; Videos about the Mission (done with TV times).

4.9 A significant gesture in the social field in each country.

5.1 ROLES IN THE CONTINENTAL MISSION

Role of Episcopal Conferences

- To provide pastoral directives in virtue of the Continental Mission (synonym and synchrony), so that all the ecclesial units go into a state of permanent mission.
- To create a central commission to animate the mission at the national level.
- To provide pertinent subsidies for the formation of pastoral agents and evangelizers for the carrying out of the missionary project.
- To revise or design General Pastoral Lines or Directives, in the light of Aparecida, in view of the formation and action of the missionary disciples.
- To prepare teams at the national level to direct spiritual retreats with a basis on Aparecida.
- To create missionary centers at the national level.

5.2 ROLE OF THE DIOCESES

"The diocese, in all its communities and structures, is called to be a missionary community" (DA. 168), and thus, the subject of the mission.

- To revise the pastoral plan in the light of Aparecida in order to give it a big missionary renewal that contemplates, as a sign of maturity, the mission ad gentes. The Continental Mission ought to open persons to go beyond every frontier.
- To create a central commission to animate the diocesan mission.
- To develop resources it deems necessary for the formation of pastoral agents and evangelizers for the carrying out of the missionary project.
- To offer preparatory courses and spiritual exercises for the pastoral agents and evangelizers in each of the stages.
- To do team work with surrounding dioceses, at the level of ecclesiastical provinces, with a great sense of ecclesial communion.

5.3 ROLE OF THE LATIN AMERICAN CONFERENCE OF BISHOPS LAEC (CELAM) FOR THE MISSION

- To support the preparation and follow up of the Continental Mission.
- To offer preparatory courses and spiritual exercises for pastoral agents and evangelizers in each one of the stages, in coordination with ITEPAL and the CEPIBAL.
- To have a team available to be invited by the Episcopal Conferences for the communication of the contents of Aparecida.
- To distribute existing resources and to develop others directed to each one of the sectors of pastoral agents and evangelizers.
- To offer information about the missionary experiences that have been held or are in the process of being held in the Continent, keeping in mind the help from the Pastoral Observatory.
- To develop catechetic and liturgical materials for the mission that will be common to the Church in Latin America and the Caribbean.